D0331809

Jungle Paths and Palace Treasures

To Mary Ellen, Roger,
Cameron -
Join me in an
adventure not to be
forgotten .

Mary L. Stickney

Medical Staff Library ~~Cannaday 1050~~

*This book is one of a donated collection provided for
your enjoyment.
To ensure that this service continues please return this
book.
A donation of additional titles would be very much
appreciated.*

JUNGLE PATHS AND PALACE TREASURES

▼

An American Woman Encounters the Romance and Reality of India

Mary Seniff Stickney

Writer's Showcase
San Jose New York Lincoln Shanghai

Jungle Paths and Palace Treasures
An American Woman Encounters the Romance and Reality of India

All Rights Reserved © 2001 by Mary S. Stickney

No part of this book may be reproduced or transmitted in any form or by any means, graphic, electronic, or mechanical, including photocopying, recording, taping, or by any information storage retrieval system, without the permission in writing from the publisher.

Writer's Showcase
an imprint of iUniverse.com, Inc.

For information address:
iUniverse.com, Inc.
5220 S 16th, Ste. 200
Lincoln, NE 68512
www.iuniverse.com

ISBN: 0-595-17275-X

Printed in the United States of America

Dedicated to my son, Dr. Dennis Paul Seniff (1949-1990), who, in his last words to me, requested that I write this book.

CONTENTS

FOREWORD

In 1960 India's population passed 400 million. During that year and the ensuing three years, the country imported more than 12 million tons of food grains annually, paying not with dollars but rupees. This money was set aside for development, and the U.S. involved itself heavily in the Indian infrastructure. This included public health, education, industry and agriculture.

By 1964, the International Wheat and Maize Center (CIMMYT) and the International Rice Center (IRRI) had developed new strains of wheat and rice that took on dwarf characteristics and could stand heavy application of fertilizer—which, when coupled with good irrigation practices, could increase yields five to ten fold. The first varieties were planted in India and other third-world countries in that year and the Green Revolution was begun. USAID, Rockefeller Foundation and Ford Foundation technicians assigned to a few dozen outposts in India led their Indian counterparts down new and exciting paths.

Back home, we heard the complaints of people about sending money overseas, yet each of us returned to our posts and went about the jobs of training new scientists, developing new facilities, imparting new technologies and encouraging new methodologies that were to transform India.

Many people ask us if it was worth it. Our reply is to call attention to the despair in India in 1960 when there were 400 million people with the spectre of starvation hanging over them—and compare it with today. There are more than one billion people in India and they are a net exporter of foodstuffs. What more can one ask of a program that was designed out of American compassion, implemented by American ingenuity, and consummated by American desire to succeed?

Those of us who shared in this bold venture are nearing the close of our lives. We have a much greater satisfaction in our contribution than all the nay-sayers combined.

In this book, Mary Stickney has taken the time to explore India in a manner that many of us old India hands can only admire. Her interest in the manners and mores of a country filled with enigmas and contradictions is evident from the beginning. She approaches each situation with curiosity and wonder, not with the righteous condemnation that flows as quickly from the pens of others. You may not understand India when you've read the book, but you will understand why she was transfixed by the country and its people.

—*Donald James Minehart, Agricultural Research Station Development Engineer with Ford Foundation, and USAID, Consultative Group for International Agricultural Research, with 13 years in India, and a stint in Iran, Bangladesh, Syria and Pakistan*

ACKNOWLEDGEMENTS

The encouragement of my children, Connie and John, and stepdaughter Whitaker Bryant, and the remarkable assistance of my editor/agent, Emily Worthy Carmain, have been invaluable in helping me bring this book to fruition. I am also deeply appreciative of the interest and support of other friends, especially Diane and Dale Olsen, Corinne Puett Giannitrapani, Rod Haynes, Rev. Kip Colegrove, Adeline Fraley, Donald and Bette Minehart, and another diplomat who must remain anonymous.

The characters in the book personify the thoughts and ideas of a tightly knit family and many new friends found along the way. Some are ruling princes of India, some are well-known names concerned in events that have figured in the public press. A few names have been altered to preserve the privacy of personal acquaintances. The incidents are true experiences of the author.

INDIA: In Madhya Pradesh is the town of Raipur, where the author and family lived—1,000 miles by train from New Delhi, in a land of thick jungles and remote villages.

NEW DELHI

1964

CHAPTER 1
"THIS IS INDIA, SON"

The blackness of the runway dissolves in the bright white beams shining from the wings of the 707 aircraft as we descend.

"Ladies and gentlemen, this is your captain speaking." The loudspeaker on the plane comes alive.

"We are arriving at Palaam Airport in New Delhi. The temperature at the airport is ninety degrees. The time is 4:33 a.m., if you care to set your watch."

"Ninety degrees!" Dennis moans, leaning over the back of our seat, and then dropping back into his own seat. "How can it be ninety degrees at this time of the morning?"

Dennis has slept very little on the trip. His teenage curiosity would not allow it. We are all exhausted. I am too excited to be sleepy

"This is India, son," Mark says.

It is May 12, 1964.

We begin scrambling behind and beneath our seats, gathering our belongings. It has been a long flight. Yet as weary as I am, I am expecting to see fascinating things. Our destination seems so enchanting, so unreal. My childhood dream is now being realized. We have at last arrived. It will not surprise me if my fantasy of seeing a flying carpet materializes in the world outside the plane.

My early years were spent in the South, where the sweet smell of magnolia blossom and honeysuckle wove a cascade of fragrant lace around my mind. I had believed that all the world could be experienced in the same manner as my recurring dream, that of flying carpets, castles and jewels. On our Alabama farm, I had known everyone in the countryside and town, yet I dreamed of seeing strange lands on the other side of the world. My mother had read Rudyard Kipling to me as a child, and those stories had enhanced my dream of India, that faraway land of romance and beauty. She also took me on Sunday afternoon walks through the woods, identifying trees by their leaves and bark, finding birds' nests and watching the chicks. I had felt the Indian jungles would be a place to see even more wonderful creatures.

Now, my first steps into the "enchanted land" come when I go through the doorway from the plane. Instantly, the intense heat strikes me across the face, making me pause. Punctuating the shock of reality, I see a dog standing a few yards from the runway. His head droops and his ribs protrude against taut skin. He shows not the slightest interest in the plane or the activities of the people. Hoping the children do not see the animal, I think about our beautiful golden cocker spaniel, Prince, that we have left with my parents.

Winnie, our 15-year-old daughter, follows me. When the hot Indian air hits, she turns as if to retreat into the plane.

"Come on, dear," I encourage. Her enormous blue eyes fill with tears, and I sense her sadness and fear as she sees the dog. I wait and take her by the hand as we walk across the tarmac.

Even though I do not know exactly what to expect, until now I had rather thought some smartly dressed American diplomat would be meeting us. The daily calls for several weeks from the Indian Desk in Washington to me in Florida had led me to believe we would be expected.

"Straighten your coat," Mark reminds eight-year-old John, our youngest child. "There is someone to meet us."

This is certainly no diplomat, judging by the looks of the man wearing a white short-sleeved shirt that hangs loosely over his dark trousers. This tall American reminds me of a Texas farmer. He grins, and I see his Adam's apple elevate a couple of times before he is near enough to clasp his rough, brown hand with Mark's.

"Leon Kiram," he introduces himself, taking another step nearer. "Namaste." Now his hands cover mine, "Welcome, in Hindi. We are glad to see you all! Call me Leon."

Mark replies, "My wife, Mary, and my daughter, Winnie. This is Mary's daughter, Connie, and sons, Dennis and John."

The introductions over, Leon takes our passports and health cards and hands them to a white-uniformed Indian standing behind him. An American flag and colors decorate the patch on the Indian's left sleeve.

"Ram, these are Mr. and Mrs. Stepworth."

While he nods his head, the Indian presses his palms together and raises them. "Namaste."

"Ram will get you through your customs and immigration painlessly. While you are with him, Mark, we'll identify your luggage."

The children and I walk across the terrazzo floor, heels clicking. We stand at the front entrance.

"Everybody is barefooted except Mr. Leon," Dennis remarks.

A black station wagon pulls up. The emblazoned eagle's wings glow silver and black in the illumination from the entrance light overhead. The Great Seal of the United States on the door of the vehicle makes me feel proud and secure as my thoughts take wings.

Our sixteen pieces of luggage are being loaded into the car, along with our guns and ammunition boxes, which we were advised to bring because we will need to hunt for our meat in the isolated places where we will live.

While we wait, Leon takes Dennis' arm. "I can see that our athletic program will benefit by your arrival," he says. "Did you ever play rugby? With shoulders like those you'll be great in the scrum."

Dennis turns his wide-opened brown eyes on me, giving a big grin. He had regretted leaving his friends and sports, so this sounds pretty good.

"More about that later," Leon adds, motioning Mark and me to his car and the youngsters into the wagon.

"It is nice of you to meet us at this time of the morning," Mark says. "Isn't this beyond the call of duty?"

"Not at all! All the planes landing here arrive at this hour."

We circle the driveway and head out of the airport compound onto a narrow black road. The beams of light seek and find a line of bullock carts extending into the shadows of the distance stretching ahead. The two-wheeled carts sway with every step of the bullocks. Dust rises beneath their wheels. The carters, or drivers, appear to be sleeping, each with blankets pulled high around his shoulders and up about his head against the night air and dust. A tinkling bell hangs around each animal's neck.

"One day," Leon tells us, "a couple of mischievous American youngsters, returning from a hunting trip in the early morning, thought it would be fun to pull a trick on the sleeping men. They turned the lead bullock around facing the opposite direction. Then they drove off and watched the other bullocks turning to follow him."

"A prank that wouldn't make friends," Mark comments.

Our trip into the city is slow. Between the carts and the people, we move at a snail's pace.

"The people travel by night. They sleep during the heat of the day," explains our guide.

The roadside scene as we near the city shows people lying on string-covered frames or mats of paper. A few have risen to build fires.

"Where are their homes?" I ask.

"Millions are homeless. They have left their villages to come here and seek work. They sleep wherever they are when the sunsets. It is dangerous for them on the roadsides. An occasional truck will go out of control and plow through them. The next day others will have taken their places."

As tired as I am, I feel that I should be trying to remember my first impressions. I promise myself that I will write every day or much of this might slip out of my memory. We drive along Ring Road to Mathura Road.

"I will show you my favorite view. This is the time to see it," says Leon, turning on Raj Path. An amber dawn colors the already impressive avenue that runs from Purana Qila, an early Moghul fort, to the Presidential Palace, which has been called the Moghuls' "Versailles."

I look through the rear window and see the faces of the children pressed against their windows in the station wagon following us. I wonder what impressions the scenes are making on the four of them, and how they will accept this new life.

   *   *   *

Besides the throng of dingily clad people on bicycles or walking with baskets, there are dozens of men and women walking on the side of the road who stand apart from the others. The women are attired in spotless white saris, the men in white pajamas.

"These are people taking their morning walk," says Leon. "I am told that you will find every profession represented. The Indians are great believers in walking. These are affluent people and live by a very set routine. They return home for ablutions (a leisurely bath and shave) before breakfast. Afterwards they leave for their office or shop work. By eight o'clock, the streets will be filled with bicycles, ten or twelve abreast, as far as you can see."

He continues, "Most of the people live in thousands of villages. You will be seeing them. You are the second family to arrive in India destined for the 'boondocks,' as we call anything outside the cities."

I ask where that family is now.

"The wife is under treatment in the States for a nervous breakdown, the husband and children are here in New Delhi. She returned once but could not take it," he says. "Cultural shock is very real here. They were hired to take the job that you will do, but they never left New Delhi."

"So we are their replacement?"

"Yes," he says, just as our car is about to pull up in front of the Claridges Hotel, where we will stay for our first few weeks.

I now understand the daily calls from the India Desk in Washington for all those weeks. At the time, I had wondered at some of the questions asked me.

"Do you realize that you will go where no other American woman has gone? There have been some missionaries, but we don't know where they are, or if they are still in the country. There will be no doctors, hospitals, no theaters, no libraries anywhere near you. Do you realize how remote that will be?"

Day after day, the State Department's India Desk had called and tried to prepare me for the life ahead. Yet I still wanted the children and myself to have this experience, regardless of the inconveniences of life in India.

A sponsor is assigned each new family arriving—an American to guide us through the orientation and obligations. Leon and his wife Martha have done their task well. The envelope that Leon handed Mark contains a few hundred rupees, (five equals one American dollar). The Kirams have stocked our refrigerator with boiled water, juice and soft drinks. Chocolate cookies, potato chips and peanuts are on the shelves. *Time*, *U.S. News and World Report* magazines lie on the coffee table in our sitting room.

All of this is designed to give us a feeling of familiarity in a land where both familiarity and comfort will be in short supply. Now, Leon leaves us. His day of work will begin soon.

As we enter the suite, I first notice a faint delicate fragrance that I cannot identify. Our bed is comfortable, and soon I am falling asleep in Mark's arms. But, hearing a noise at the door, I raise my head and look in that direction. Two silhouettes are framed against the light coming from the hallway. The figures wear scarlet turbans, with tall plumes sticking up from the folds. Their beards and mustaches are twirled, drawing the hairs tightly against the skin, and the twist is pulled up under the turban.

They look menacing, and I utter a little gasp. Mark sits upright.

"Very sorry, Sahib. We will clean your room."

"Oh no, not now...no, no." Mark and I lie back down. "They are Gurkhas," he tells me.

I remember reading about the men called Gurkhas—Indian warriors renowned for their bravery in wartime. Called "The Lions of the Punjab," they finally controlled Punjab, the richest state in India. They are said never to unsheathe their short, curved knives, worn in their belts, without drawing blood—even if it is their own—before returning the knife to its sheath.

Reassured that the men are servants of the hotel only trying to do their job, I pull the covers up over my shoulder and go back to sleep.

CHAPTER 2
THE WAY IT HAPPENED

How our life has changed, I think, as we get up and start dressing on our first morning in India. A little over three years ago, I had ended a marriage that left me with three children, John, Connie and Dennis. It was about three years before I met and married Mark. An Alabama native, he is tall, athletic in build and has blue eyes and curly salt-and-pepper hair. He is quiet and soft-spoken, with a heavy Southern accent, and he has been a successful scientist for some years. From the start, I felt confident that whatever happened, or wherever we went, we would be in safe hands with him.

Like all parents, I feel our children are pretty exceptional. Mark's teen-aged daughter, Winnie, has lovely, naturally wavy brown hair with lights that glow in it from hours spent in the sun. She has an attractive suntan, is bubbly and active in her interests, her schoolwork and friends. There's much I need to learn about Winnie as we have had such a short time together. She has been the only girl in a family of boy cousins and is excited about having a sister and brothers.

John is a small boy, blonde and sensitive. His teacher declares that he will be either a poet or a priest. He is quiet and has never been talkative. Perhaps he has felt outnumbered.

My daughter, Connie, is just entering her teens. She excels in her studies and is vibrant, happy, and beautiful with flashing dark brown eyes, nearly black hair, and a slim, curvaceous figure. Dennis, who is now 13, took top grades in the state when he was tested in his high school. He is interested in history, math, languages, music and sports. Besides being an athlete, he loves to pore over maps.

Both divorces— Mark's and mine— now seem to have been a blessing for all, with the opportunity to begin anew and the exhilaration of sharing in this new adventure. I am 38 years old, and I want something beautiful to fill the void of the past several years of unhappiness, when my former husband and I could not work out our problems.

The freedom to travel will educate our family. We will explore strange places, taste different foods and have a lifetime of memories. The children and I have enjoyed each other already, and the experiences ahead should bond all of us as nothing else can.

                    *   *   *

We have come to India to assist in a program of country building. We are optimistic, hoping that we can extend America's concepts of technology in agriculture, animal husbandry, water management, and credit management. The training we will provide is with the U. S. State Department

As we start this new chapter in our lives, I recall the last months before we left home. Neighbors and friends wanted to know how we got this job and how our work is funded. Our qualifications for the Foreign Service, as I told them, come from Mark's educational background and experience, along with my background and our family interview. The fact that we have nice children is important, too.

On the day of our official interview last November, a Foreign Service Officer had visited our home in Florida to meet the family and discuss with us some of what we could expect, the conditions we would encounter.

Dennis was mowing the lawn around the house that afternoon. He continued to mow up to each window so he could take a peek inside. He grinned at me from ear to ear, and I rolled my eyes. He was so excited he could hardly contain himself. The girls and John had gone into their rooms to wait.

The interview lasted two-and-a-half hours. We drank iced tea and answered the questions put to us by the officer, who had a vast knowledge of South Asia. Although he personally had never been to our post— Raipur, in southeastern India— and knew no one who had been, he had traveled through many parts of rural India.

Finally, he announced that we had been approved for the position, and we were overjoyed.

"We are going!" Mark and I exclaimed in unison. We went to tell the children, and we all hugged and laughed.

Word spread throughout the town that we would be leaving for India. Everyone was excited about our plans, and farewell parties began. Ours is a small town where friendliness and social graces are the standard behavior.

I had looked forward to discovering a new country as much as the children did. Growing up on a farm with my boy cousins, I had been a real tomboy, who explored the woods, learned to shoot a rifle and could ride horseback or on a mule or whatever I could climb on. When I married an Air Force captain, we went to Columbus, Ohio, for his graduate work and my bachelor's degree. It was there that our three children were born. The children spent their early years in Ohio, except for summers on my parents' farm in Alabama.

After my divorce we had moved back to Florida, where Mark and I met and were married. I have always taken the children on camping trips, for cookouts and exploring in the parks. The love of adventure is in our blood.

We understand that our work will be in the Deccan. We will make our home at the scene where fierce, bloody battles were fought between the Moghuls, the Rajputans and Hindu kings until the Emperor Babar's demise in the 16th Century.

*   *   *

There is a saying in the Foreign Service that with a husband and wife team, the Foreign Service gets two for one price; although I am not allowed to work at a paying job, I must do whatever will enhance our mission.

The program comes under Public Law 480, which came into being for the purpose of disposing of excess grain to needy, developing countries. The law provides for repayment to the United States in almost all types of aid under this law.

Like most people, in the past I had felt our foreign aid programs were "giveaways." Since we have been involved, I've learned much about loans made by the U.S. government. I now know that much of our money going to these other countries is used to purchase U.S.-made materials, supplies and equipment.

Under Title I of the Agriculture and Trade Act, the underdeveloped country keeps its money and "borrows" the food from the United States. This way, the needy countries can use their money on schools, roads, dams and other projects. They repay the loan to the United States over forty years with a very low interest rate.

Another part of the law, Title II, is for famine and disaster relief, and Title III provides commodity grants to U.S. agencies: i.e., The Catholic Relief, CARE and UNICEF.

Title IV requires money for commodities to be repaid in American dollars to the United States government.

The amount involved in Title II and III combined is less than ten percent of Title I sales, which are in the form of a loan to be paid back eventually.

It reminds me of a quote I've always liked. In Mark Twain's book, *Letters to the Earth*, he said, "I don't know why they hate me, I have not loaned them money lately."

CHAPTER 3
THIS IS A BIT OF AMERICA ABROAD

Today, we began our official calls, registered and left our calling cards at the Embassy. After introductions to Embassy employees, whom we will see often and work with, Mark left me to begin his work.

Before I returned to the hotel, I was shown around the building, an impressive structure, said to be our country's most beautiful embassy in the world. Located on land owned and controlled by our nation, it is maintained as our "bit" of America abroad. A huge bronze and silver eagle, wings spread, looks down on the massive steps from its mount on the front of the Embassy. From the flagpole before the building flies a very large, beautiful Stars and Stripes.

A high fence protects the American Embassy in New Delhi. The gate sits fifty or so yards from the building's wide steps, and the green lawn is well landscaped with plants and flowers. Uniformed Indian guards are stationed at the guardhouse and gates.

The building itself has two walls—the inner one solid, and the outer decorated with ornately cut blocks to allow air circulation over the water that flows between the walls, for cooling. The office doors are built into glass walls opening onto the apron of an Olympic-size pool for beauty rather than swimming. Fish dart among exotic flowering plants rising from the tropical pool. Mallards sit grooming themselves on the stones that crisscross the pool. The roof is covered in glass, so visitors have a lovely view of the sky with birds flying by. The affairs and interests of the United States are conducted inside the rooms that surround the pool.

After my tour, I went back to our suite at the Claridges, a five-star hotel where we will live until our house is finished in Madhya Pradesh. I found an invitation for all of us to have dinner with the Hinkleys, new acquaintances from Oklahoma, but "Old Indians" in Embassy terms. There were other invitations for other days, not only for Mark and me, with special ones for the children.

We learned that first night that news travels slowly from the States to India, so everyone wants to catch up on the latest happenings back home. They want to know about politics, sports, fashion, music and ordinary events that take on a very extraordinary interest here. Only one newspaper brings American news, The *New York Herald-Tribune*, which is published in Paris. Otherwise, we will wait for weeks for magazines that are delivered by American pouch to the APO address at the Embassy.

*　　　　*　　　　*

I think I am beginning to adjust to the crowd, the odors, and the fragrances of flowers, incense, and spices. I can take this, I believe. But the truth is, I have no idea what lies ahead of us.

After having breakfast in the hotel a few mornings, John, with his cherubic face, blue eyes and blond hair, has become an immediate favorite with bearers and waiters. Once after dinner when the band played, he was invited up to play the drums. He was game, and the Indians love him for it. Wherever he goes, he is called "Baba Raj," Boy King.

Dennis draws his share of attention as well. He has already been approached about joining sports teams and is meeting young people his age. The two girls have begun making friends. After breakfast, they often spend part of each day around the hotel pool.

We are learning to arrange our day around the weather as the locals do. When the sun rises, tennis players are waiting to take advantage of the courts while it is reasonably cool. Being golfers, Mark and I soon learned that we must reserve a tee-off time, meaning we too can experience a break-of-dawn round. Here, no carts are allowed. We must have two caddies each.

"Why two caddies?" I asked Mark. "I've never had one caddy, much less two!"

"You've never had a large bird swoop down and take your ball, or a monkey run away with your ball," said Mark dryly.

"Of course not!"

"That's the reason we have two caddies. Those are the conditions," he informed me.

The caddies were beaming as the staff master introduced us on our first day at the course. Slim but strong-limbed, they knew their game. They observed every stroke we made and suggested clubs for each shot. "This is great, I might even have a decent score with this kind of help," I said.

Late in the day, people who are not working lounge on lawn chairs placed beneath large umbrellas outside the hotel. White-coated bearers move silently serving lemonade from trays. An air of luxury accompanies this gentle activity. Life goes on for the children much as it would have on a summer vacation back home, except that now home is Claridges Hotel in New Delhi, India.

*   *   *

Today is Sunday, and this morning was our first opportunity to attend a church service. We inquired and were told that, as we are Episcopalians, the Cathedral of the Holy Redeemer, an Anglican Church, would be our service. When we told our driver, he said, "Oh, the Wiceroy's Church." (V's are always pronounced as W's.) The streets were as busy as usual.

People were riding to work on bicycles, always ten or twelve bicycles abreast.

We dressed in our Sunday clothes, the girls looking fresh and sweet in their flowing dresses and sandals, the boys wearing ties with their short-sleeved shirts. Mark was in a light summer suit, and my own outfit included a crème leghorn hat with scarlet silk poppies marching around the wide brim. My sleeveless dress was the color of my poppies, and beige pumps and a small bag accompanied it.

Upon entering the church and taking a few steps, we realized that the entire congregation had turned around to look at us coming down the aisle—my heels clicking noisily with every step I made. It was only when we were seated that we noticed everyone else in the Cathedral was barefoot—including the priest and acolytes.

The beautiful voices sang in harmony at the rear and soaring high under the towering ceiling. Yellow and blue parakeets and numerous other birds flitted from magnificently carved pillars to posts within the cavernous building.

When the choir processed down the winding stairs and into the chancery, I realized they too were barefoot. They wore white saris with one end covering their hair.

I hope to join the choir in time, as I've sung in choirs and on other occasions all of my life.

Following the service, we were driven past the *ghat* (an elevated concrete slab) where Mahatma Gandhi, or *Gandhiji*, as the Indians refer to him, was cremated following his assassination in January 1948. The term "ji," added to the last name in respect, means "honored person." The ghat is covered with leis of marigold blossoms, so thickly that I can't see the concrete they lie on.

Every night I open my journal and continue to write. There's so much to say. How can I describe the beauty of the antiquities, the statues of strange, many-armed gods and goddesses, the vivid red, ochre, blue and green hues on the pictures of gods and voluptuous figures of women painted on buses, buildings, carts and every conceivable spot? This colorful setting seems interwoven with the pungent, delightful fragrances of the spices in the market. The strangeness and excitement of it all makes me want to record everything that happens. I am hoping for a typewriter.

The author at one of the Embassy functions she attended in New Delhi as a representative of America.

Safdarjung's Tomb, from the 1750s, is one of the last examples of architecture from the great Mughal empire. We passed this monument of white marble and pink limestone daily, driving to the American Embassy in New Delhi.

CHAPTER 4
LIFE IS SEEN IN THE OPEN

We have soon learned that New Delhi branches off from India Gate, where everything that is best in official New Delhi begins. Large white houses with Paladin facades stand behind stone walls on spacious, tree-lined avenues. Flowers in orange, yellow and red are placed within borders in attractive groupings. Glimpses through open gates reveal well-kept lawns and servants' quarters clustered behind the main houses. British civil servants once occupied these homes, now assigned to high officials, government ministers (equivalent to U.S. senators) and senior officers of the armed forces.

Yesterday, Mark and I wanted to get out on our own. He reserved a vehicle from the embassy garage and we headed for Old Delhi, former capital of the old Moghul Empire.

Leaving the area around the hotel and embassy and entering the old city, the contrast was startling. We moved through milling crowds, bullock carts, stubborn cows wandering untended mingled with bicycles and trucks on mean streets. Brass horns sounded, as drivers squeezed a rubber bulb to make the horn blast. Lorry drivers yelled when they couldn't get past. Bicycle riders with raspy buzzers contributed to the clamor. Oblivious to the commotion and the human stream swirling past, the children laughed as they tugged at kite strings, maneuvering fluttering wisps in the form of birds and butterflies high in the air.

The stench of urine, added by billions of gallons over thousands of years, clutched our throats. The fumes permeated the blasts of hot air. I held Mark's knee and the car's doorframe as we lurched along.

We came to a stop, surrounded by the hordes. I felt the pulsation of humanity. Life goes on here in the broad open daylight. The natives seem unperturbed by the lack of privacy. Men and boys urinate openly, standing with their backs turned, facing a post, a fence, tree or building. The women squat. Bowel movements are managed in discrete ways, in corners or in bushes or woods. No one goes inside a bathroom, for there are no toilets. Besides, the people cannot go near members of another lower or higher caste. No one pays any attention to the personal activities, and there is never any laughing or snickering about them, for they are as commonplace as breathing.

Intimate glimpses of everyday life can be seen as one drives past. There is an openness that invites the casual passerby to become knowledgeable about the people's lives, as there are no closed doors or screens.

Finally, our car moved on, passing old Moslem tombs, British gardens, historic Hindu temples, Protestant churches, old Mughal battlements, British barracks now used by Indians, ancient mosques, towers and the Old Delhi wall. As Mark and I continued to inch forward toward our destination, in the hot, dusty atmosphere, I became conscious that a single drop of sweat was trickling between my breasts. I began laughing and he gave me a quizzical look. "I have water on my chest." The rest of my body was dry, as perspiration evaporates instantly in the arid heat.

We reached Chandni Chowk, called the Silver Street. Having searched in vain for buttons for a dress I am having made, I have taken my friend Goshen's suggestion that I buy silver studs. Orthodox Hindus shun anything that is made of bone, such as buttons or utensils. We have learned quickly that Hindus do not eat from china or porcelain, as it may contain bone meal. They use metal dishes or eat from a communal metal pan.

While looking at the silver items, I was being pressed into the counter that separates customers from the merchandise. A miniature set of scales, aged, dented and worn, was set out. Studs in the shape of peacocks and a lion were placed in the tiny cup to be weighed.

The salesman was calculating the cost, and when I felt pressure on my shoulder and back, I paid no attention. Then I realized that someone was exploring my body, caressing my waist and buttocks with a hand. Startled, I turned to see a naked man, thin as a rake, with protruding bones and wrinkled skin. I'm sure I had a surprised look. He responded with a weak smile. In a moment someone drew him away, saying, "Nay, nay, Baba (No, Uncle)."

On the same streets, in the shadow of the Jama Masjid, the world's great mosque, goldsmiths and silversmiths sell jewels as their forebears did in the days of the Mughal Emperors. Now, brash vendors also offer roasted kabobs and Coca-Colas. In the alcoves of the ancient walls, on the steps that go down to the Jumna River, Brahmins chant Sanskrit verses as other Brahmins have done for more than three thousand years.

We finished shopping and drove out of the old city, inching along. It had been a most interesting experience. We chatted between the horn blowing. By the time we returned to the hotel, we were ready for a hot, soaking bath. Covers had been turned down on our beds and water drawn for baths. At least there was privacy for us here. We realized that we take so much for granted in our life, organized traffic, air-conditioned cars, and a place to sit for a drink.

Connie rushed in from her adjoining suite, laughing. She is getting to be a grown-up young lady and what a beauty, I thought.

"Listen to this: We were dressing for bed when a rap came at the door. Before we could reach it, Winnie saw the door knob turning."

Winnie entered and interrupted, "Connie was not dressed, so she dived into the closet, pulling the door closed behind her."

"It was the bearer taking orders for our morning drink," added Connie "He didn't understand Winnie, so I spoke up from inside the closet." Winnie continued the tale, "He started creeping towards the closet as if a ghost were there. I thought he would open the door, so I grabbed a towel and shoved it through the door to Connie."

"You should have seen him when I walked out with the towel draped around me. He probably never moved so fast," Connie finished.

They eventually went off to bed. Mark and I were so tired we decided to forego dinner and have crackers and cheese with a drink.

CHAPTER 5
BACK TO COLLEGE

After being here one week, Mark and I have begun classes on The Delhi University campus, at the Institute of Economic Growth, Old Delhi. A faded red bus, battered by years of service, pulls up in front of our hotel to transport us. On the first day, we took the seat behind the driver, against the advice of the assistant who had pointed to seats farther back in the bus. We soon discovered that this was a mistake, as each time the driver depressed the brakes, a great hissing, popping noise was emitted into the bus.

At the campus, we study the complexities of the country, past and present. The walls inside the lecture rooms are saturated by heat. An overhead fan plods on throughout the day attempting to cool us. Flies are free to seek their food and comfort, as window screens are unheard of in India's lifestyle. By lunchtime I find it difficult to hold my eyes open. I rub them, rub the back of my neck and move my shoulders. I'm sure the professor sees this entire maneuvering going on but says nothing. I am still out of sync with the clock—a day and a half different from that at home.

The director, *Shri* (educator) Rameshwar Dayal, wears an *achkan*—a long coat of fine, heavy silk—with a white silk turban wound around his head. He seems energetic far beyond his seventy-two years and is full of enthusiasm.

All the lecturers hold graduate degrees, and some have studied in England. One, whose specialty is human geography, takes each area of

India and weaves the seasons, climate and terrain into a patchwork-picture of her country.

India is unique, differing from other lands in history, climate and religion. It forms a gigantic triangle, 1,900 miles long and as broad as from the Atlantic Ocean to the Mississippi River. Yet this section of earth is a peninsula. The northern end of India, where the Himalayas are, is so high that if the Pyrenees were piled upon the Alps, the Himalayas would tower above both by 4,000 feet.

Below the snowy peaks of Kashmir in the north, down on the plains of central and southern India, the heat at times reaches 130 degrees in the shade, exceeding that of almost any other place on earth.

We learn about the life of Mahatma Gandhi from Shri Annasahbe Sahasrabudhe, who was with the renowned leader for the last twenty years of Mr. Gandhi's life and has intimate knowledge about him. Sahasrabudhe, who had been imprisoned with Mr. Gandhi, also literally walked over India with the great man as Mr. Gandhi directed the land to its national identity and independence. Bengali poet Rabindranath Tagore bestowed the title Mahatma or "great soul" on Mr. Gandhi. I am touched by the personal insight offered us by Shri Sahasrabudhe.

Indian grammar, law, architecture, sculpture, painting, music and arts, such as metal casting, enamel work, jewelry design, precious stone cutting, ivory and wood carving, all are highly developed, as are the sciences and mathematics.

To better understand the culture, we are studying significant beliefs, learning how animals are held sacred and play a part in Indian religions. Other elements of nature can also have significance. The peepul tree, for instance, is still held sacred today, as the tree under which Buddha sat to find enlightenment, although some legends say that it was a fig tree.

A few days ago, we joined an official from the National Museum on Janpath, New Delhi, to adjourn to the dark, cool basement auditorium where we watched slides of national art treasures. Unlike our own treasure housed in temperature-controlled buildings, India's art works mainly remain scattered about the country where they were carved and painted. We were told that in centuries past, the greatest artists and sculptors were blinded or maimed, after completing their work, to insure the originality and avoid duplication.

"How could they?" was all that I could ask, stunned by such waste.

*   *   *

As days follow each other, we jiggle and bounce to and from the University, the bus horn blowing repeatedly to make a path through masses of people walking in the streets, surrounded by lorries (trucks), other vehicles and animals. Buffalo and goats wander freely and feed on anything that catches their eye. Bicycles pass with several people clinging to them, pedal carts also have riders hanging on, and flatbeds are pushed along, piled high with sticks, wood, pots, pans, whatever needs to be moved.

The delightful aromas of many Indian spices, most of which I'd not known—ginger, turmeric, peppers, fenugreek seeds, tamarind, mustard, dhanna jeera—add to the exotic fragrance that is so rich, pungent, and uplifting to mind and body. The beauty is that the seasonings are available, freshly ground and extremely inexpensive, so that everyone uses them daily in varying combinations for taste and for enhancing appetites. The salvation for counteracting the ever-present stench of urine in the streets is to pass shops bursting with the aroma of roasting coriander and cumin seeds, along with cinnamon, cloves, nutmeg, and cardamom being ground together to become *garam masala*.

*   *   *

Archaeologists reveal human activity here as far back as 400,000 to 200,000 BC. A long period of slow evolution resulted finally in the spectacular Indus Valley civilization in 2400 BC. Remains of small agricultural sites and isolated villages were found in the lower Sind and in the Baluchistan Hills, centuries ago rich in rivers but now a waterless desert.

The urban Harappa Culture centers in two cities in the Mohenjo Dara and Harappas that runs from the Arabian Sea north to the Himalayan foothills and east to New Delhi. It shows evidence of advanced civic planning and organization, with strict uniformity of features such as weights and measures, size of fire-hardened bricks and architectural plans of cities. These well-fortified citadels had buildings that rose as high as five stories.

Archaeologists' findings show that Harappa houses had indoor baths and privies connected by drains and water chutes. Sewers ran beneath the main streets, with openings allowing city inspectors to enter. The people grew cotton, wheat, barley, peas and sesame. Artisans, working in silver and gold as well as carnelian, a grayish yellow agate that changes to an orange-red color after baking in a kiln, turned them into exquisite jewelry and sold it in the areas of the Persian Gulf region.

From that era also comes India's gift, perhaps most valued by the world, the domestic fowl. Ornithologists agree that all domestic fowl descended from the Indian jungle fowl—larger than a fully-grown parrot and splendidly colored in yellow, blue, red and green. Archaeologists have found Indus Valley carnelian in Mesopotamian tombs.

Archaeologists were confounded at Mohenjo Dara when they discovered a curious decline had taken place. Mansions had become tenements; large rooms were divided into small ones. Streets were no longer maintained. Artifacts and pottery, once delicate and colorful, were now produced from plain clay. In the span of a thousand years, the Indus Valley Civilization disappeared. Whatever happened, indications were that the downfall had come suddenly and violently.

Much of the civilization of China and Japan originated in India, we are learning. The language of the early Hindus was Sanskrit, which scholars such as Max Mueller called the most artistic in the world. This language ceased being spoken three hundred years before the birth of Christ. Its best thoughts have, however, crystallized into magnificent literature whose epic poems are the "bible" of the Orient: *The Mahabharata*, an epic poem of 10,000 verses describing the great battle between the Pandavas and the Kurukstra, not far from modern New Delhi; and the *Ramayana*, concerning Rama's realm. Rama was the seventh incarnation of Vishnu, the god of preservation. The "Reg Veda," part of the Mahabharata, is the oldest of the Vedic works that form the basis of Hindu thought.

Western explorers discovered India and America practically at the same time. For ages, other countries and conquerors looked on India with longing eyes. Alexander The Great, the great Mughals, and Great Britain were among many who saw this as a land of wealth, the object of the world's cupidity for centuries.

With this skeletal understanding of the nation, we Americans are to go out to face the situation as we find it.

Dr. Prekash, our professor, turned to a topic not entirely popular when he said that Europe, as it became more modern, has regarded India with great disdain. The attitudes toward India have been so indifferent as to be reprehensible. Indian friends are well aware of this. As one said to me, "India became on one hand a spiritual refuge for European intellectuals, who came here to escape their materialistic European lifestyles—and, on the other hand, a land to be commercialized and exploited."

British historians of the 18th century, fascinated by the rise and fall of dynasties and empires claimed that India was considerably enriched by the British Raj rule. Indian historians believe the glorious period of India's history occurred before the British came. European scholars had as their classic background the ancient Greek civilization where they felt the greatest achievements were made. Hence, the British measured India's achievements and found them wanting, compared to the Greeks. The idea of assessing the civilization on its own merits came much later.

European scholars of Sanskrit realized with some surprise that Sanskrit is related in structure and possibly in sound to Greek and Latin. That ultimately led to the theory of a common language, for after all India had grown as a flower when Greece was but a seed.

CHAPTER 6
A YOUNG HERO

Life in Delhi has brought us more adventures, and the latest one involved Dennis. I was typing at our desk this afternoon, when the door rattled. The thick mahogany doors of this old hotel are quite soundproof. Opening the door, I found Dennis standing there, wearing his wet swimsuit, his shoulders quivering,

"A little boy…." he stammered.

"What is it? What has happened?" I said, putting my arm around him and drawing him inside the room.

"He was lying on the bottom of the pool…." Dennis stopped to catch his breath. I brought a towel from the bathroom, draped it around his shoulders and sat by him on the sofa while he told me about the last hour's events.

"I thought he was playing at first. He had been down there a little while, I don't know how long. Suddenly I realized he wasn't moving. I dove down and took hold of his arm and pulled him up. When I got him to the edge of the pool, I called for help. Several people looked, but no one moved. Then I screamed. A man jumped out of his seat. We got the boy onto the apron of the pool and both worked on him till he revived."

For a time we sat in silence, our separate thoughts unspoken. "It would've taken only a few more minutes— and it would have been too late, right, Mom?"

"Yes, son, just a few more seconds, perhaps," I said.

He compressed his lips. It was Dennis's first life-threatening situation. I put my hand on his arm, and we hugged each other for a brief minute. "He'll be all right. He's a lucky boy to have had you act so quickly. I am proud of you. Now, let's have something to drink."

I took a Coke out of the refrigerator and was pouring it when the phone rang. It was the hotel manager, asking about Dennis and commending his part in the rescue.

"He is fine, thank you," I said. "Yes, I am glad. The little boy was French, you say? Thanks for calling. Goodbye."

Dennis was lying across the bed. The door opened, and Mark, Winnie and Connie came in. "Hey, Dennis, we've got to get ready to go," the girls said.

In a happy flurry, the teen-agers changed clothes, combed their hair and rushed out to meet their new friends for an evening and dinner. Mark rose from his chair and, reaching out with his hand tapped Dennis on the shoulders as he went by. "Good man!" he said.

"Better finish dressing, Doll, the night lies ahead of us," Mark told me. While I applied my makeup, he read aloud the names of the guest list for the reception we would attend in the evening. The names were Indian and difficult to pronounce.

As in Latin, the "a" sounds like "ah," while "i" is pronounced "e." and "e" is our "a" sound. We repeated the names.

Our nights here have been as filled as our days, a change for us, coming from a quiet suburb in Florida. We have been here only a matter of days. I have not been able to overcome the jet lag, am wide awake at midnight and sleepy at noontime.

*   *   *

Weeping mourners filled the streets yesterday. It was the morning of the memorial service for Jawaharlal Nehru, Prime Minister and Hindu political leader of India. Our first official duty was to attend the memorial service.

Mr. Nehru had brought the country into a democracy following independence from Great Britain. He was and is greatly loved. It is felt by many that he would have been more effective as a benevolent dictator, because India's problems are so great.

The service, in the Cathedral Church of the Redemption, was filled to capacity with leaders from around the world, Indian dignitaries, families and friends, and the diplomatic community was well represented. Brigadier S. J. Mukand read the beautiful poem, "Wisdom of Solomon."

"We took our fill of the paths of lawlessness and destruction.
And we journeyed through trackless deserts,
But the way of the Lord we knew not.
What did our arrogance profit us?
And what good have riches and vaunting brought us?
Those things all passed away as a shadow,
And as a message that runneth by;
As a ship passing through the billowy water,
Whereof, when it is gone by,
There is no trace to be found,
Neither pathway of its keel in the billows,
Or as when a bird flieth through the air
No token of her passage is found,
But the light wind, lashed with the stroke of her pinions,
And rent asunder with the violent rush of the moving wings,
Is passed through,
And afterwards no sign of her coming is found therein;
Or as when an arrow is shot at a mark,
The air disparted closeth upon again immediately,
So we also as soon as we were born, ceased to be:
And of virtue we had no sign to show,
But in our wickedness we were utterly consumed.
Because the hope of the ungodly man is a chaff carried by the wind,

And as foam vanishing before a tempest;
And is scattered as smoke is scattered by the wind,
And passeth by as the remembrance of a guest that tarrieth by a day.
But the righteous live forever,
And in the Lord is their reward,
And the care for them with the Most High.
Therefore shall they receive the crown of royal dignity?
And the diadem of beauty from the Lord's hand;
Because with his right hand shall he cover them.
And with his arm shall he shield them."

These age-old words appeared to console, give comfort and peace to the people who are so saddened by their loss.

CHAPTER 7
"WILL WONDERS NEVER CEASE?"

An urgent message for me was delivered to our suite today. I assumed it was from the Embassy. It did not mince words. "Be at Room 1502 of the International at 3 p.m." It was signed "Helga"— a young woman I have met only once, at an Embassy reception upon our arrival here. About 25 years old, she had impressed me as a very serious young American with a terribly serious young husband.

The Sikh doorman was standing at attention as I arrived at the entrance of the International Hotel. His lifetime growth of hair was bound and held tightly beneath his turban. His uniform was of crisp white cotton with a red and green cummerbund.

I felt conspicuously out of place going into the hotel alone. My husband and I have been in India only two weeks. His time has been spent in meeting officials and travels about the country, while I've taken over the chores of meeting Embassy people and Indians.

I did not know what the message meant, but I thought this was probably a showing of saris or jewels arranged by the hotel. I was not prepared to make any purchases, but consoled myself for this indulgence of looking. After all, I want to get acquainted with the community of Embassy people.

As I walked down the corridors, the thick carpet muffled the sounds of my steps. I stopped at room 1502, but no sound could be heard from inside. Perhaps I was early, I thought, as I tapped on the door.

The man who opened it was of slight build and shorter than me, with a dark complexion and green eyes. He said, "Mrs. Stepworth, come in please." I walked inside.

A taller man, more American in looks, stepped up and said, "I am Paul Caraway. Mrs. Stepworth, we are glad to see you."

"Yes," I said. "We met at one of the receptions."

The others in the room introduced themselves, but I didn't really hear a word that was said, as I wondered what I was doing here. Two of the men sat on a chartreuse couch. They pointed to a blue velour chair for me.

I wondered where the women were. There was no sign that it was a reception or display of any kind. A table separated us. Mr. Caraway asked me if we were settled and if I liked what I have seen of New Delhi. I listened and said everything was fine.

"Oh, yes, you are the Floridian who sails and plays golf," Green Eyes said.

"There's not much chance for sailing or golfing in India, I've been told, not where we will be." I replied. That subject was dropped.

"Mr. Parprath is with Interpol," said the man with dark hair and eyes.

"Interpol?" I exclaimed. "Goodness! What could I have done in two weeks' time to get involved with Interpol? Does my husband know about this? I don't like the idea of keeping anything from him."

"I'm afraid not," said Green Eyes. "We need your cooperation in this matter, not his."

I looked around. "Where is Mrs. Harper? Aren't there any ladies coming?"

"No, just you. You must be an adventurous lady to have agreed to living in remote areas of India. Have we drawn an incorrect conclusion?"

"Well, I never really thought of myself in that light. I am intrigued by the prospect of seeing India. I understand we will be near Rudyard

Kipling's area. Kipling's books and E. M. Forester's *Passage* got me started on this dream," I said, trying to make sense of my interest in the country.

"What would the world be without dreamers," Mr. Caraway said.

I found this conversation incredible, and asked again, "I am to talk with Interpol alone?"

"You are talking to Interpol now," he said. "In this case, it is absolutely necessary. There is a vast ring of jewel thieves and precious jewels have been stolen. We think you will be able to help us. You will understand more as time passes. Go about your life here, as you would do normally. We wanted you to know who would be contacting you if it became necessary."

Still puzzled, I told him I thought Interpol existed to find terrorists and the like, rather than being involved in jewel thefts.

"You are correct, but one thing can lead to another," he said.

After a little more conversation about the jewel thefts, he said, "This meeting must be kept strictly confidential. I will be in touch. Thank you for coming."

I rose and walked out of the hotel with questions and thoughts tumbling over and over in my mind. What is going on? I wondered. Why has this been added to my "plate"? We have enough just to assimilate our own tasks. It seemed this land was already living up to its image of adventure, intrigue and mystery that it had in my long-ago dreams.

*   *   *

It has been several days since since my strange encounter with Interpol. Mark is away again for a day or two. Yesterday, I received another invitation from Helga— this time, to have dinner with a group of people and spend a night in the hotel.

"It is a new and gorgeous hotel with a great chef. The next day, have a sauna, a body wrap, your nails and hair done. You can sleep as late as you want to, bring a book. Doesn't this seem inviting after having the children under foot and your husband at home all the time?"

I didn't tell her that my husband was out of town. I do have good servants; the children are quite capable of me being away for the night.

"Will you be present for dinner?"

"No, but my husband will join you," she said.

I called the embassy security information department and asked if they knew the couple. After a brief time when I heard papers shuffling and steps, the embassy official came back and said, "Yes, he is a successful American businessman." I thought best not to tell him of my meeting and the conversation about the jewel thefts. It is to be a secret and I don't know if I should talk or to whom. There is nothing to say at this time. I turned it over in my mind.

Finally, I called Helga back and said, "Let me check with my children's plans, I'll call you." I feel there is no way for me to make a decision without giving it much thought. Am I going to get deeper into something if I go? All I can say is that she is a pushy little thing.

CHAPTER 8
PALACES AND PURDAH

The day arrived last week for our trip to Udaipur, Rajasthan, for a conference bringing together all Americans involved in planning India's agricultural and assistance program. This was our first trip out of the city.

We had been advised of the need to make special arrangements for traveling. Necessities were purchased and packed by staff—extra gasoline, oil and auto parts. Service stations are hundreds of miles apart. We took food and water, supplied by the hotel's kitchen, and we also packed toilet supplies to use for the call of nature.

Don and Bette Michaels took us in their air-conditioned Mercedes. A specialist in wheat, Don came to India eight years ago. He completed an assignment in the development of a new strain of wheat in Mexico for the Ford Foundation. This trip would be an opportunity for us to become acquainted and learn from his experiences, while getting insight on living in the countryside.

Americans usually travel in a convoy because bands of *decoits*, or bandits, roam the isolated areas and many instances of thievery and murder have been reported. However, Don felt secure without the convoy.

Our destination for the first day's drive was Jaipur, 134 miles from New Delhi and located in the desert of Rajasthan.

As we traveled into the desert, the sun fused the sky and desert into a dry, still brilliance. I leaned against the car door, gazing across the barren vista, allowing my mind to wander. This was called the Country of Kings,

I recalled. For centuries it had been ruled over by descendents of warrior princes. Blood, violence and splendor colored the history of this harsh desert. The only living things that I could see were vultures and buzzards circling over something dying.

It was a depressing sight to watch the untold number of vultures everywhere circling, waiting for death to come. Then they swooped down, and, along with predatory animals such as hyenas and dogs, began playing out the circle of survival. They paid little if any attention to us as they were put in harm's way on the road. No one kills anything in India—cows, goats, wild animals or birds. All are sacred.

There was no greenery on the mountains we passed. The stunted trees and bushes were brown and gray. I saw nothing but emptiness on all sides with the exception of dust and dervishes that whirled across the flat brownish-grey landscape of sand and stones. At lunchtime, we were still speeding through the desert.

"Do you see the tree in the distance?" Don said. "We'll stop there and have the few branches to protect us from the sun when we stretch our legs and eat our lunch."

We no sooner got out and opened the trunk than we were covered with black flies, stinging us despite our flailing arms. Each of us grabbed a box lunch and jumped into the car, swatting and shooing them out. In all this commotion, I did not notice the group of Indians approaching. They came and stood by the windows and looked down into the car. Bette lifted a sandwich, but they ignored her. Mark held up a banana. The man walked away, and the woman and child followed him. We may be considered non-touchable, I'm told, or else these people show pride that is stronger than hunger.

From the plains we came upon Jaipur, encircled by rugged hills with fortifications and walls snaking over the contours. Called the "Pink City," it was founded in 1726. The ruler from whom it took its name, Majaraja Jai Singh II, came to the throne at the age of thirteen in the 18th century.

He distinguished himself as a mathematician and astronomer, constructed an observatory here and designed his own instruments.

We walked through the city with its crenellated walls of pink and orange creating a magical effect as the golden sun lowers. Hawa Mahal, meaning home, is called the "Palace of the Wind." With its oriental honeycomb design, it looked like a decorated cake.

Women here wore long skirts in red, magenta and daffodil yellow that swirled about them as they walked. "Each skirt takes from ten to twenty-five yards of material to make. Aren't they graceful?" Bette said.

*   *   *

Our reservations were at the Rambagh Palace, home of one of the Maharajahs. Gravel crunched beneath the tires as we drove through the garden, bordered in jasmine, frangipani, roses, poinsettias and *baku,* which has white star-shaped blossoms with a strong fragrance. Peafowl strutted and fanned the manicured lawn with their tails, rustling their quills to our admiration as we watched them at close range. Surely the peahens saw them, but they were coy and continued to peck at the grass. Green doves, yellow and blue parakeets flitted about. The fresh air smelled sweet.

At dinner, the waiters wore gold cummerbunds and handsome turbans with starched, white muslin fans attached to the scarlet and gold crowns. Wearing white gloves, they served us from silver trays onto silver dishes and poured water into silver goblets. We ate steaming dishes of curry with piquant chutney and spiced vegetables. For dessert there was a nutty cream covered with thin, fragile layers of silver foil, all edible. We dipped our fingers in silver bowls, as we have come to expect in India's fine restaurants. We adjourned to the veranda for a picture-taking session as we viewed the mauve and blue hills in the distance before nightfall.

The sounds of crickets and birds calling to their mates were our lullaby as we went to sleep.

The cries of peacocks woke us early the next morning. Although we would have relished another hour of sleep, there was much ahead of us, and all was forgiven when we were brought the dark, cocoa-like Indian tea laced with rich milk and *gur*, dark, raw sugar. Our breakfast consisted of a heart-of-wheat cereal with honey, cream, almonds flavored with a touch of cardamom.

*   *   *

Back in the car, we drove another two hours to reach Ajmer, "City of Jewels."

"Jewels," I thought suddenly. "My gosh, I forgot to call Helga. Oh well, it doesn't matter now. This is what I have waited to see."

We were in a familiar territory for the Michaels, who had lived in Jaipur and Ajmer. Offering to show us their "hometowns," Bette said, "We lived here for eight years, so we do feel an attachment."

We followed her over a cobblestone path winding between yellowed square stone buildings surrounded by a lackluster garden, obviously needing water. Coming to a gate, we entered and climbed a few stone steps to a veranda with its own garden. The small sign offered an insight into what we would find; Bhuramal Rajmal Surana, Manufacturing Jewelers.

"This jeweler and goldsmith created the official gift for the Queen of England and for Mrs. John F. Kennedy, commemorating their visits to India," said Bette.

From this remark, I expected to see something quite splendid. When we entered, we found a simple, unadorned shop with a few wall hangings.

"Remember, I'm here just to look," I whispered.

All of us were warmly welcomed. Bette, who loves jewelry, had studied stones while they lived here. A cloth was spread on the table in front of us. A young man served us Coca-Colas. A large wooden tray was set on the table, with an array of star rubies, diamonds, opals, jade, garnets, and pearls lying on the black velvet cloth.

"I must confer on our budget," I said. "Are these precious stones?" Looking at them, I decided I could not resist a champagne topaz.

Bette told me that the cost of some of the semi-precious stones would surprise me, and, in fact, the jeweler asked the equivalent of thirty dollars. They took my ring size and said the ring would be mailed to me. I bought rings for my daughters, too—small garnet and jade stones surrounded by diamond chips, at a very attractive price. The clerk was as gracious as though I had spent much more.

We then visited shops selling cloth for saris and skirts and enjoyed the delicious aromas of spices in other nearby shops.

Ajmer has long been a point of pilgrimage for Moslems. The artificial lake rises past a vast embankment between two hills, called Anasagar. The scene was such an inspiration to Mughal Emperors that they subsequently embellished their landscapes with gardens, long parapets, and reflecting lakes and pools whenever they put up a special building. .

After looking at Ajmer's ancient temples, we sat in the shade in silence, reflecting on the exotic beauty. "In this land, anything that you can prove, the reverse may be proven, poverty, beauty, wealth, sorrow and peace," I thought.

A great emperor of the Middle Ages, Akbar, came to mind as we visited this area. Born in 1542, Akbar ascended to the throne at the age of thirteen with uncanny skill. He ruled the middle of India, two-thirds of the country, and won over the proud Rajas who controlled this desert. He blended India's Moghuls, Persians and Armenians, and the result was even to integrate the harems in the households of wealthy men who had several wives. Harems previously had been segregated by religion.

Emperor Akbar was a liberal leader making changes that raised Hindus to be on a par with Moslems, and he virtually became the whole country's religious leader. Although unschooled, he had an intellectual curiosity and surrounded himself with scholars. He became a genius at conciliation. It was an ethnic beehive that Akbar walked into in 1556, when the Moslems were a minority in the midst of the Hindus. It was said that he hypnotized the Hindus and the Moslems and welcomed the Christians. At a time when nationalism was unknown, he welded the heroic clans of Rajputans, the bearded, strong-bodied Sikhs, and the Jains. The Jains are believers that life is so sacred that they wear gauze over their mouths so as not to injure a gnat that might fly in, as it might be a reincarnation of a loved one.

*   *   *

"Do you think India will keep afloat?" Mark asked Don, thinking about India's past struggles, its fight for independence and its present need to survive so people can have a better life.

"It is a battle with time. India has been described as a 'functioning anarchy.' If that is true, it probably functioned best after the establishment of the British Raj in 1858. We are needed here, our programs, our know-how and money. What they will do with it after we do our work here and leave is yet to be seen," said Don.

"Our programs depend upon a distribution of water, not only for people but also for irrigation. We need a network of canals and deep wells and that will take time. We must face the reality of an uncertain water supply."

Magnificent carvings and fabulous statuary adorn the many Hindu temples built centuries ago throughout the country.

CHAPTER 9
THE LAKE PALACE

After hours of driving through the desert from Ajmer, we saw a fantastic city ahead. We entered Udaipur, called the "Venice of the East." Named for Maharana Udai Singh, who founded the city in the 16th century, Udaipur has many palaces and temples, beautiful, extravagant and some whimsical. As it sits on a lake, water is plentiful. Soon, we arrived in front of a palace that stands on the crest of a ridge overlooking Lake Pichola.

Glistening white in the distance was Jag Nivas, now called the Lake Palace. Sitting like a floating mirage in the center of the steel-blue water, this palace is the work of the designer of the Taj Mahal, Shah Jahan. We took a launch and soon reached the island ramp, where we climbed steps leading to the three-story building of yellow sandstone. Surrounding the palace was an emerald garden where mynah birds, parrots and parakeets fluttered and perched in lacy shrubs among brilliant flowers.

We entered a room decorated with arabesque stones and splendid in every aspect. In our suite, paintings of beautiful maidens, cavorting erotically, covered the ceiling. The maidens' breasts, full and luxuriant, their waists small and extending into well-rounded hips and buttocks, were voluptuous and suggestive, creating a longing for intimacy. The colors ranged from blazing red to delicate lavender, pink, yellow and green. Some of the bed frames were made of crystal.

A further romantic addition was the swing in the large bay window. A gold-colored chain was attached to the seat piled with silk and velvet pillows in red and gold colors. Legendary beauties had swung there— among them, the ruler Hymayan's wife, the fourteen-year-old Hamedu. Others had been Muntaz Mahal, wife of Shah Jahan, and lovely Hermian, called "the fairest of all flesh on earth," whose death had led to the first and most terrible battle Sack of Chitor.

            *   *   *

Throughout the next days, this impressive building has been the setting for the meeting of the American specialists from many fields. Along with Mark, the soil scientist/agronomist, there were economists, bankers, credit specialists, administrators, environmentalists, engineers and management professionals.

Together, the group wrestled daily with the problems of India's hunger. The term "Green Revolution" was coined at this meeting. Discussions dealt with food production and irrigation. We heard the shocking report that a world famine will begin in Africa and move through South America and continue through India unless plans can be formulated and action taken to halt it.

The weight of the responsibility showed on Mark, and in the evenings after his day's work was done, I held him close. "I only ask that you not worry about it now," I told him. "Let's enjoy this place."

Meanwhile, in New Delhi, the newspaper headlines screamed for more industry, even as reports went back to the government on what was transpiring at this conference.

The exploding population is called "the most significant terrestrial event of the past million millennia." Every week there are one-and-a-half million additional mouths to feed on earth. If the rains do not come soon here, we will be in the midst of starvation and death.

For centuries fathers have passed their fortunes, skills, and knowledge to their sons. Now, to feed the millions in India, the hoe must be replaced by modern equipment, and the fields need more than a wooden plow and bullock.

Mark's plan is to use a package of programs including the finest seeds, fertilizer, irrigation and pesticides—and to ensure training so the programs may be extended from the district level to the farmers, and from the university, through the students, to the farmers.

*   *   *

At dusk, we joined friends for a walk on the stone ramparts that led to minarets overlooking the water. We watched the rare birds feeding their young. They showed no fear, as they have never been threatened. Indians stand by their resolve to kill no living creature, regardless of being on the brink of starvation themselves. Exceptions are Moslems and Sikhs. Dr. Singh, Mark's Indian counterpart, is a Sikh and wants his sons to learn to eat meat. He marvels at Mark's stamina, which he sees as related to a diet including meat.

In the beautiful Lake Palace, everything surrounding us represented the Indian culture, with one exception—the classical music, Bach, Beethoven and Mozart, that was piped throughout the building.

"It was brought here by an American with duty-free privileges that were at that time unlimited," Don told us. "He rented large amounts of farmland, hired peasants to work under his supervision and then imported all the stereos, refrigerators, and automobiles he could afford."

"That is the reason we are strictly limited now to what we can use personally," Don said. "Those days are over."

*   *   *

It was a beautiful dawn yesterday. Mark and I sat on the balcony overlooking the lake and discussed plans for the day. The other ladies and I were going to visit the city ruled by the Maharani of this foremost Rajput State. The Rajputans as a group are clannish, we are told.

Our trip included a visit to the City Palace and tea. The Maharani was in Paris, so an official hostess gave us a tour of the palace. We passed the

Zenana quarters, where the women of the palace live. We couldn't see them, although they could watch us. They dress in *purdah*, totally covered in *bourkas*, except for their eyes. When they travel outside their quarters they are in curtained vehicles. The Maharani dresses in the latest fashions when she is in Europe and is included on the list of the ten most beautiful women in the world.

*   *   *

Finally, the business meetings ended— and with them, our exotic interlude. We returned to the real world as we headed out across the desert, back toward New Delhi. After several days away, I was looking forward to seeing our children. This was the first time I had been away from them for this long.

In the long hours as we traveled though the desert, our conversation turned to many topics. With encouragement, I reminisced and talked about the family farm in Alabama.

When I was a very small child, we lived three miles from the nearest town. There were no neighbors nearby. I had time to think, and I wondered about the world and what my place would be. At night on the farm when there was only the blanket of stars overhead, I felt small and insignificant. Yet when the next day came, I felt strong and capable of doing many things, as my parents encouraged me to do.

I told Don and Bette about how I had grown up as a 4-H member, which required that the members have projects. At age 11, I began raising thoroughbred pigs, cattle and poultry. A Duroc pig, which was given to me, was the beginning of larger projects. When I sold some grown hogs, I could afford to buy White Faced Hereford steers, and after raising them, I bought white leghorn chickens.

I had taken great satisfaction from these projects throughout high school, and the experience created an interest in economic development and planning. In 4-H, we were meant to make a profit, so record keeping was important. I had been invited around the country to talk to civic organizations, encouraging their interest in supporting farm children in similar projects and the promotion of sound farm practices. The Governor's wife, who was responsible for some of my travels, had encouraged me in important ways.

"You are the farmer," said Bette, smiling as she listened. "I thought Mark was teasing, but it's true."

I laughed, but then confessed that my life hasn't centered entirely on farming. In fact, I have had many interests, from music to theatre. I had spent a few years as assistant to the cultural director and auditorium manager of a "Big Ten" university in Ohio, where we offered varied programs to students, faculty and citizens. That was among my favorite jobs— and, in a way, I think, also good preparation for some of the responsibilities in our present activities abroad.

The 16th-century Lake Palace in Udaipur, Rajastan, appeared as a floating mirage in the center of a lake. It was designed by Shah Jahan, who also designed the Taj Mahal.

Chapter 10
COMMUNIST SPIES?

Upon our return to the hotel yesterday, the doorman, splendid in his turban, matching cummerbund and starched, spotlessly white uniform, greeted us like returning family. Khaki-dressed bearers streamed indoors with luggage and a water cooler, while another offered us glasses of *nimbupani* served on a tray.

We hurried up the circular stairs, eager to see our youngsters. When the door opens, they were all accounted for, except the youngest.

"Where is John?" I asked. With a sad look, Connie said, "John is in bed with fever. He became ill two days ago. I gave him cool packs and all the fluid that he could take. I didn't want to frighten you and I hoped he would be well right away."

I put my arms around her and we both sat on his bed, where I kissed John's cheek.

"The bug again? I'll call the doctor."

Soon afterwards, a diminutive woman wearing a sari came through the door. Introducing herself to us, she donned a white coat. Her stethoscope and thermometer were in her bag. Her fingers, as tiny as a child's, probed and measured glands.

"I'll need a specimen for the laboratory," she said. "You can send it by my bearer who accompanied me. I will return tomorrow. At the moment I would say your little boy's symptoms are standard for stomach problems. However, he complained of a neck ache. I think you will see improvement by tomorrow when he can take some soft food. In a day or two he will be his normal self."

I was worried about the neck ache, which I knew could mean something more serious. I didn't want to dwell on that fear. The doctor talked with John, though, and he responded.

I thanked her, and as she was preparing to leave, I said, "Are there many lady doctors?"

"Oh, yes." She turned her head first to one side, then to the other, which I had learned was the Indian's version of our nod for the affirmative.

"We have women obstetricians, gynecologists and pediatricians—women are in every field of medicine." Pausing, she held her head down in thought, then continued. "Our people are very peculiar, you might say superstitious, totally unaccustomed to your ways. In New Delhi there is only one male obstetrician. Women are shy, and the husband won't allow another man to see his wife. Midwifery has always been our way to have births and follow-up treatment. Now, modern Indian women want women physicians."

Shortly after the doctor left, my friend, Dorothy, the Ambassador's wife, came in. This family has become our friends. Like us, they attend The Cathedral of the Holy Redeemer, and we all live in the same hotel.

"Mary, Pamela is very sick and we are worried. This is the fourth time she has had these high fevers since we arrived," said Dorothy, looking very concerned.

Pamela is a beautiful, Dresden-like child, slightly younger than John. "We have taken every precaution. The same thing could happen to your John," Dorothy said.

"It has. He was running a temperature while we were away. Do you think our water is contaminated?" I asked, alarmed. The glass bottles appear in the refrigerator daily, a chore of the man responsible for the rooms.

Dorothy replied with a question. "You do know that there is a large Communist element in this country?"

I could not fathom why the Communists would have an interest in us. "I suppose it could discourage us from wanting to subject our families to life here," I said finally. "If you are continually sick in the best hotel, what will life be like elsewhere?"

"What better way to stop our husbands' work?" Dorothy reasoned. "Anyway, my husband has ordered our intelligence to look into it. Look, my dear, don't drink another sip of that water or let your family drink it. Not until you treat it with these." She reached in her purse and brought out a container and poured a number of pills in my hand. "Let it dissolve and stand for twenty minutes at least."

Thinking about Dorothy's concern, I realized our period of adjustment to India had sealed our friendship. But there was something else I needed to do. I called a car and walked back upstairs. Mark would not be home for a week, and I had to act on my decision. This last occurrence was scary. What were we to do? I had been expecting this life to be educational and interesting, with the exception of some discomforts—but life threatening? No!

I was driven to the Embassy, where I raced up the broad steps and through the glass doors, to stop at the information desk attended by an Indian girl. Two Marine guards, in full uniform, stood looking at a manual to my left. Their presence had a calming effect.

I asked to see the Housing Officer, and after a brief phone call, I was directed into his office. He invited me to sit down and waited politely to hear what my errand was. I described my son's illnesses, and I said we need a place to live where I can control the food preparation, especially the water we drink.

"Housing is very scarce in New Delhi, very expensive. We will do our best," he promised. "In the meantime, we will bring you a hotplate for boiling water."

Next, I went to Mark's office and told his senior officer about my fears. As my story unfolded, I watched him rotate one thumb around the other while his hands lay in his lap. When I had finished, he looked at me directly and said, "I will relay this message to our officials. Do what you must."

He had spoken very calmly. He rose, came around the desk and took both my hands in his. I walked out the door, thinking about how safe I'd felt until this turn of events.

I appreciated the directness of the Housing Officer's promise and felt confident he would see his orders were carried out. Sure enough, a small table, electric hot plate, a kettle, hot pads arrived at our suite the same afternoon.

*   *   *

I have taken no chances after that frightening experience with John. Beginning that day, and on each morning for a week, I boiled kettles of water in the dressing room, which was already cramped by a refrigerator. I took precautions to sterilize the bottles and cool them, before placing them into the refrigerator.

John has recovered, his crimson cheeks paled to a normal shade, his blue eyes have brightened and he once again meets his friends by the pool daily. His friendship grows with the small girl whose fate paralleled his own.

*   *   *

Early this morning, as I sat in our hotel room with my morning tea, I wrote on a borrowed typewriter. I was pondering the Hindus' belief that the world has been here for hundreds of millions of years, but the time will come when it cannot be maintained and must be destroyed. Another world of the same material will be created to take its place, they say.

Mark, entering the room, broke into this thought.

"Sorry to interrupt, Doll, but we are on an errand and wonder if you would like to join us. I want you to meet someone. Al Rafiq Kahn, may I present my wife, Mrs. Stepworth." (We are never called by our first names here unless the person speaking with us is a friend.)

A young man dressed in white work uniform stepped forward, placed his hands together and bowed slightly. "Salaam, Memsahibji."

I was pleased, as I had been told we would have an interpreter and driver. His broad smile showed white teeth. He was handsome with black hair, a strand of which fell over his forehead; he pushed it back in place. There was neither a look of arrogance nor one of servility about him.

"You have a surprisingly accurate American accent," Mark commented.

"I have been with the American Embassy for four years. I see the movies sometimes. All of it helps me," the young man said.

"I didn't know there was a theater here," I said, surprised.

"Memsahibji, it is no theater. A screen is set up on the lawn, and chairs are brought out a couple of nights a week before the monsoons come."

We learned that Rafiq grew up in the palace of the Nawab, the prince of Ripal. His father held the position of chief *shikar*, or guide, an authority on hunting. This is an honored position in his culture, as Moslems eat meat. Rafiq was educated with the children of the Nawab and Begium. He speaks several of the fifteen major languages and some of the four hundred dialects of this country, as well as English, Arabic, French and Persian.

Besides, we discovered, he is reputed to be the best *shikar* that can be found. We will be the envy of others. Soon, he is going to take us on a hunt.

"Do you expect us to have trouble finding meat?" I asked.

"No, where there are animals you would kill it. Sahib tells me that you are a good shot."

"I haven't picked up a gun for years," I admitted. "But I grew up on a farm, and we all knew how to shoot. We had tin cans placed on a wall and would practice shooting, especially on holidays. My mother is accurate with a rifle. I hunt with my grandfather, father, and brothers. We hunt birds, quail that are plentiful there."

"Only you and Sahib will be hunting. If there is meat, you two will have to kill it, as I am not allowed to hunt," said Rafiq.

Beef is outlawed in all of India. However, as Americans, we have licenses and government permits that will allow us to hunt game within certain areas of the jungle around the town where we will soon be going. There is a limit on each type of large animal and also on birds.

Chapter 11
NEW HOUSEHOLD MEMBERS

Now, things are changing again. We have left the hotel and moved into an apartment on Birbal Road. With the Housing Office clerk's help, we now have a modern stove, fueled by butane, and a refrigerator crowded into the postage-stamp-sized kitchen. The apartment is on the first floor. In Indian houses, thanks to British culture's effect, the first floor is called the ground floor, and what to us would be the second floor is called the first floor.

American friends moving to Turkey have bequeathed us three servants and an ash-blonde Alsatian dog named Gillie. Our newly inherited cook, called "Joe," arrived with a packet of credentials. He has been with numerous families. He is short and exudes strength. He wears a saucer-sized handlebar mustache, his salt-and-pepper hair curls on his neck, and gold studs are in each ear lobe.

We greet Joe with "Salaam" as he is Moslem. Another Moslem servant, named Seit, boils our water.

It is difficult to communicate when the only statement ever made by Joe is, "OK Madam, please." He does speak English but obviously does not think much of talking to women. When I come in the kitchen to see how the meal is progressing, he gives me an absolute scowl. When I talk about the meal, he doesn't answer me. I say, "We must have this or that, please." I get the usual brief retort or no reply.

It has taken a few days to get our phone installed. We are grateful to have one, as phones are difficult to get. The Embassy made all the arrangements.

Once again, we do not discuss our business on the phone because of the likelihood of a tap being put on it.

We also do not leave important papers out on tables, in case there are curious eyes around. Spies abound, from several countries. We've been told to protect any information about our work or personal business. The Chinese Communists forced their way across the northeast frontier in 1963, threatening India.

*   *   *

Joe, without informing us, has set up a "pecking order" for family members: first Mark ("Sahibji"), John, and Dennis, then the girls and I follow. I have learned from friends that in the majority of Indian homes, women do the cooking and all of the work. If Mark is present, I get second place.

Joe's enthusiasm for his job varies by the calendar, too—the nearer to payday, the more attention he gives Mark. This all came to a head yesterday, when he served Mark's entire breakfast before even serving the rest of us a beverage.

Goughram is our second servant. We have nicknamed him "Gomer," for he reminds us of the television character, Gomer Pyle. He squats all day long, waddling about with his straw broom or scrub brush. Squatting is the position Indians commonly use while working. He seems to pay no attention to any of us. Dennis, observing this, is making a special effort to give him attention.

Goughram is of the sweeper caste, so he cleans the bathroom, floors, porch and yard. He is not allowed to touch anything we eat from, nor the table we eat on nor the seats of the chairs. He cannot wash our dishes or touch our beds. I occasionally hear Joe yell at him, but never hear a word in return. The other day I went to Joe and asked, "Why do you yell at Goughram?"

"He is the sweeper, Memsabji, I am the cook." With that remark Joe turned and left the room. The kitchen is his domain and he makes it known.

The servants' families live in villages and so far they have not mentioned visiting them.

We have a gardener who clips the grass with shears. I am told he sells it for fodder to herdsmen who own cows.

Our *darsey* comes and takes the boys' measurements to make shorts and shirts for them. He owns a Singer sewing machine that has no legs. It is placed on the floor on a cloth spread out large enough for him and his material. He uses his toe on the left foot to slide the cloth through, leaving both hands free, one to turn the wheel for propelling the action, the other to pull the material.

Our clothes are washed by our *dhobi* who comes daily and takes the many changes, washes and irons them and returns them before sunset

> *   *   *

At night we all gather in the living room to discuss our day.

"Where are the 'holy cows'? All I see on the streets are either water buffalos or scrawny cows," Dennis remarked last night.

"The big bulls are more scarce," Mark said. "You may have seen one of those. They are called free bulls. They are the big, rangy, muscular ones and are allowed to go around unimpeded—or free ranging. We will see them more on holy days. People paint their horns and hang leis around their necks."

"What are we eating for meat?" Connie wants to know.

I told her it was undercut, the filet from the water buffalo, which is available in the market.

"I wish you hadn't told her," said Winnie.

"It doesn't have the flavor of our beef, but it is protein," I said.

Dennis had gone to visit a *chowk*, a market square with shops bordering it. He elaborated on the way people bargained over everything, and described the unusual sights he had seen.

"I saw a little girl with lovely curly hair collecting fresh cow dung in a pan. She must have been no more than five years old. I hear they sell it—for fertilizer maybe? Then there was a woman cleaning out the gutter of excrement. She would empty this into a container, put it on her head and dump it into a larger container, and a man lifted it onto a cart. Ugh! I felt like I was going to be ill and began walking towards home."

"Please, Dennis, not at the table!" Winnie said. "That almost made me sick to my stomach."

"We're not at the table," Dennis replied.

"You could have been," Winnie snapped back.

"Okay, now, enough!" Mark said.

He told them, "The people you are talking about are the untouchables. No one except people of their caste goes near them. Imagine how we would feel if people would not come near us. How demeaned we would feel."

Dennis had the last word. "Cleaning those troughs would make me feel like an animal instead of a human being."

CHAPTER 12
A BUBBLING VOLCANO OF RACES AND RELIGIONS

We have become so immersed in this culture; it seems hard to believe we were in America only a matter of weeks ago. I still attend classes at the New Delhi campus, learning more of the country's past and present.

India's history is as fascinating to us as her geography. One cannot escape the vast influence of religion in this society. Almost every step one takes every glance one makes fills the eye and ears with the rhythm and heartbeat of this culture. This land is the cradle of the two most widespread religions of humanity—Hinduism and Buddhism. Hinduism boasts thirty centuries of existence, while Buddhism was ten centuries old even before Great Britain emerged from barbarism.

The beginning of the Indus civilization has been fixed in the middle of the third millennium B.C. There were Paleolithic and Neolithic people here many centuries before Christ. Several different races arrived in waves, one after the other, to settle India— from the darkest Negritos to the lighter-skinned Nordics, who arrived last.

The conquering Aryans, descendants of the Nordics, who arrived around 1500 B.C., made slaves of the Dravidians, a mix of the darker races, in the Gangetic Plains. The Dravidians fled south where they, in turn, enslaved the Aborigines. Brown Aryans, black Dravidians, and blacker Aborigines—there lay the roots for establishing the caste system.

We have studied India's history, cultural heritage, sociology, caste and economics with several professors. In legend and religion, from Purusha's breath came the Brahmans, the priestly caste, they told us. From his arms came the warriors, or Kshatriyas; from his thighs, the Vaisyas (agriculturists and traders); and from his feet, the servile caste, the Sudras. Each caste can identify which caste other individuals belong to, by the names, the work and appearance.

Many factors played important roles in the creation of this unique system. Small groups and tribes were divided from each other by mountains, rivers, jungles and deserts as well as social barriers, restricted marriages and dietary habits. But by 1500 BC, Central Asia was the home of "new people."

The Aryans, which means "noble ones," swept in and rang the death knell for the Indus Valley Civilization. The acts of the Aryan invaders were anything but noble. These nomads ravaged the country and ended a civilization far more advanced than their own. They worshipped Soma, a cult god of fire and war. Soma was also a potion considered a sacred drink, used at ceremonial times when sacrifices were made to the gods. It is believed to be the first mind-expanding hallucinogen. The Aryans were seen to be rude meat-eaters and drinkers. Their habits were very different from the present-day Indians.

Customs changed over time and ritual triumphed over the sword; the Brahmin priesthood gained an ascendancy over the Kshatriya rulers and established its caste supremacy.

Meanwhile a third system, the Vaisya, developed, and then the Sudra, a completely new caste. Diet restrictions were associated with ideas about purity and pollution. The dangers of internal "pollution" were already evident in the status assigned to children. When the father was of higher status than the mother, they retained the status of the father. If the mother married into a lower caste, she was defiled by her low-born mate.

Below the four castes is a fifth, the "untouchables," who have no caste advantages or benefits. Members of each of the four castes lead the lives set down for them, with their own situation, occupations and inherited benefits. The "untouchables" have none of these privileges. Their very presence is seen as defiling and they perform the most menial jobs.

The caste structure was related to complex theories about the universe and the nature of man, and profound philosophies developed in a country that was divided into numberless kingdoms, principalities and chieftainships large and small.

Indications of caste are often clear even to us. We have learned that if a man wears a sacred thread looped around one shoulder, he belongs to a Hindu high caste. The Parsees, who came to India from Persia centuries ago, also wear the thread. They are often wealthy businessmen and merchants.

Ideas infiltrated from various Brahmin centers of learning into the different peoples and tribes—each with its own ancient traditions, customs and religious beliefs that account for the diversity of the Hindu caste system.

A bitter opposition to reform, which resulted in the martyrdom of Gandhi and other leaders since his time, is deeply rooted in beliefs that have withstood alike the assaults of the Aryan nature worship, of Islam and of Christianity—now under attack itself here.

By the end of the fourth century BC, estimates set the population at 181 million. India became a bubbling, human volcano—throwing off streams of human lava. For thousands of years, a movement of migrants continued—all different kinds: white, black and yellow races. Rather than acting as a blending machine for the races, the government refused to meld. Instead, the people lived side by side, staunchly living out their customs and beliefs. Today, India has over 900 million inhabitants.

*   *   *

One of the younger religions of the world is Sikhism, founded in the 16th century by Nanak, a native of the Indian state of Punjab. His parents were Hindus. He constantly associated with Muslims and felt there must be a True Name for God different from Brahma, Allah, Vishnu, Shiva, etc. One day while in the forest he had a vision of "the one God whose name is True" and began to preach on the theme that if men follow the True Name, they would cease to be divided. He taught that man has been ordained by God to be served by the lower creation. Nanak condemned idolatry, but accepted reincarnation and the Law of Karma. He did away with taboos against eating meat, and he taught that one True Name predestined all creatures, clearly a Muslim teaching.

The first four teachers who succeeded Nanak as the leader of Sikhism followed his pacifism and quiet philosophies. In the 16th century, however, the emperor Jahaingar was determined to constrain the Sikhs by force. The resulting warfare led to the Sikhs becoming a more militant religion. Their leader added a war cry, a Baptism of the Sword, militant chants and an honorific title.

*   *   *

Other changes have come to India over the ages. Buddhism is now a relatively minor factor here, yet when it was founded twenty-five centuries ago it was a revolt against the tyranny of Hinduism. At first it superseded the old religion, but Hinduism rose again and finally drove Buddhism out. Today India's major religion is Hinduism, with Moslems, Buddhists, Jews, Parsees, and Christians insignificant. Christians make up only about two percent of the population.

Day by day, I listen and observe. It occurs to me that Buddhism and Christianity are outcasts from the lands where they originated—India and Judea. The Indian religions and their ceremonies attract all ages to explore, experience, and reach for the divine. Young people of the West are coming in droves to study the Eastern religions.

The Indians' profundity, their apparent knowledge of things human and divine, their maturity, dignity, and sensitivity leave me filled with wonder. In the midst of staggering poverty, filth and conditions that seem humanly impossible to check or correct, they demonstrate a personal peace, tranquility and patience with each other.

How this can happen, with living conditions that would appear to put an enormous strain and frustration on the vast sea of people, is beyond my explanation. We Westerners rarely, if ever, broach this subject to each other, indicating that we spend little if any time thinking about it—or else believe it to be unfathomable.

"Perhaps there will come a time when we better understand the culture," I said to Mark one evening. He only shrugged his shoulders.

CHAPTER 13
THE AMERICAN
INTERNATIONAL SCHOOL

The three older children are now enrolled in the American International School in New Delhi, a different experience from their schools back home. About a quarter of the teachers are internationals, as are the pupils. Foundations finance it, along with private corporations operating in the country and the U.S.

We are very proud of the school. A grand white house stands beside it, now used as a hostel for the school children that are boarders. Children over nine years old whose parents do not work in New Delhi live there; some pupils are from Burma, Ceylon (Sri Lanka), Pakistan, India, and France.

We had given much thought to the education that our children would receive. I had talked with the staff of the India Desk at the State Department numerous times with questions before we left home.

With the three older ones there, it leaves me to teach John. The school ordered a home study course from the University of Maryland—the Calvert's system of study. It has been the method of teaching children the world over who will return to an American curriculum later.

Not all foreign children attend the American International School. Our children have become friends with children who go to the two outstanding mission schools—the Anglican Church schools in Srinagar, a city in

Kashmir, far to the north at the foot of the Himalayas. It is a long drive from Rawalpindi, Afghanistan, where some of the families live who send their children to Srinagar to school. The road runs through red rock gorges that catch echoes from the river below. It is a cold place, Kashmir. Many want to get their education there to escape the heat of the plains. It is understandable that the British have always sent their children there, as did the Anglo-Indians. Thank heavens our school in New Delhi is air-conditioned.

In the mountain school, the curriculum is strictly British. I am told three reviews a year are given for each child on body, mind, and soul. Gymnastics is important, counting 400 points, with English and math, 100 points each. The grades are given in order of importance. Pluck and unselfishness count 300 points. Sports grades are not given for excellence of performance, but to those who try the hardest. Four honor boards award special honors, and this year, we heard, one award went for pluck and endurance, three to youths who risked their lives for others and another was posthumous, to a boy who drowned while saving his brother.

*   *   *

Going by grades and reports, our children are doing well in many ways. Besides their normal enthusiasm to see and experience this country, they have entered into the spirit of our mission.

Wanting to perform some service, they learned of a need for help that would frighten most American parents at the mention of it. It did not stop the parents or children here from pursuing the project. They built simple stone houses for lepers. Every Saturday morning, Connie and several other children gathered to accompany supervising adults to the project. Not only did this give the lepers a home that they needed badly, but also the children appeared to be pleased.

"They are truly the forgotten ones, Mother," Connie said, having just returned one day. She and the others have witnessed sights that are truly unforgettable.

          *   *   *

My new friend Goshen says to make a friend is to know happiness. If that is true, I have great happiness in my life, as I have made many friends here.

Outstanding among them is Marge, who has taken me under her wing with concern and experience. The wife of an American official—my husband's senior officer—Marge is a professional educator, married after working many years in her field. Her husband is cousin to our nation's vice president. Her twinkling brown eyes, graying hair and the smile on her face give a sense of confidence and peace.

She organized the first school for American children living in New Delhi, which later became the American International School. Until then, the children had been taught by wives and mothers, some without proper credentials, in a garage of one of the homes. The Ambassador declared that the American children deserve the best possible education, and finally the new school was built. Then he sent a representative to the U.S. to find the best teachers available.

Marge worked with the organization from its earliest beginnings. Meanwhile, in her spare time at home, she was learning Hindustani from her cook. She in turn taught him English by writing a sentence each morning on her kitchen blackboard.

Marge has taught me to use Indian recipes that she's collected using local products. There is a small commissary in the American compound that brings over a small selection of canned foods, bottled items and supplies for young mothers and girls. All vegetables and rice must come from the local market.

I have added dozens of wonderful recipes to my collection since we came to India. Among them is Mulligatawny Soup*. It is my favorite soup, which we first tasted at the splendid Ashok Hotel on Panchaheel Marg in New Delhi. Mulligatawny is a Tamil word, and one might deduce that the dish originated in the Madras region 100 to 300 years ago. It is a great favorite with the British and meat-eating Indians. *(See recipes at the end)*

Another friend who has special meaning to me is the wife of our American Ambassador, Chester Bowles. She demonstrates all that a Foreign Service wife should exemplify—service, kindness, patience, firmness, and leadership.

These qualities help her to bridge the distance between the East and West. She wears a common, thin, white cotton sari with a blue border, the same kind worn by the peasant woman who repairs the streets, and the same as that worn by Mother Teresa.

CHAPTER 14
QUTAB MINAR AND THE RED FORT

John has returned to his normal enthusiastic self after his recent illness, and he has been excited about our promise of a family outing. Today, the big day began with him up first. His enthusiasm came under attack by his "sibs," who wanted to sleep later, and it all ended up in a pillow toss. We rallied, finished breakfast and dressed. We crowded ourselves into two mini-Ambassador taxis that rumbled up to take us to the seven cities of Delhi. The drivers were bearded, turbaned Sidars, or Sikhs, wearing pajamas that originated in India.

Soon, we reached the ancient cities that stand between the sacred Jumna and an outcrop of the Aravalli Hills on the Delhi plains. Indian families with their lovely dresses and saris were walking around, full of curiosity about us as we are about them. We explored the crumbled walls of Indraprastha that had been built in the 10th century B.C. and Lal Kot, dating to the 11th century B.C. We saw ruins of the Siri, Tughlakabad, Jahnpannas and Firuzahad, built in the 1300's A.D.; Dinepannah, from the 16th century, and 17th-century Shajahanabad, crumbled now but with parts still standing. Old Delhi and, now, New Delhi, followed all these.

From here, we went to appraise an architectural Wonder of the World, or what would be known as one if it were outside of India. Outside Delhi, we found the Qutab Minar complex. Qutab Minar is a

234-foot-tall marble and sandstone tower, with its first three stories of red sandstone, and fourth and fifth stories of marble and yellow sandstone. It is thought to be the world's most perfect specimen of ancient Afghan tower architecture. It dates to the era after the Third Kingdom was defeated. Qutab-ud-din began the construction in 1193, and his successor, Feroz Shah Tughlag, completed it, rebuilt the top story and added a cupola.

At the tower's foot stands the first mosque to be built in India. The Might of Islam Mosque was built on the foundation of an old Hindu temple.

Merchants sell their wares along the roadside here, where dust rises with any movement. Bushes and flowers are covered in the dust, but it does not appear to interfere with the sale of papayas, bananas, mangoes, squash, tomatoes and cucumbers. The vegetable *wallas*, wearing flimsy pajamas, squat on their haunches, awaiting a sale to some of the prospective buyers that stream by.

As we approached the Qutab Minar, we could see the red soil of the grounds, topped with loose sand. We noticed a crowd gathered on one side and went to investigate. A *walla* squatted by a basket where a cobra lay coiled. The man held the leash of a sleek, burnished mongoose with one hand, allowing enough rope so that the animal could antagonize the reptile. It responded by rising, spreading its hood and, as fast as lightning, striking at the alert animal. The mongoose strained, muscles undulated. The creatures faked and struck again.

Excitement rose amongst the crowd; bets were made and *annas*, coins worth about a tenth of a cent, hit the dust encouraging the walla. The cobra was no match for the mongoose. Sensing that the owner was preventing an outright attack, the mongoose wearied of the fight and the snake coiled itself.

The owner extracted a rat from a nearby sack. He pulled the mongoose's leash and allowed the rat and the mongoose to face each other. When the rat was released, in a flash, the mongoose nabbed the rat with a vigorous whip-like snap, and the rodent lay dead. The reward for the cobra was the rat, which slithered down the snake's gullet. The crowd dispersed. The walla's child hurriedly gathered the tiny pieces of change from the dust.

Rats are sacred to the Indians, although they carry diseases. When our government agency offered to pay for eradicating each rat that was caught, Indians captured rats, put them in cages, took the pay and released the rats on the other side of the river.

We moved on to the Iron Pillar, a twenty-four-foot black shaft of solid iron standing at the base of the tower. A Hindu king, Chandra Varman, erected it in the fifth century. A six-line Sanskrit inscription indicates it was built outside a Vishnu temple and raised in memory of the Gupta King Chandragupta Vikramaditya, who ruled from 375 to 413 AD.

A challenge is to stand with your back to the shaft and put your arms around the pillar so that your fingers touch. They never do, to our knowledge, but if you can do it, you are to have good luck!

We walked on to the tomb of the Tughlagh king who built the city of Delhi. Amid the flowering trees and pleasant scene, people wandered, examining relics. We did not notice that John had wandered off, until suddenly there was a yell.

We recognized John's voice. He was frantically trying to escape from a family of monkeys pursuing him.

The monkeys' leader screeched. We began yelling, as did others, and waving handkerchiefs, purses and hats. We finally captured the attention of the male monkey, the apparent leader, and they all scampered away after him.

"Do you allow monkeys to run free?" Mark asked an Indian standing nearby.

"Yes, it is our way. Monkeys are sacred to us," he said.

"But doesn't anyone ever get hurt?" John wanted to know.

"Maybe. These were bad monkeys," the Indian admitted. "But killing a monkey or anything that is living is unthinkable. To the Jains, one of the many religious groups, even a gnat might be the reincarnation of the soul of a friend or relative. You see them there." He pointed to several Indians wearing cloths over their noses and mouths.

We all listened as he went on. "We have a beautiful temple in Hanuman at the top of Jakko Hill in Simla," he said. "Hamuman was the leader of the monkeys. One legend has it that Hamuman saved a prince's life. In the jungle we see the langur monkeys. They are slender with long tails. The *chetal* (deer) stay near them on the ground while the langur monkey eats leaves, nuts and fruit from the treetops and warns the deer of danger. The monkey has piercing black eyes and looks very intently at the surroundings. Every animal depends on others for its existence."

India also has many legends about a parrot who laid down his life to save his friends, the other birds and animals of the jungle. When he made a futile attempt to quench a forest fire with the drops of water that he had collected on his wings and scattered, he perished from exhaustion.

We thanked our new Indian acquaintance, and said our goodbyes.

*   *   *

Our next stop was the Red Fort, a site we have looked forward to visiting. The Red Fort, lying between Old Delhi and the River Jumna, is named thus because it is a copy of a massive red sandstone wall built for Shah Jahan's grandfather at Agra. The fort was the hub of the Shah's empire, where he received reports of the life and work of his subjects from departments of government, dispatches arrived from provincial governors and replies were made. Intimate details were recorded on the activities of the emperor and his chief nobles. From bleedings that had been administered to dreams that had been dreamed, all were brought out and recorded in this open court.

Since there are no metal screens, the windows are covered with delicate, lacy relief work carved in white marble. In long-ago times, the ladies of the court sat behind the marble screens and watched the *durbar*, a procession, on either side of the three-tiered marble gallery in which Shah Jahan sat.

Even today, it takes little imagination to hear the orchestra booming and to see the *nautch* girls dancing, slapping their bare feet on the marble floor while attendants sprinkle perfumed water on the throng. The girls

are being served betel leaves, a stimulant. The smell of musk and amber-
gris fills the nostrils. Princes and noblemen march by, placing right palms
to their foreheads and bowing their heads out of respect to the Shah.
When the formalities begin, there is strict silence as the performance and
pageantry get under way. Shah Jahan sits on his famous peacock throne
that he had commissioned to be built on his accession. A pearl-fringed
canopy held up by twelve emerald pillars that surmount the throne. At the
top are two peacocks on either side of a tree set with rubies, diamonds,
emeralds and pearls. This triumph of the artisans' talents, mellow with
graven gold, is encrusted with diamonds, rubies, emeralds and sapphires.

As we wandered around the Red Fort where the Shah once reigned, I
wished the jewel-encrusted throne, which long ago disappeared, were still
here for 20th century visitors like us to see.

Qutab Minar, outside Delhi, dates back to the onset of Moslem rule. The five-story tower of red sandstone and marble was started in 1193 celebrating the defeat of the last Hindu Kingdom. An iron pillar in a courtyard of the complex was there long before the mosque's construction. The iron is of such purity that it has not rusted in the 2000 years that it has stood. A Sanskrit inscription indicates that it was initally erected outside a Vishnu temple.

CHAPTER 15
MONSOON

The long awaited monsoon has come to New Delhi in a form I did not expect. We were playing golf at the Delhi Golf and Country Club a few days ago, when suddenly a black curtain of dust moved towards us like an impenetrable gray screen had descended from the heavens. Following this was a torrent of wind that came across the horizon to engulf us.

"Grab the towel," my caddy called.

He took the other end of it, and with our heads down we ran to escape the dust. I didn't know what direction the clubhouse was and would have been lost, had it not been for the caddy, for I was blinded by the dust and couldn't see three feet ahead of me.

The dust that comes at the beginning the monsoon blows off the Rajasthan Desert. Finally, sheets of rain arrive and daily pound the dust, turning it to brownish-gray mud. The mud slides into ditches, where the water washes the human excreta along with it, as it pours through the *nullas*. These man-made canals run through the neighborhoods and empty into the rivers.

Enormous concrete sewer pipes have been placed about the city and are used for housing. If not used yet for culverts, they await the untold numbers of street people searching for a dry place to stay. Families move into these government-owned open-ended, dual-purpose pipes. Their little fires appear inside the dry edges night and morning, to warm their thin bodies and cook their food.

Death comes more frequently to the weak and the aged during the monsoon. Pneumonia, tuberculosis and fever, diseases waste the already weakened bodies. There is never any indication that exposure to germs gives immunity. People die in unknown numbers.

A doctor at All-India Medical Centers told us that record keeping is impossible. Virtually all the dead are cremated. He told me that the cremation, for an adult, takes three hours, and for a child, one hour.

"The red cloth you see is used to wrap bodies of young, unmarried girls," said the doctor. "The white cloth is the cover for older people. Gandhiji preached that to eliminate disease we must burn all personal belongings, not even keeping the hemp string-wrapped *charpoi*. But the people are too poor to burn possessions now."

*   *   *

Mark is away from home for a week. Last night, I was sitting at my desk writing after the children went to bed. There was a knock at the door. I asked who it was, through the door, and a voice said, "It is Goughram, Memsabji."

The servants have quarters attached to our house and bordering the alley. Goughram never comes after the dinner has been served and the kitchen floor swept. When I opened the door, to my surprise Goughram indeed was standing there. His hair had been freshly cut and was neatly combed, his shirt pressed.

"He is a nice looking young man," I thought for the first time. He is always sitting in the corner of the kitchen on his haunches with his head lowered except when working or if I entered the kitchen, when he stands up. I had not given any thought to his looks or age.

I assumed he spoke no English, and I greeted him with "Namaste." Behind him stood an older man, a sage, wearing a white Gandhi cap and a spotless *dhoti*, a cloth that reached his ankles, with a Nehru jacket over that.

"Good evening, Madam," the stranger said. "I am Rampat, here to speak for Goughram." His English was flawless. "Goughram hired me to speak for him about a matter of utmost importance."

I motioned to a chair but they remained standing, Rampat holding his hat in his hand.

"Goughram is distressed at the events that have transpired in your household. He is prepared to go with you to the police."

"Police? What is going on? Tell me!"

"Madam, we are here to tell you that your servant whom you call Joe is a thief. Every day he fills a bag with your stores; soap, sugar, tea, powdered milk and oil for cooking. And, he threw your meat in the dirt of the alley, and the dogs ate it."

I thought of our anticipation of a dinner of pork chops. An American friend, who worked at the Alligarh University, where our agricultural program under way sponsors a piggery project, had brought this meat to us. It is a great rarity as no pork is ever on the market. Our friend had brought a ham and chops, and none of it had been prepared for our meals.

Yesterday, I had noticed that the staples had dwindled. When I asked Joe, he said, "I make cookies, cakes, bread, they go." I had not argued.

I thanked Goughram. "Say nothing to Joe. We won't go to the police. Here, take these four rupees," I told him. From that time on I relied more on Goughram as I have seen that he is honest and dependable. Joe doesn't like this, but I ignore his scowl.

Today, I called the Embassy and asked that a carpenter come to place a lock on the pantry door to secure it. Nothing was ever mentioned to Joe. From now on, I must ladle the food out each day, which is a nuisance, but it can not be helped.

CHAPTER 16
THE MADMAN OF BUSTAR

For a time, a startling headline in the papers has overshadowed all the controversy concerning the economy and government policies. "THE MADMAN OF BUSTAR CUTS OFF THE HAND OF A THIEF. The Maharaja of Bustar in Orissa State had cut off the right hand...." the newspaper story began.

"My grandfather would have used him for tiger bait. He had no sympathy for a thief," the Maharaja is reported to have said.

The Maharaja's act not only bespeaks the onerous agony of losing a limb, it represents something that goes much deeper than physical pain. To every caste it has a special meaning. If a man found guilty of stealing has this punishment carried out, he will never again be allowed to come to the family circle to eat from the common bowl. The people eat with their fingertips of their right hand, gathering the rice in a ball and lifting it to their mouths.

The custom is to always use the right hand for eating and the left hand for personal hygiene, or for labor, but never for eating. It is a realistic custom, because there is no toilet paper for the millions. Instead, they carry a small container to scoop up water and pour on themselves. My servants save and sell every can emptied in our kitchen.

*   *   *

Yesterday, Rafiq and I rode down Link Road, a major thoroughfare of New Delhi that leads to residential sections. Smoke curled from behind a high gray wall along the road. I had seen bodies being carried on top of a charpoi,as they processed down the narrow street with family and friends following. Rafiq had not commented, taking for granted that I knew what they were and where they were being taken.

I had not made the connection between what I was seeing—obviously corpses—and the evidence of fires. Finally, I asked, pointing to the columns of smoke swirling high above the wall, "What are those?"

"They are called *ghats*, or raised places," Rafiq said. "This is the crematorium. The ghats, which are bed-size concrete slabs, are lined up in rows inside. The bodies are placed on wood, then more wood is piled on top. The oldest son applies fragrant oil as he walks around the body seven times, sprinkling it with the fuel."

*   *   *

Today, despite the searing heat, I took a taxi down to Cannaught Circus to meet my friend Bette, who promised to walk with me through the shopping center. Whoever arrived first would look for the other in the lobby of the hotel. The weather is its usual 117 degrees, and one is always looking for a cool and comfortable place to stop. I learned early to prepare a bottle of boiled water and freeze it for each of us to take with us on any outing. I looked around, window-shopping, while waiting for Bette.

"Pardon me," said a man standing in the doorway of a nearby jewelry store. "Do you live at Claridges Hotel?" When I looked at his face, I did not recognize him and turned back to the display.

He spoke again, "I recognize you from the description given me by my cousin who works there. He says your son saved a boy's life."

"Yes, that's true." The news of the incident at the hotel pool had apparently reached farther through Delhi than I had thought.

"Would you honor my store by coming inside?"

"It is very kind of you, but no, thanks," I replied. "I am not in the market for jewelry today. I am waiting for a friend who will be along soon."

"I will not think of your waiting outside. If you choose to, you can look from the inside, or perhaps I can show you my office."

Looking around, I saw several young ladies in lovely saris working at the counter. It was obviously a popular shop.

"We'll tell your friend when she arrives," the man assured me.

Inside, there were cases of carved ivory, necklaces of jade and pearls strung with pear-shaped droplets, sparkling displays of diamonds, rubies, and sapphires. He led me slowly across the room to his office, furnished in walnut and leather. It was obvious he was very proud of it.

"Coca-Cola!" He clapped his hands, and within minutes, a young man appeared with a tray holding a Coke and a glass.

"We have many Americans, British and Europeans coming to our store," said the shopkeeper. "This business has been in my family for several generations. You must come back and meet my wife and family. I have two sons and two daughters. I would like for my sons to study in America."

"Unfortunately, we won't be in New Delhi very long. We will be moving on. But this has been a most interesting time," I told him, as I saw Bette approaching and rise to meet her. I introduced her to the friendly merchant, before we departed.

Leaving the cool building, we walked in the direction of Cannaught Circus, the hub of the business district, where all streets converge like spokes of a wheel. We wove in and out of the crowd, passing Tibetan stalls where baubles, trinkets and treasures intermingle.

"Memsahib, see, buy!" Hands reached out, offering objects of all descriptions as the vendors followed us along. One stone, egg-shaped and opaque, combining midnight black, forest green, earth brown and azure, caught my eye.

"That's a worry-stone," Bette told me. "It is held in the palm of the hand and rubbed between the fingers. Indians contend that doing this will make anxiety disappear. Come on, you have many choices."

The bargaining that goes on here is fascinating. Customers make a ridiculous offer, far below what I imagine the asking price to be, and the merchant refuses, acts indignant and makes a counter-offer. This goes back and forth until each feels he or she is getting a bargain.

"A person capable of hard bargaining is much respected," said Bette.

We looked at an amazing selection of wares, and I decided on a pair of earrings. We continued making our way through the crowd.

"Baksheesh, baksheesh (alms)," the little beggar women cried. One held out a child with twisted, deformed limbs and withered skin. It was heart-rending to see the pitiful child, almost devoid of flesh, and held in a dirty rag serving as a blanket. I reached for my coin purse.

"Keep moving," Bette urged. "The woman might have maimed the child so that it will forever be a beggar as she is. If you give her anything, you will be surrounded," she warned me. "It encourages begging."

Nevertheless, I pulled a rupee note out of my bag and shoved it into the woman's hand, then shook my head and plunged into the crowd that was now more demanding, insistently pleading.

"Nay, nay," Bette spoke up to the beggars. We pushed ourselves through the mass that had gathered, holding out their hands and trying to look in my bag.

"You can't do that, no matter how much you want to," Bette reminded me as we hurried along.

I realized more than ever what children mean to so many of the parents, who actually use them to make a living. For these, children are their social security, their retirement benefit—only something to be used as their parents used them themselves.

Finally, we reached a store and escaped indoors. While outside the throng milled and moved like a turbulent river, inside the cloth shop were row after row of shelves and tables holding elegant materials. The Indian women were dressed in fine saris made of the sheerest silk. They scrutinized each piece of the delicate silk or linen. Chubby tots, eyes blackened with tar, held onto mothers' skirts or sat eating sweets.

We threaded our way to the cotton material for Bette, who does the sewing for her daughter. Having learned to look for flaws before buying, she spent an inordinate amount of time examining every inch of the material.

"Do you think your driver has arrived with the car?" I asked finally. I was tired and by now disinterested. The heat and odors of heady perfumes were becoming tiresome.

She looked at her watch. "He was only to be gone briefly."

I walked outside and spotted the driver leaning against the fender. He opened the door and I sat down on the rear seat. I opened the pages of the *New York Herald Tribune* I had picked up in our mail at the Embassy.

"May I speak with you, madam?" quietly asked a man who stood by the car window. A clean-shaven, middle-aged Indian, he had bluish-black skin and very black hair under a white Nehru cap.

"Yes?" I couldn't refuse to reply, he was so courteous.

"Excuse me, please, you will be leaving New Delhi soon?" he asked.

I raised my hands with the palms towards him. "I do not want my fortune told, thank you. No!" I turned to my paper

Undeterred, he said, "You are the last of four children, two brothers and one sister. You bore three children, one girl and two boys."

I lowered my paper and looked at him in surprise, but I could not recall having seen him before.

"In the future you will encounter many obstacles," he went on. "Do not give in to them. Move steadily, but very gently ahead. If you do this, life will flow from problem to solution. Gather strength from those you will meet. You will find them to be in many colors and by many names. They will sustain you as its tributaries strengthen a mighty river."

Lowering my head, I closed my eyes, thinking about the man's words and this strange encounter.

"What are you doing, falling asleep on me?" asked Bette, as she sat down beside me.

"Where is he?" I said.

"Who?"

"A man who was talking to me."

He had simply disappeared. I looked out the rear window, but he was nowhere to be seen.

"He told me a number of things about my life," I told Bette. "I want to give him something."

"There are many men out there, take your pick," she said, smiling.

"Don't tease, I am serious. Honestly, do you think I have had too much heat? I believe Jesus could walk out there and we might miss Him."

I told her about the mysterious conversation, and neither of us could find an answer to explain what the man had known about my family. Could he have been a spy? I became more cautious. If he is a mystic that is one thing, but to have information about me to keep track of me for a reason is entirely different.

We have heard many times that the spiritual elements of life here are explored and given great consideration. Indian people study and meditate upon events that appear mystical, and their thought cannot be compared to our Western ways of thinking.

CHAPTER 17
JUNGLES OF MADHYA PRADESH

It is August, and the monsoon has been dumping rain daily in New Delhi since mid-July. We have been notified that our home is finally complete in Madhya Pradesh, so we will be moving there next month. The state is geographically and culturally isolated from the rest of India. It is located in the part of the country called the Deccan, which lies between the Plains of Hindustan to the north and the Plains of Deccan to the south.

The Deccan remains the most backward and impoverished part of India. Wild, thick jungles surround its villages. This is the area where we will live and work. Although we will travel to other districts, this will be our home.

We will live in Raipur, a town in the southeast. It is located halfway from Shrinigar in the north to Nagercoli, the southernmost city in India. Life there will be far different from the city environment of New Delhi.

Last night, our international friends in New Delhi invited us to their national day festival dinner. Streams of cars made their way through torchlights set up to border the driveway.

The word has passed around the fifty people attending that we are soon going to the "boondocks." As we were being introduced to the guests, others greeted us heartily and with varying reactions. More than once, we heard, "These are the people going off into those dreadful places."

One woman said to me, "Why don't you stay here in New Delhi, darling, and let your husband come to you?"

I heard a man speak up. "Don't worry, you will like what you are going to do. I have been out in the boondocks, as they call it, and find that it is terribly civilized. I understand you will be traveling a great deal. I wish I had more time for it."

He paused, then said, "Forgive me, I did not introduce myself. I am Callan Gruen."

"Mary Stepworth," I replied.

"Yes, our hostess Patricia was telling me about you and your husband. I envy you. I wanted to meet you. As a matter of fact, I came from Bombay for the party tonight hoping you would be here. Surely you are not a stuffy American."

"Stuffy American? That is news to me," I said.

"I find a patina of friendliness and openness, it's true. There are exceptions."

"That is what we say about British and Europeans," I replied. "Let's close the direction the conversation is taking and tell me about yourself."

I recognized his name, as Callan is well known in India. I had been told that he lived here many years as head of a large corporation. He is called "the Last White Raja."

He has fought for the rights of groups to pursue their occupations when they have been threatened. An example is the *dhobi* classes that have washed clothes by the river's edge for generations. The government had planned to fence the river off, but the plan was stopped. Callan has influence. Besides, he has charm, with his blue-green eyes and blond-streaked curly hair, and he listens closely and attentively.

On his lapel, Callan wore a perfectly formed yellow rosebud. He hardly left my side during the evening, with Mark on the other side. Callan served as our interpreter for the program. It was a delightful evening, with lively people talking on many topics. It was my first experience of an Embassy party other than our official receptions.

     *   *   *

As we drive through the city each day, we see multitudes of archetypal images within arm's length. Small women wearing saris sit on the pavement on mats selling bananas, coconuts or vegetables. Each woman has her own vegetable or fruit basket.

Barbers are shaving and cutting the hair of men and boys. In small stalls women pierce ears or noses, placing studs of silver in the holes. Groups of beggars with babies huddle in the shadows, and boys play shell games.

Even though the people are thin and often in dingy clothes, they hold their heads high with dignity. Their posture is so straight, in part because they carry large bundles on their head. Whether it is a bag of sticks, a bundle of clothes or another object, it sits on a ring perched on the top of the head.

The colors of turmeric, orange and red mark the men's faces. The elderly *sadu*, sacred priests who dress in saffron robes, wear markings of saffron and white, while the women wear a red dot on their foreheads to denote that they are Hindus.

When a girl is married, a red line marks the center part in her hair. Women's nails are stained as are their palms and the bottoms of their feet. They wear rings on the nose, and, if wealthy, a cluster of diamonds on one side of the nostril. They are given bangles of gold for their arms and wear a glass bracelet if married and the husband is living. If a woman is widowed, the glass bracelet is broken. Rings are worn on the toes, and bracelets of silver on the ankles. The peasant woman traditionally wears heavy bracelets to keep her from running away from her husband, I am told.

The culture is extremely sensuous. The people's daily lives are filled with intense colors, sounds and smells—all rich, expressive and exciting to experience. The people move around each other, as do the vehicles and animals, in a sort of silent dance, as the flowing saris sway gracefully with the slightest movement.

*   *   *

With all of the beauty, however, there are enormous problems. In these surroundings we cannot expect life to be like ours back home. This country, we are informed, has little notion of public order, common honesty, or sanitation such as our Western society demands.

One of the old customs, *sati* (suttee), the burning of wives on the husband's funeral pyre, has long been outlawed, but I am told that to outlaw a tradition is not easy. Female infanticide, mutilation and torture were prominent in the culture here for centuries. When the British came, long periods of struggle against such enormities invariably brought scorn and dislike of the new rulers. Nevertheless, many English and Indian acquaintances have overcome cultural differences and developed intimate friendships.

CHAPTER 18
TAKING OUR LEAVE

We are already packing our clothes, readying ourselves for our move. Dennis, Connie and Winnie will stay in New Delhi, as boarders at the American International School. We each are responsible for our belongings, except Mark. I am taking care of his, as he is out working in the countryside.

Yesterday, I received a call telling me of an appointment to meet some American wives of our mission. The Minister's wife called for me in her car. The Minister is second in the hierarchy of our diplomatic mission.

While driving, she asked me how I felt about moving so far from the three older children. "Of course, I do not want to be separated from them," I replied. "We discussed this as a family, and we know that our separation is part of the conditions of our work. I am looking forward to seeing them as often as it can be arranged."

We arrived at the yellow stucco house with a broad veranda. A liveried servant was standing by the door. As we entered the room, the hostess greeted us and led us over to a familiar looking woman. I recognized her from pictures although I had not met her before—Madam Vijya Pandit, sister of the late Prime Minister Nehru. She was former Ambassador to Moscow and Washington, Governor of Maraharashtra and Member of Parliament.

Madam Pandit wore a white flowing sari that matched her hair. Chairs were emptied so that my hostess and I could sit beside her. A Delhi resident, she had heard that we would be leaving for the Deccan and would travel about the country.

She told me that it would be good for me to wear a sari, the dress of her country. "In India we simply do not show our legs. Besides, they are very cool in this terrible heat. The heat must be hard on you."

She enjoyed talking about her years and experiences in the United States, and I could hear a kind of yearning in her tone of voice as she spoke of life in New York.

Speaking of the Deccan, she said, "You will find people very kind and hospitable. They are not wise in the ways of city dwellers. I expect you will like them. Come and talk to me about your experiences when you return to New Delhi."

I thanked her for the invitation and told her she'd get a call from me. I expect to keep notes on happenings and what we encounter. I feel greatly honored to have talked with this leader.

*   *   *

The day will soon arrive when Mark and I will leave our children, except John, and the comfortable community of friends we have come to enjoy and our servants whom we have come to rely on and like. We have discussed our needs of foods and supplies to be shipped with us or to be ordered. The order will be sent to Denmark, according to government agreement, and will eventually come to us by ship and goods train. We know that we will have to hunt and kill wild animals in the jungle if we have any fresh meat. To Mark and the boys, meat is a must.

The list of supplies ranges from medicines to food, which has grown to nearly a thousand dollars worth, including canned ham, bacon, coffee, peanut butter, flour, mixes, and jelly, and tuna. We will particularly need cleaning supplies, things that I cannot purchase here.

*   *   *

"Mother, may I have a pet?" John asked several days ago. "Can we get a dog or if not, a cat—or both?" He must be thinking that he will be missing his siblings.

We saw an advertisement in the embassy bulletin for a Siamese cat to be given away. "Let's visit the family and see the cat," I said. We drove up to the house, and a young man answered the door wearing a towel about his waist.

We told him we had come about the ad for the cat, and he invited us in. He was an official of an American bank in New Delhi, but did not appear to be a very friendly sort. When his wife came in, she told us how much the cat meant to them and how they still loved him, even though now they had more on their hands than they could care for. They didn't appear willing to give him to us.

"We'd like to have the cat. However, it appears that you have made up your mind to keep him," Mark said. Finally, they told us we could take him.

Back at our home, we named him Chase after the bank where his master worked. Chase wandered around the house, smelling his way from room to room, becoming acquainted. After a day or two, he tired of this and seemed lonely. Joe, who is in the house all the time, doesn't like cats. We decided that Chase needs something to play with. At the market, there were no balls or cat toys, but we found a pair of brass cats, life size. He loves them and spends his time rubbing against them and purring.

*   *   *

The day has arrived for our departure from New Delhi. This morning, the embassy station wagon crept away from our flat on Birbal Road loaded with bags and boxes.

One of our recent acquisitions is going along with us—Gillie, part Alsatian, part questionable, a gift from American friends who had been transferred to Turkey. Chase, our other newly acquired pet, is traveling in a woven basket. Lazarus, our newly hired cook, will be in charge of her.

I am bringing tranquilizers to be given to the pets once we are in our private compartment. Mark had inquired about bringing the animals and was told that since they would be in our compartment there would be no extra cost.

The railway station swarmed with people. The smells, the dust and the many hundreds of travelers, looking like piles of rags as they sat or lay on the floor, overwhelmed us. They were all thin, gaunt and old looking, even though many of them must be young.

Lazarus was overseeing the bags, and numerous porters were hauling boxes on the train. It was a first-class, air-conditioned compartment of the Grand Trunk Line to Madras. This would be the first leg of our trip. We will disembark in Nagpur and take another train there to Raipur.

Joe, our former cook, who will stay in New Delhi, came to see us off and help load everything into the train. He had Gillie on a leash.

Someone let out a cry, and then others followed. Chase had escaped from the basket. Lazarus looked puzzled. Finally, we spied her. "Gently," said Mark.

Chase was leaping from one side of the platform to the other, over and around people, as Lazarus tried to get to her. Just then the train whistle blew. I was walking toward our car, when I heard a man nearby laughing. I looked around and recognized him— Callan, whom we'd met at the Embassy party a few weeks ago.

"It is not so funny. This is the cat we promised to give the most loving care. If the former owners find out she got lost, they will be enraged," I said. "Oh, I'm sorry, but you can see we are in a bit of tizzy."

Seeing Callan was a surprise, as he lives in Bombay. Apparently, it is a courtesy to see people off and bring a gift, when friends move from post to post. This was our first experience of such a move, and I never expected him to appear like this.

"I have a few good secretaries who got your schedule," he said. "I had to see you off on this adventure. You are rare, you know."

He offered me a long-stemmed yellow rose. "I want you to remember that there are roses in this country. You may forget it where you are going." Callan leaned over and gave me a touch of his lips on each cheek, a custom of the Europeans.

Mark came up and shook his hand, said a few words, and then it was time to go.

"It was nice of him," said Mark as we entered the train car. "I hear that if anyone knows India, it is Callan. A cable just addressed to Callan Gruen, India, will reach him."

The children had been with me all the time. We had talked too little, I now realized, dreading to say goodbye. We hugged each other for a long time and tried to assure each other that we would be fine and be together in a couple of months.

"I'll write very often, and don't forget to answer me," I said to the three older children. They got into the station wagon with the American emblem on it, and we watched them from the window of our compartment as they drove away.

I felt very sad leaving them. It helped somewhat that we had been promised they would have good care. We gave the servants money and said our good-byes to them with sincere thanks.

CHAPTER 19
TRAIN TRIP TO THE UNKNOWN

We are taking the Grand Trunk Line, a splendid railroad, India's best. As the train speeded up, once out of the station, we felt that we would be on schedule, but the idea was short lived.

John and I looked out the window. We passed storage buildings, open shops, and shack-like houses with postage stamp sized gardens. Goats wandered about. Small trees grew by the edge of the crops planted since the monsoons had waterlogged the fields.

A knock came at our compartment door. "Hello, you are Americans?" said a man as he stepped in. He introduced himself as "Mr. Engineer." We had already learned that Indians take the name of their college degree, whatever they majored in.

"Do you mind if I join you for a little chat?" he asked politely.

Mark motioned him to the only seat available, and we introduced ourselves. The man told us he had graduated from Syracuse University in New York. "I am a mechanical engineer with the American Company where I have worked for five years," he said.

Another knock came at the door, and a uniformed man, who told us he was assistant to the conductor, opened it. "Do you own the dog here?" he asked. Gillie was now lying on the floor, drowsy from his pill, and did not stir.

"You did not pay to bring your dog on this trip," said the man. "You owe the railway 95 rupees, and there will be a penalty cost of 20 rupees." The total of 115 rupees ($26.50 U.S.) would be more than most Indians earn in a year.

"I am afraid you are misinformed," said Mark. "I made inquiries from the train supervisor in Delhi and the express people. They both said that since the dog will remain in my compartment there is no charge. Let me speak to the conductor."

"It will do you no good to speak to the conductor. I am carrying out his orders."

At this point, Mr. Engineer spoke up in Hindi. When he stopped and the conductor's assistant left, our new acquaintance translated what he had said to the fellow: "Why are you being so rude to these people? Can't you see that they are not lying? This is the Grand Trunk Line, not a goods train."

Mark said, "If he comes by again, please tell him that if he will cable me from the rail supervisor in Old Delhi, I will pay, but not before." We had been advised to watch for people making demands.

We resumed the conversation about our stay in New Delhi over a pot of tea that had been brought to us.

"I am from Andhra Pradesh State," he said. "You must have heard of the giant dam being built there. When it is completed, this dam will back up the Krishna River into a reservoir of one hundred and ten square miles. We hope to have electricity for homes and industry, and that the land will blossom and be productive."

Mark answered, "Yes, we had heard that this dam is being built inch by inch, with sheer muscle power. Some 125,000 workers swarm over the dam. Women in ceaseless streams carry up pans of mortar on their heads. Using this labor allows the government to spend money on machinery, I understand. Is that true?"

"Yes, it is a fact," said Mr. Engineer. He said he had not traveled extensively over India and was interested in our impression of his country. Few Indians travel great distances from their homes. "Do you like India?"

We both told him we find it to be different and fascinating. "We have been taken to see the Red Fort, Hermian's Tomb, Rajastan Desert—many places," said Mark. I mentioned the market place in Old Delhi and the impressive buildings in New Delhi.

"The fate of our country and the legacy of the British rule here was to leave the task of unifying India to the Indians. That must be our future," said Mr. Engineer.

"I must go and do some review. It has been most interesting speaking with you," he said as he left us.

John and I must have slept, finally.

CHAPTER 20
ON THE TRAIN TO RAIPUR

It was three o'clock in the afternoon when we arrived in Nagpur, in central India. The trip of approximately 1,000 miles from Delhi had taken twenty-two hours. We were in a private room and actually quite comfortable. We made this part of the trip slowly, since there is the possibility of flood damage, washing away railroad ties.

We stepped down from the train, stretched our legs and walked around while our men checked the luggage to be sure that it had all arrived. We were tired and hungry; although we had our cook prepare food for us, it was some time since we had eaten.

We hurried to the restaurant on the second floor of the station. A few men were sitting around the porcelain tables eating food with the fingers of their right hand, in the Indian style. A waiter led us to a table, then left and returned with a white tablecloth. The man who said, "A tablecloth restaurant is one of the great rewards of civilization," would have appreciated the fact that this was the last tablecloth we would see and the last restaurant for many months to come.

The waiter suggested that we order no green chilies, as they are extremely hot. Most Westerners cannot eat them. He served us a platter of rice with mutton curry on top. There was a bowl of curds, along with *puris*, unleavened bread fried in *ghee*, Indian butter. The curry smelled of exotic spices, exploding with heat when it hit my throat.

We have been warned that curry can be tested for hotness in three ways: One, When the heat is felt in one's throat. Two, When beads of perspiration stand on the forehead. Three, when you have the hiccups. This curry was in the first, coolest category.

We had a pot of hot tea, and we practiced teeming the hot tea over the edge before placing the lips on the cup, so as to clean away any bacteria. This was a suggestion coming from our Indian friends.

We thoroughly enjoyed this meal. It takes awhile to become accustomed to the spices, but with good chutney, nothing is better than Indian food. We would have every opportunity to experience it in the next few years.

Outside, Lazarus had found a corner of the platform and fallen asleep. Soon it will be time to get started on the second leg of our trip. We expect to arrive in Raipur tomorrow morning. With luck we will find Rafiq waiting for us.

                    *   *   *

Upon entering the new train car in Nagpur, I looked for pillows and linens. None were to be found. The porter came around before the train left the station and said to Mark, "Sorry, Sahib, no pillows, no linens." Our first class accommodations did not meet any standards for first class known to us.

The travel section of our embassy had ordered this private car, and we had an entire coach. Two long seats ran the length of the car on the sides, one upper and one lower. One of the hinges was loose on the upper seat over my head. When the train gave a jerk, this situation became evident as the seat flapped. I jumped up, thinking it might fall on my head. Mark inspected it but could only shrug, as there was no prospect of it doing anything but rattling for the next two hundred miles.

We three, along with Gillie. were alone in this large car, with no way in, no way out until the train stops, and no service. We were locked in from the outside. Our belongings were stacked in the corner. Gillie was sleeping.

A noise came from the toilet. The seat had slammed shut and the door was slamming back and forth. Mark tried to get it to stay closed— a bad idea, as there was no hook, no lock or handle. The water was sloshing over the sill of the toilet door as the train gathered speed. We looked helplessly at each other.

"I will find someone in to clean this mess up when we stop at a station," he said, but with little enthusiasm. Mark was catching on, as was I.

We lay on the green plastic benches, each on a towel that we had packed. Dark screens covered the windows. The windows were open. It was black dark outside, not a light or lamp to be seen.

The window covering afforded no protection from the black smoke billowing in from the train stack. Each time we went around a curve, the smoke seemed attracted to our open window and came directly in, filling the car. I drifted off to sleep but bolted upright when a puff of smoke came in through the window smelling of oil and coal. The whistle let out a shrill sound. Suddenly I longed for the long, comforting sound of the American train, although it was years since I had ridden one.

Finally, the train began slowing down, the brakes catching. Dim lights could be seen on the boarding platform, and people were waiting. It was still black outside. Mark had the helper open the door, and John stepped down and walked to the platform looking for a porter, a bathroom and a drink. The tea walla was presiding over the boiling tea, and others were selling chappatis. There was no one willing to tackle the job of cleaning the toilet.

Much of the remaining part of the night was spent waiting for sleep. "Doll, are you all right?" Mark asked as he settled on the seat.

He reached out to me, holding a glass. It was a whiskey, or Scotch to us. There is a time for all things, and we decidedly felt we deserved a three a.m. drink. Mark had added some of our remaining water to it. We carefully passed the glass back and forth, each taking a little sip, hoping the result would be that we sleep.

We lay during several stops, listening to commands, chatter, hawking of food and tea, without comment. The train slowly pulled away. Finally the sweat began disappearing from my body.

The desert of the Deccan had slipped by us during the night. We had spent nine hours coming two hundred miles. Gillie rose and stretched, coming out of the tranquil state that she has been in. John kept his eyes focused into the morning haze with his head against the glass window, looking for wild animals. He occasionally glanced at me and gave me a smile. He declared that he had seen a panther. Then he pointed out the five-foot conical shapes that Mark identified as termite hills where the insects nest.

The train began slowing down. The sun broke over the horizon as we pulled into the station. A rosy glow settled in over the whole place. Indian skies have some of the most remarkable colors anywhere on earth, possibly because there is not the pollution that is found in some places.

As we stepped down from the car, Indians surrounded us. They appeared inquisitive about the very tall white man, the tall white woman, and the blond, blue-eyed boy. No doubt the news has circulated through the grapevine.

John pulled Gillie out, and suddenly people began falling over each other giving the dog space. Gillie's sense of power finally overcame her tranquil state. She gave a lusty growl, causing chaos.

John said, "Nay, nay. It's fine. She won't hurt you." It was obvious that they spoke no English. But the people clearly were still frightened and unwilling to be so close to a dog, because there is so much rabies among the wild dogs of India.

Raipur, Madhya Pradesh

1964-65

Chapter 21
GODWANA

At the Raipur station, Rafiq was nowhere to be seen. Mark spotted a bicycle rickshaw over to the side and climbed onto the seat. The little man operating it had a very hard time getting the wheels turning; they kept spinning in place. Mark is a big man. Finally they set off in search of Rafiq. Mark had been through this town before, but not on a rickshaw.

John and I sat on our pile of luggage and supplies, and he held tightly to Gillie's leash. The little Indian boys were hugging their daddies' and mommies' knees, not taking their eyes off Gillie.

For the last two hundred miles of our trip, we had traveled across the state of Madhya Pradesh, meaning Central Province. In an earlier period, princes of the Rajput dynasty and minor chieftains of the Ghone Tribe had ruled it. Even though this state now has a different name, people in the country still refer to it as Godwana.

Before we left America, the person on the India desk of the U. S. State Department had called me daily, trying to describe this remote region of India where we would be living. He'd never been here himself, nor did he have first-hand information.

However, he told me of the isolation and desolation that we would find here, that there are no doctors, no laboratories, no hospitals, no libraries, movies, clubs, shops or pharmacies. There will be no other Americans for many miles.

In my interest in our having this Indian experience, his words registered only faintly. Besides, at the time I had nothing to use as a comparison. I thought about my early childhood, when Mother would prepare food for a sick woman on a nearby farm. Mother took me once and I saw lying on a rumpled bed in a dark, hot room, a woman, her arms like that of a skeleton. It was the waning years of the Depression, and she was starving. Surely it would not be that bad here, I thought.

*   *   *

I remembered, now, how the news of where we were going had been spread around our Florida hometown, and our friends had become worried. Two of them, a doctor's wife and a nurse, decided to do something to help us, and they began collecting samples of antibiotics and other drugs from local doctors. I was given instructions of all kinds: "For upper respiratory infection, 3x daily; if there is no improvement, switch to box 4, or 5, or 6." Assorted instructions were clearly laid out. There were parties and wonderful words of admiration and encouragement from our family and friends.

We took a supply of drugs in our airfreight, and then packed other boxes in the sea freight. Malaria is rampant throughout this part of the country. The American Embassy doctor in New Delhi added to our supplies boxes of quinine and anti-venom, snakebite remedies with syringes. Finally, Mark's physician brother, Stonewall, had said, "We could cure anything that you get. Go in peace."

*   *   *

As I sat on the boxes waiting, I thought about what I had studied about the deities and spirit worship here. I had learned about Khermata, goddess of the earth or the village, and Marhai Devi, the goddess of cholera. There was also Sitala Devi, the goddess of smallpox, Nagdoe, the cobra, and Bjaomsa Sur, the buffalo. Many strange legends came into my mind, were they real? Dulha Deo had been a young bride who was killed by a tiger. Hardaul was a young Rajput prince, poisoned by his brother on the suspicion of loving the brother 's wife, and Bhilat, a deified cowherd.

Whether the legends were real or not, we knew the cobras and vipers were. As Mark had said while we were on the train, "Is it any wonder that American Foreign Service people won't venture out here?"

I had replied, "Let's keep our eyes open and enjoy everything that we can."

We will certainly see much wildlife. We have been told that Madhya Pradesh has large reserves for animals. Kanha Park is a park that is being set aside to protect a unique type of swamp deer, barasingha. There are large herds of chetal (not cheetah, the predatory animal, but a type of deer), nilgai, blackbuck, barking deer, spotted deer and gaur, a kind of true buffalo, along with elk, unlike the kind we know in America. Leopards and hyenas also roam the park.

Another is Shivpuri National Park, en route to New Delhi, near Gwalior. A lake surrounds the forest. It is home to charwsingha, nilgai and other varieties of deer, as well as tigers and leopards. We will be traveling through these areas.

*   *   *

A jeep finally pulled up with Mark and Rafiq, and an onlooker opened the door. I smiled and nodded, and we left the crowd standing looking at us.

"How many people live here?" I wondered as we drove through the streets of Raipur.

"There are thousands; we don't know how many," said Rafiq. There was not many shops open, but some had pushed their accordion doors and grills to the side.

"They call this a city?" I said.

"There are not as many houses as you might expect, since in the extended families here, the parents, grandparents, sons and wives and children live together. People sell their goods on the street, so one does-n't see many businesses. You haven't seen anything until you go to other villages. The masses live in the villages."

We drove onto the Revolutionary Road that took us past two large stucco buildings, the Municipal and District Administrative Office, the largest buildings to be seen. None of the buildings had window or door screens.

Rafiq seemed to read my questioning look. "I think we all want all the freedom we can get. That includes insects, birds and animals," he said.

We turned onto Civil Line Road, and then he pulled off the metalized road as we saw our home for the first time. The house was painted pink!

"Pink!" I exclaimed.

A mosaic of flying white birds took off against the blue sky. The birds swept toward the roof of the curved, fully screened porch. Evergreens had been placed in the garden. It was the most spectacular house I had ever seen in India, and I learned later it had begun with the foundation that was to become a school but there were not enough funds to build it.

A young man in uniform stood by the gate, then two other men ran and stood at attention. They were dressed in sharply pressed clothes and had wonderful smiles showing very white teeth. I love the Indians' white teeth that show attention to them—how, I don't know since I've never seen toothpaste here.

We entered a wide center hall running from the screened porch to the even larger L-shaped back veranda. Everyone was watching for my reaction.

"I love it," I said quickly. Smiles came on the faces of all the servants.

"How does the bedroom lock? I don't see any locks on the doors," I said.

"There is a lock outside. You will have a guard standing outside."

"This is Prem Das, Memsabji," said Rafiq.

"Namaste, Prem Das," I said. He gave me another warm smile, then ran over to open my door.

Standing at attention dressed in khaki shorts and a shirt, both with a razor-sharp crease, knee-length socks and highly shined, military type shoes, was Prem Chan, our number-one servant and chokidar, or guard, who will oversee our other servants except for the cook. We are so pleased to have him on our staff. His hair was shining black and he was obviously in fine physical condition. He had been a paratrooper during World War II with the Indian Army and had been captured in Singapore. Prem Das is his son. Their salaries will be entrusted to Rafiq, who will pay them for services.

                    *   *   *

I am delighted with my new home and thankful to be in it. The exterior looks more like the outside of an elegant resort inn than anything. It is a happy-looking house with artistically inserted swirls of color—sky blue, pea green, mauve, and lavender.

Our five large bedrooms have double windows that have screens. They must be covered with heavy drapes to keep the sunshine and heat out. The drapes will be hung when we get rods for them. Each room has single beds, except ours, which has a king-size bed, a writing desk, a large closet and chairs.

The living room is large enough for a table that will seat ten. The china press and buffet stand at one side of the room. There are three groups of sofas, chairs, coffee tables, and lamps—all required for entertaining. I like it! I think of our paintings and artifacts, pictures being brought from home that will make it a home.

                    *   *   *

The day after we moved in, the water pump stopped working. The deep well had been dug so water might be pumped throughout the house. The gray pump stands in the corner of the compound near a large bush, which conceals it.

I asked Prem to write a note and sent Das with it to our neighbor's head servant asking for the name of an electrician. Ravi is head of the biggest Oil Company in India and has many employees at his bidding. However, the return note said they had called their engineer in Nagpur, two hundred miles to the west, and it would take five days to reach us. In the meantime, our helpers are transferring water in huge jugs. Mark is especially handy at some tasks, but plumbing and electrical work are not among his specialties.

Enormous teak and peeple trees stand within our home's high-walled compound that is the size of a city block. Grand old trees stand throughout the grounds. I can imagine having tea served to my guests while sitting beneath them.

*   *   *

Tonight, Mark came home and said, "I tell you, this heat will get you down. I want a shower and a drink. Then perhaps I will feel like a human being. Let's have a bottle of our precious champagne. This is a night to celebrate. It is really our first night in our home."

We gathered in the living room. "Here's to a wonderful, useful, and happy life in India," Mark said as he raised his glass. He talked of his plans to meet with various officials and eventually talk with university officials and landowners to discuss his plans.

With our refills, Ram brought in a tray of stuffed, deep-fried pastries called samosas. We lingered over our food and discussed the happenings of the day.

"It is good to have something so special as champagne," I said. "Do you recall the U.S. Senator on an inspection trip to the little commissary in New Delhi saying to the manager, a retired Anglo-Indian military officer, 'You have quite a sizeable supply of alcohol here, don't you, Brigadier?' Do you remember his answer?" I asked.

"Yes," said Mark. "Senator, this is not alcohol, it's medicine and you are in India." We both laughed.

"Das, help bring our porch chairs out on the lawn," Mark said.

We three gathered beneath the sky, brilliant with enormous stars and the wispy Milky Way, all nestling on blue-black velvet darkness.

When I was growing up on a farm in the South, if the weather was clear we had a nightly ritual of watching the stars and looking for shooting stars in the summer. Looking back, I felt that was nothing compared to the display that we see here in our new home.

The first time that we heard about the stars in India was when the dean of Florida State University's College of Education visited Connie at our home offering her a scholarship if she wanted to stay in Florida. When she said she wanted to go with us to India, he told her that she must look at the sky if she wanted to see the most magnificent display of stars anywhere. We sat watching as we emptied our glasses of champagne and listened to the calls of the night birds enjoying the quiet time in India.

*   *   *

This morning, the squawking of birds awakened us. The compound wall was covered with crows. A servant tried to shoo them off using towels, aprons, and brooms. John decided a scarecrow would do the trick. With rags and a shirt, he built one. They paid no attention and would sit there until someone came out of the house, then flutter up in the air, circle and land when all was clear.

"Memsabji, people think if a person commits suicide, their spirits will return in the form of a squawking crow," said Prem Chan.

There must have been many suicides; there are surely many crows.

We have used the kitchen today. As all the other rooms are large, so is the kitchen. The walls and shelves are white, and there are no doors on the cupboards, just space for the dishes. The dishes, utensils, pots and pans from the Embassy loan have been arranged. Indians use stainless steel platters, concave skillets for cooking chapattis, and pots for rice and curried vegetables. They own few utensils. The white and gray marble countertop running the length of the room is most attractive and wonderful for kneading bread. The propane stove with its tank of fuel sits in a corner.

We were served Masala chai* as our morning drink today. This tea is flavored with cinnamon, cardamom, and cloves. It is good cold as well as hot.

After breakfast, Rafiq came in and said, "I'm sorry to bother you, Sahib, but I need to show you something."

Mark went with him and saw that a group of people had entered our compound through a hole in the concrete wall. They have been using the corner of our yard for their toilet.

Rafiq had Prem tell them if they did not stop using our garden they would be punished by being shot by the gun filled with salt. Nevertheless, the same situation went on for a few days. There was never a shot aimed at them, although the gun was fired into the air finally, and that ended their practice.

*   *   *

On our arrival in Madhya Pradesh, Mark paid a visit to the local bank and deposited rupees that he had exchanged for dollars at the Chase Manhattan branch at our Delhi embassy. He met the bank manager. Within a week, he dropped in to withdraw more rupees. We needed window drapes and rods; material for drapes is available but rods must be carved.

Mark proceeded to complete a draft and handed it and the bankbook to the teller. "I stood and waited, and waited and after slowly reading and re-reading the documents, the teller moved the draft along the way handing it from one teller to the other," Mark told me afterward. "Stamps were placed on the draft. It proceeds to the next station I went with it. The same process continued through seven more tellers. I was doing a slow burn by that time. I asked to see the Managing Director."

"'But Sahib…' the last teller began.

"I want to see him now! I won't wait another minute."

The man went through a door, then came back out followed by the Manager.

Mark said, "What is going on here? I have all my documents and you have my money. I want this draft cashed. It is apparent that they do not want to relinquish the money."

"The manager looked at me with sad eyes. 'But, Sahib, what will I do with them?' He nodded toward the many young men working as cashiers at the windows.

"It finally became apparent to me that the bank is required to find work for these young men. There are so many trained young men who do not have positions. The salaries are miserably low, but the government controls the bank and must offer jobs."

*   *   *

Before we left New Delhi, Rafiq had told us that he was planning to be married soon, and would move his wife to Raipur with us. We asked her name and he told us it was Sadiq.

"What a lovely name. How old is she?" I asked.

"She is very young, Memsahibji, and very shy."

He appeared to be too self-conscious to tell that she is probably only a couple of years into womanhood.

"I will be looking forward to meeting her," I assured him.

Today, Sadiq finally arrived in Raipur, and Rafiq is bursting with pride. She is dainty with black eyes and long, shiny black hair that is a perfect frame for her face. She looks no more than twelve to fifteen. It is difficult to tell. She wears a salwar, a dress cut round at the neck and reaching well below the knees, with a long scarf worn against the front of her neck with the ends on her back. Beneath the dress are long pants with a band at the ankles. On her arms she has bangles, a glass one and gold ones.

They told us they would bring her niece as company for her while Rafiq is traveling. Sure enough, a tiny little six-year-old is now here too. She is too shy to speak except to say, "Salaam, Memsabji."

Prem Chan, our honored senior staff member, supervised servants and helped manage our household in Raipur. An Indian paratrooper who served in World War II, he guarded our family and belongings with dedication.

Rafiq Khan, our Moslem interpreter and shikar (huntsman-guide), with his wife Sadiq and her little niece, who came to keep the young bride company while Rafiq worked. Our Raipur home is in the background.

Chapter 22
A TREK TO THE SOUTH

As we drive through the villages around Raipur, I watch the many activities going on in the mud-filled streets, where children slip and splash in the puddles. In the midst of this downpour is a scene of poverty, dirt, disease, yet the children laugh and chase each other. I think to myself, "The mind is a wondrous thing, accepting, readjusting, growing, and facing all adversity."

There is a unique aroma pouring from the burning cow-dung patties, the fuel for the fires over which meals are being cooked. The smell of the fires is fused with the many pungent spices used on the food. It causes me to feel this is a primitive smell of life, as I watch the ribbons of smoke swirling skyward.

*   *   *

A week has passed. The problem now is mosquitoes. The screen door to the kitchen is black with them, and the servants have begun spraying. The water had allowed them to lay eggs and now they are swarming. It is a good thing that we have taken quinine.

The monsoon has already ended here in Raipur, after only a few days of rain. People murmur their fears of a drought ahead. The torrential rains we experienced in New Delhi have not reached this area. The red earth is barren except for a few spots of grass. Shepherds are herding goats to these spots. Instead of chewing grass off above the ground, the goats pull it up by the roots, so it won't have new growth.

I remember June 23rd, when the monsoon rains arrived in New Delhi and the deadly grip of the hot weather relaxed its hold. There, the warm rain fell from a dun-colored sky in sheets of water that turned the parched dust to rivers of mud. The rain brought a fantastic wave of green, growing things where only the day before there had been nothing but burnt grass.

Here, hot winds blow again, the mud cakes over, and the sun blazes savagely down, turning the caked mud to iron and covering it again with thick layers of dust that whirls up into dust-devils. These dance across the scorched plains until the next rain. If the rain does fall, the ground is once more turned into liquid mud and a green steaming jungle begins to grow.

Herds of camels have reached our area. They are searching for water. Their shepherds are walking beside and behind them. A baby calf was born on the 1,500-mile journey from the Rajasthan desert.

We are constantly having the electricity go off. I am sitting in the living room today with a fan in my hand and a glass of water by my side.

*   *   *

Having lived in the South, back home in Florida and Alabama, we are now traveling farther southward in India. Mark is examining the potential for his program throughout the country. Our latest trip has taken us at least several hundred miles from Raipur, as we toured India's southeastern and southwestern regions.

We traveled to Madras, Pondicherry and other cities and towns in Tamil Nadu. Then we went across and up through Karnataka to Goa. Not only is the scenery different, the cuisine here also has a tropical flavor. The curries, for instance, are made with coconut, cashews and exotic fruits, unlike the dishes we have had in the north of India.

Each place we have gone, I have made a habit of taking a handful of dirt, to get a sense of what those who had passed before us might feel. The soil is of grave importance to the farmers.

After traveling for a few days, staying in dak bungalows, rest houses, with our limited staff, we arrived in the state of Goa, located on the Arabian Sea in the southwest. Goa is one of India's jewels and is a place we did not want to miss.

Its history goes back to the 3rd century BC, when it was part of the Mauryan Empire. It was refreshing to look on the beautiful waves rolling in as we drove alongside. The main reason for its popularity is the magnificent palm-fringed beaches and the people.

Goa's character is different from the rest of India. The Portuguese colonized Goa and brought Roman Catholicism with them. Whitewashed churches with Portuguese-style facades can be found through the land. English is spoken, as are Konkani and Marathi and French. Some older residents still speak Portuguese.

Women wear skirts that outnumber the saris. An easygoing, relaxed attitude is prevalent, and the people have a sense of humor. We found that many American young people come here to disappear from Western life. Although on certain beaches nudity is allowed, that doesn't mean people can go nude where families are relaxing. There is a sensitivity and civility here that must not be breached.

*   *   *

Looking back at the history of India's South, it is interesting to reflect on the Dravidian kingdom, which was established here when the Aryans drove the Dravidians out of the north. They developed a highly civilized country, although not much is known of the region before the Christian era. The Dravidians were prosperous and developed trade with Asia Minor and countries to the east of India.

Today we travel in caravans of cars and jeeps. Then, the caravans were camels and pack bullocks carrying jewels, spices and manufactured articles from the interior to the seaports. There they would be placed on ships and sail to their destinations in the Orient and Asia Minor.

When the Aryans came to South India, as Brahmins they kept their class or caste name, and the Dravidian priest-teachers took the same class name. The Brahmins even today call the Dravidians outcasts, meaning outside of society. Yet the Dravidians themselves feel that it is the Brahmins who were the real outcasts, since they did away with the Dravidians' culture and imposed their ways upon them.

South India maintains its own languages: Tamil, Telegu, Kanarese, Malayalam, taking into them Sanskrit words. Sanskrit has not been used since before Christ's time. Aryan Sanskrit was called the educated man's language. It is so rich and full that the important books, "Ramayana," "Mahabharata" and "Puranas," were translated into the language.

Following a huge migration to South India in the Christian era, this region is where the majority of present-day Christians live. We followed the steps to where St. Thomas was reportedly stoned to death. A magnificent church has been built at the spot where it was believed he died.

There are also tens of thousands of Buddhist monks in over a hundred hermitages in the country. History is rich with recordings of the Madura, a beautifully planned city located here in the early seventh century.

A great king of South India, Rajaraja, built a highly organized government in the 11th century. Each village had its own assembly, called Sabha, which exist today. The people's opinions were part of the decision-making. Records were kept of land surveys. There were vast irrigation systems, and roads were maintained.

We have seen many works of art that were constructed during the reign of Rajaraja, such as the many Chola temples. Traveling through Tamil Nadu, we saw the Brihadeshwara Temple, the main attraction in Thanjavur, Tanjore. On top of the 63-meter-high temple, a dome encloses an enormous Siva lingam, a replica of the male sexual organ. This statue is constructed from a single piece of granite weighing an estimated 81 tons. The dome itself was hauled into place along a six-kilometer earthen ramp.

Inside the open-air temple, guarding the inner courtyard stands the figure of Nanda, the largest sculpture of a bull in India. The statue was carved from a single piece of black granite twelve feet by sixteen feet in size, brought four hundred miles to the temple. Inlaid jewels encrust the ceiling of the temple.

One traveler wrote of the ancient city of Vijayanagar, "Eye hath not seen or ears heard of any place resembling it upon the whole earth." The Hindus annexed the city, which fell to the Moslems in 1327 and in 1346. It has changed hands until today it is within Bijapur, a small city packed with mosques inside a wall.

All of the kingdoms of India were similar to those of Europe in the same eras—the nobles lived in luxury while the common people suffered hardships.

Yesterday, we completed our exploration of India's southernmost states and returned to Raipur.

Nanda, the sacred bull, sits beneath a bejeweled ceiling in a Hindu temple in Thanjavur, Tamil Nadu. Carved from a single block of black marble, it is India's largest bull statue.

Harvesting grains: In Tamil Nadu, South India, called by some "the most Indian part of India," the work begins at daylight and is still done as it was for centuries past. Oxen, on tether, move round and round stomping the grain from the chaff.

CHAPTER 23
HOME AGAIN IN RAIPUR

We look settled, but I won't feel settled until our personal things arrive. I am beginning to meet people. One of my new friends, Lolita, has taught me to meditate, a form of self-hypnotizing. The hot air of the Deccan feels as though it will sear our lungs when we inhale. At times I find myself gasping for breath when we are out riding. I am learning self-hypnosis helps.

Mark is making day trips into the country now. We are very concerned about the food situation here, even with our agricultural project. We see what is being done with the food. The farmers are keeping it for their own families' use. They aren't taking it to market, therefore city dwellers will be the ones to suffer. What will happen now, we wonder?

Mark wants to get water to the land, as this is the only way the intensive program can work. There is a project— although here, they call projects "schemes"—to do this, but it moves so slowly. He has invited an American friend from Poona who is an irrigation specialist to come over and give suggestions. Mark says that the man has headed some of the great projects in the United States. If something isn't done soon, there will be starvation and thirst on a scale the people here have never known. The country has been overcome by one invasion after another. Now it seems that the next one will be from starvation.

*   *   *

My first caller at our Raipur home was a man in need of parts for his Czechoslovakian tractor. I gave him the address of the All-India Tractor Institute, where tractors from all countries are sent for tests before they are sold. Corporations are entering the Indian market.

The next caller was the secretary to the Collector and his wife, a maharani, or princess, leaving an invitation for dinner. The Collector, who holds a high rank, is now well within the system that could take him to the post of Minister (Senator) of his state one day. The positions that must be filled, I am told, take the most talented and weave them throughout the fabric of the Administration process on their way up.

The Headmaster of Rajkumar College and his wife invited us for tea, and we accepted their invitation first. We went to their home yesterday, and the wife stayed in the back until she served tea and a variety of treats.

"She is very bashful," the husband commented.

Today, a white fish arrived from the kitchen of our neighbors, the Mukerjis. Fish is rare here. I surmise that it comes from a private pond. Their servant delivered it with a little note saying the fish was caught this morning. The note also said, "Do you play bridge?"

This is a joyful discovery. To have a friend to pass the time with and play bridge with is beyond my wildest dreams. Sonu and R.C. Mukerji live in a private compound diagonally across from us, bordering on our block compound. The two houses and gardens each have a huge fence dividing us. I asked Rafiq about them. Talking with neighbors, he was told they are a well-educated couple who met when they were both students in Paris at the Sorbonne University. The husband has studied at Sandhurst, the West Point of England, as well. He was the pilot of the first Indian Airline before going with his present position. She is said to be beautiful and he handsome. He is an Olympic Gold medal winner on the Indian soccer team—as his father had been twenty-five years earlier.

Another note, hand carried, arrived today. It is an invitation to visit the Maharaja and Maharani of a kingdom some 75 miles from us. The secretary, a bright, handsome young man in spotless white uniform, said he would wait for our answer.

I looked at the calendar and wrote a note. "I see that we can't possibly leave for now, and possibly in a month. We are expecting a guest from Poona to arrive here this week. It may be several weeks at the earliest before we can take advantage of it. My sincere thanks."

*   *   *

The first few weeks here were difficult for John. He became quieter. He misses his brother, but his sister Connie even more as she always gave him lots of time. He and Dennis have always played, wrestled, or argued in a give-and-take manner. Now, in our house there are only servants who pad about the house silently, barefooted.

No one wears shoes indoors. We do not want to bring the shoes we have worn outdoors into our home, since human urine and excreta are expelled outdoors, mainly near trees, or by fences, behind bushes. There is little opportunity for the dogs to run loose outside.

At last, John has found two little buddies and it is making such a difference with him. Ages 10 and 11, the sons of Indian families, they are precious children, jolly and mannerly. They attend Rajkamar College, a prestigious college for sons of Rajas who live all over the country. They speak the "King's English," as they say. They are required to pass the Oxford (England) English test. It is said to be the most difficult English language course there is anywhere.

One of John's new friends is Gatum Mukerji, our neighbors' son. Abraham, his other pal, is the son of the District Engineer for power for a very large area of India. His family is Christian. These friends have come to accept Gillie, and even play with her, which is unusual, as Indians are so deathly afraid of dogs.

Mark spends very little time at home, and we can't always go with him on long trips. When the trip is for a few days and we can go along, John and I load up his schoolbooks and papers, pack a bag, plenty of water, and beer to use if our supply of water gives out. We have often sat in the shade of a Hindu tomb, or beneath a peepul tree for John's "class" while Mark met with whatever group his appointment entailed.

It is difficult to remind John to watch where he walks or runs. A fall causing a skinned knee or arm is no small matter in India. I try to keep infection down. It is not easy since there are millions of people, and as many cows as people. It takes weeks to get a scratch or skinned knee healed. It is hot, and the air is filled with dust that carries germs. The nearest doctors practicing are in Tilda, where there is an Evangelical Reform Hospital—thirty miles away, and a two-hour drive. I watch our diets and vitamins closely. John is well aware of his responsibility to be careful.

*   *   *

I sat on the veranda this morning, thinking of the distance that we are from my three other beloved children, my parents and my country, and today it weighed heavy. My parents are elderly and unwell and are missing us. Mark's parents miss us as well, I expect, but their daughter lives with them and is company. My heart felt heavy, as I have never had it do before. My stomach was in knots. I asked myself if what we are doing here is worth this separation? Shouldn't I be back where I can be of assistance and comfort to our parents?

I don't know how long I sat there. There was no interruption. Finally, I realized that the afternoon sun was low and soon Mark would return from his office. John should have finished his homework. I decided I wouldn't mention my feelings, and I said a silent prayer asking for help. I rose and walked into the kitchen.

Das came rushing in, saying, "Sahibs, Sahibs!"

"Show me." He hurried to the door ahead of me, and on the veranda stood two young American men, whom. I invited in. Tea and water were served. They are Peace Corps men who have been sent to start a piggery over a hundred miles to the northeast.

"Piggery?" I questioned.

"No one eats pork in this country except the tribal people and Soviets. We are not getting along very well with our project or with our health," said one of the men who introduced himself as Hank. The other man, Ivan, looked flushed and feverish.

"Go with Prem, he will show you to the shower," I told them. "Get cleaned up and we'll have some food for you."

"I haven't been able to eat for some time. I am nauseous and have an upset stomach," Ivan said.

"I'm not feeling well either," Hank said. We gave them some medication followed by broth and tea. They spent a week here, recuperating. It was dysentery, which hits most people in this country, especially foreigners.

While here, they talked for hours about the difficulties of being in India. They told us the Indians think they are too young for the type of project they're involved in, and pay no attention to them. "Yes, age has its advantages here as no other place that I know," I said.

My advice was for them to go to the head person of the village and present their credentials, which are not much—a short course in Boston on raising hogs and bachelors degrees from a university. If they can't do anything else, I felt, they could see the country and meet the Indian people. I did not see them again.

*   *   *

The furniture in our home has been sanded and varnished. It had seen heavy duty with other American Embassy families in Calcutta. I selected the fabric in colors of blue and mauve for the cushions that go in the chairs, with throw pillows in chartreuse and pale blue, to freshen the appearance of the room. The two large carpets are off-white. I expect the color will deepen after a month of dust accumulates.

It is time that I return some of the social invitations that we have accepted. I have sent out the invitations by Prem Das.

We have discovered that tea is the drink of India. It is said to be 2,500 years old, and some Chinese claim that it was drunk as long as 5,000 years ago. Although it may be indigenous to Tibet and northeastern India, Darjeeling and Assam, the craze for tea transformed the British social life, along with visitations and the elaborate calling-card protocol required in navigating them. It has proven its worth to us, as we enjoy it and Indians prefer it to any other drink

My cook, Lazarus, prepared a tray of tarts, cookies, almonds and chocolates. A problem had arisen in the kitchen when he was going to make the cookies—he found the five-pound bag of sugar from our commissary is as hard as a brick. He couldn't melt it, so I sent for a mortar and pestle. Prem Chan had the idea of where to find a makeshift pestle—a railroad spike of iron to use in an iron straight-sided vessel. It served its purpose—crushing the sugar into powder.

Mrs. Baroda, a Brahmin's wife, who lives in the next house to our garden, came to tea, along with Mrs. Penidra, Mrs. Mukerji and Mrs. Singh. Their husbands are in high positions: commissioner, head of international corporation, and educator. The women are all of the two highest castes and it is acceptable for them to be together. They arrived wearing flowing, wispy saris in lovely colors and many gold bangles, and each wore one glass marriage bracelet. Their earrings were heavy gold, requiring a small gold attachment hooked over the top of the ear to carry the weight of the long, bejeweled ring.

During the afternoon, Mrs. Baroda rose, walked to the china cabinet and opened the door, then proceeded to inspect our china. She pulled open the drawer and was inspecting the linens, when I asked if I could show her anything. "No, I want to see what you have," she said.

I told her I didn't have expensive things, as our things were being shipped to us by sea freight and had not yet arrived. Until then we would use those supplied by the Embassy.

We were on our second cup of tea when John came through the door, with Gillie at his side. When the ladies saw the dog, they leaped out of their chairs and raced across the room. Two of them jumped up on a chair. John and I grabbed Gillie, but not before her wagging long tail had knocked the contents of the tea table onto the carpet. I threw a tea towel down. Lazarus came running and rushed out to get more cloths for the carpet.

"She is okay, she won't hurt you. She likes company," John said.

"We are so terribly afraid of dogs. There is soo much rabies in this country; we never go near dogs," said Mrs. Singh.

"Gillie is harmless. She has had rabies shots and all other shots to keep her healthy," John said.

The local fear of dogs became understandable to us, though, when a pack of wild dogs were found rummaging through the yards and streets one night, killing and eating everything in sight. Neighbors rushed to ask Mark to come with his guns. He and Rafiq killed eleven.

Raipur was far from a modern city. Its dusty streets were crowded with colorful throngs and permeated with the aromas of Indian spices.

CHAPTER 24
THE HUNTS

Mark and I both have permits to hunt. We own a .357, a shotgun and a .27-gauge rifle. We brought our shells and other hunting supplies. They are a necessary part of our equipment as there is no fowl, pork, nor beef available unless one considers dirty goat that can be found in the market occasionally.

Many cows are seen being herded along the road with dust rising beneath their feet to fill the air. When the dust settles and we see the sorry state of the animals, we would not want to eat their meat. If the cows and bulls are too crowded to pass, they run into the side of the car. If we try to force our way through the herd and frighten them, they panic and try to climb onto the jeep. The driver ends up leaning on the horn. Ours is the only motor vehicle on the road.

The headmaster of a nearby village paid us a visit last week, complaining that a tiger had been injured and dragged old men and women, and even babies, out of the village. The people are terrified. The Indians do not own guns to hunt with as they are expensive, and the laws of their religion and the law of the land prohibit killing.

Mark asked the regional Forest Officer about the tiger, and he verified the story as being true.

Usually when we hunt, there are a variety of animals to choose—nilgai, deer, wild boar, antelope and birds. This time, we would hope to find the man-eater. There would be beaters furnished by the village headman and the Forest Office.

Yesterday, we drove through an area of undulating ground covered by scrub and rock outcrops. The occasional villages that we passed looked barren, the ground was hard packed and there were no flowers about. As is the habit, the driver asked three people for directions and took the two that agreed. The Indians do not stray far from their village.

It was getting hotter. The cook and bearers with us had seen to it that we had enough boiled water, lemonade, and loose tea so that we could have *chai* when we wanted it. The guard would build the fire.

The Forest Officer and villagers met us. Mark inquired about the situation and the tiger attacks. A villager tilted his head from left to right, and sadness came into his eyes.

Rafiq translated for us: "Yes, Sahib, the father of one of our families was taking a rest underneath the neem tree where the earth is cool and the breeze whispers through the fan-shaped leaves, when a tiger grabbed him. We searched for him even though the sun was down, as we carried torches and sticks. The following day we found some remains."

"Sahib, you must help," the man said. "We can call on no one else as there are no guns in this village or anywhere near."

"When did this happen?" Mark asked.

"At the time of the last full moon," the villager answered.

The Forest Officer spoke up, "The jungle here was once thick and would support many animals, so that the large animals had smaller animals to prey on, but things have changed. Now the wood has been cut and sold. The trees have not grown to replace the ones cut. The cutting is illegal; soon there will be no forest or jungle. The summer is the worst time, since it is dry, there is nothing to eat, the animals turn to eating village goats, when they are gone they turn to people—the weak and slow."

"Has this problem been taken up with the politicians, to start programs of reforestation?" said Mark.

"For years, these politicians have been writing reports, referring, deferring and inferring. It goes round and round, but nothing happens," said the officer sadly.

When we arrived at the edge of the more dense woods through which a bone-dry ditch ran, eighteen villagers were waiting. They had obtained a bullock and had tied it to the trunk of tree. We left the animal as bait, with the understanding that we don't want the tiger frightened away by our being there. We were traveling on a dirt track.

We finally jolted to a stop as we had reached our destination. We parked and stood behind large neem trees, where we could get a good shot when the tiger appears.

Despite the drought, the flame-of-the-forest was in full bloom with its salmon colored, waxy blossoms and few leaves. The banyan tree, enormous in height and spread, looked mighty with its roots extending from branch to soil. I wished for a gentle rainfall. I was hoping to see the earth burst forth with color and richness. I love the renewal of nature, and I await it eagerly here.

*   *   *

We were here now to meet a killer. I did not feel comfortable, as I was to be part of the safari with a gun to operate. The beaters were armed with *lathis*, stakes made of branches, and spears. Two men had drums lashed to their bodies with leather straps, others had two short sticks and lids to bang together. They appeared happy and expectant, ready to rush the animal into our path for Mark and me to shoot.

The Forest Officer gave them final instructions, and I rested on a chair that had been brought. Mark and I took a drink from the clay jug held in a woven rattan carrier that held our water. I felt a drop of sweat running down my chest. We had put on insect repellent so although flies swarmed, they did not light on us.

The cicadas began chirping. It sounded as though there must be millions, all beginning in unison. The noise was so shrill it was piercing to the ear. Men slapped their hands together, but it did not stop them. They covered every inch of the trees, trunks, limbs, and leaves. As suddenly as they began, they stopped, as though their voices had been an orchestrated choir.

Our two rules in hunting, which we had discussed thoroughly, are that we will not kill anything that we don't expect to eat, unless it is a threat to lives. The second is that if we hit an animal, and it gets up and runs, we will hunt it down and not leave it injured.

The men divided and went off in different directions. Pugmarks had been found in the ditch showing the direction the animal had traveled and where we expected him to come again. Mark was getting restless. When we are hunting, and we cannot speak, the tension builds. The sound of drums and metal could be heard in the distance. The animals of the jungle were now alerted to the threat and running. First came the deer, samba, and nilgai.

Then, the tiger broke through the main outlet and bounded over the clay wall, heading across the dry field.

The men pursued it, shouting and making noise. Just as the tiger got in our line of fire, three beaters darted across, obscuring our view. Mark yelled, as did our driver. The beaters looked back, saw us and fled in another direction. They had obviously forgotten where we were stationed.

During the entire melee, a bear trotted by, birds were screaming, peacocks and peahens were making a great noise. The man-eater fled, and not a single shot was fired. The Forest Officer, my husband and the villagers were infuriated. They all yelled at the poor fellows who were too excited to know what they were doing.

The little bullock that was tethered escaped with its life. We returned home to rest for another day, and to explore what the next step would be.

Hunt for a man-eating tiger: In the jungle, villagers held stakes and spears, and others carried noisemakers to flush out the tiger that had killed several people. Bears, wild boars and small animals fled before the men. Mark and I sat in a platform in a tree, our guns ready, and waited for the killer tiger in total silence.

A jungle village, typical of most of the ones we visited in our travels through the heart of India.

CHAPTER 25
WHITE TIGERS

Sonu invited me to come and meet several ladies at her home yesterday. The conversation moved from clothes, saris that have borders of gold and silver, to the latest purchase of jewels, a big topic.

Sonu told them of the tiger hunt that my husband and I had gone on last week. Then she turned to me and asked, "Have you heard of the white tigers?"

"No," I said, "Where are there white tigers?".

"The white tigers were discovered several years ago in forests owned by our friend here, Geta, and her husband in Rewa," she said, turning to Geta.

"Your forests, Geta? This is wonderful news."

"The tigers are not albinos, according to our veterinarian and the forester, who have done studies of these tigers," said Geta. "They have multiplied, and now, we are sending a few to zoos around the world so people will have a chance to see them."

"I would certainly like to see one," I said.

"Come and visit us, and you will be assured of seeing them," said Geta. A few of the animals are also in zoos in England and America, as well as the one in Delhi, she said.

Since tigers are such a part of our life here, we often discuss them, their whereabouts and habits, with interest. Rafiq's father is the *shikar* for the princely kingdom of Bhopal, so Rafiq knows and tells us a great deal about wild animals.

We've seen tigers in various places, even though they lie well hidden in grass that is nearly the color of their fur. We always try to place ourselves up wind from them so they can not smell us. Strong and ferocious preda-tors, these huge cats demand respect. They rely on the element of surprise, essential for their success in making a kill. They have a role to play in nature, to keep it in balance. For instance, we have learned that tigers feed in a area of one hundred square miles, and it takes that much area for them to survive in the open jungle. The tiger is said to get one in ten ani-mals that it stalks, depending on the type of ambush.

The cats have amazing power. A tiger can throw a 1,200-pound bullock on its back and has strength to jump, clearing a fence as tall as the animal's height. Cubs remain with their mother for two years, and by that time they have established their territory. The male tiger has nothing to do with raising his offspring. However, father tigers have been seen playing with the cubs, appearing to recognize them even after not seeing them for long periods of time.

*   *   *

We have only hunted a tiger once, as we usually hunt only to supply our own food. We hunt for deer and nilgai, most often in Derumsilli, because it is near home.

Last night, Rafiq and Mark both climbed onto the roof of the jeep while I took over the driving. The nightjars were out and for me it was easy to mistake these birds for animals, since their eyes showed brightly in the darkness. It was late, and my job was to concentrate on driving with the two men on top of the Jeep. I didn't want to hit something that would cause them to be thrown off. Still, after the long ride into the jungle I was ready to get home, get a bath and get into bed.

The spotlight, attached to the frame, was ready to be switched on when Rafiq spotted their prey. I slowed down to ford a stream, changing gears as the vehicle slowly ascended the bank. I was grinding up a bumpy incline when I saw a hyena running in front of me. Another joined him. They lurched ahead of the headlights, occasionally stopping to look back. Despite their menacing look, they are scavengers, not predatory animals. I continued to drive slowly while the men each took a side to search for animals. Then came a tap on the roof. Mark whispered, "On your left!"

I could see dozens of animals. They were lying on the ground with their heads raised, their eyes shining, looking at us and showing no fear because they are never hunted. Mark took aim and hit one of the nilgai. Rafiq jumped off and ran like the wind, opening his knife. He said a prayer over the animal before slitting its throat. Now, as a Moslem, he and his family will be able to eat of the meat.

I drove the Jeep over the terrain to where the nilgai lay, while the other animals moved out at a distance and innocently observed us. Our hunting license permit specifies the limit we may take. We were only taking this one, as our rig on the front was secured for the journey home.

Back at the house, the men were tired, so conversation was at a minimum. On the patio outside, the animal was skinned, washed thoroughly cut into quarters and refrigerated. Once it is thoroughly chilled, it will be cut into cooking size pieces, wrapped in market paper and placed in the freezer for further use. We will give some of the meat to our servants, friends, and to people of the lowest caste, the untouchables, since they are allowed to eat it. In our kitchen here, we have found one of the favorite ways to cook a haunch of our kill is to slip buds of garlic into slits, salt and pepper, wrap slices of bacon around it and bake slowly, bastingwith olive oil and red wine. We also make curry and meat loaf of the venison, since it is our mainstay.

Rare white tigers were discovered in Bustar, Orissa, on the land of my friend Geta, a Maharani. The tigers, originally thought to be albinos, were later seen to be authentically white with dark stripes. Their numbers have increased and white tigers are now in zoos in New Delhi and in other countries.

CHAPTER 26
FRIENDS AND NEIGHBORS

The Mukerjis, our neighbors, have invited me to visit, sending a calling card that said, "Drop in anytime." Today, I took them a piece of our venison, very cold and wrapped well.

Their servant assured me that Memsahibji could see me. Sonu and a friend, Raji, were standing side by side in the library, laughing and obviously enjoying each other's company as they covered hardback books. I began helping them as they made and placed new covers on the volumes. Books are hard to come by and must be protected.

She introduced me, saying Raji was architect for the project for the Oil Company. I later learned that he is the permanent architect employed by the company.

Although this was a casual call on my part, I felt that the apparent warmth of their friendly attitude toward each other indicated something more between them. Sonu has been a helpful friend to me. The Brahmin couple next door are older than we are, and we see little of them.

*   *   *

The Maharaja and Maharani of the Kingdom of Kiwarda have sent us a second invitation. It appears that they are eager to have us visit them at their palace. I am appreciative of their thoughtfulness. We have no mutual acquaintances that I am aware of. However, word travels so fast by the

Indian grapevine that we wouldn't wonder if the whole of the district has some knowledge of our being here.

The secretary who brought the note from the palace said he would wait for an answer. I offered him a seat, but he would not sit down. Looking at my calendar, I saw that we couldn't possibly leave for perhaps two weeks.

"Sahib has plans, and he will need to be consulted. I thank your Majesties and when we have a clear calendar, we will come. My sincere appreciation," I wrote quickly on a note and sealed the envelope.

"Lazarus, give him food and water for the trip," I said. "You say it is seventy miles?"

"Yes, we say kilometers, Memsahibji. Thank you," said the secretary as he left. "My Master thanks you."

*   *   *

We have had other social engagements lately, as members of the Board of Regents of Rajkumar College are in town for meetings. We were invited to the Chairman's home for dinner tonight. We arrived at the large, stone house located beneath enormous old banyan and large-leafed peepul trees. Arbors of bougainvillea and jasmine were a colorful relief and the fragrance was breathtaking after the bleakness and scalding heat of the dusk.

We had dinner around a long table. The ladies were lovely in their native dress, elegant silk saris, which are six yards of material, wrapped around the body several times, with the last couple of yards pleated and tucked in at the waist. Never is a pin or button used. The silk is often woven with gold thread on the edge, and the gold is meant to be their wealth if they were kidnapped or held for some reason and needed the gold. The dress could then be burned and the gold would collect in a mound. With the sari, a woman wears a blouse with no sleeves or tight elbow-length sleeves, a rounded neckline and fitting just below the breast. Ten to fifteen gold bracelets and gold earrings complete the outfit.

The men wore raw silk *kurta*, shirts closed at the neck with gold studs. Seeing all the silk shirts and saris brought on a remark about the variety of silk found in India, and a lively conversation ensued.

"Aristotle mentioned silk weaving in the fourth century before Christ," Maharaja Kumeraj spoke up. "But silk had been brought here even earlier than that. The Chinese had taken precautions to guard the secret of their profitable silk culture, and attempts to steal the secret from them provided plots for many stories of adventure."

"How did you become interested in silk?" I asked him.

"Silk trade is my business. It has been handed down for generations and now I am the owner of the trade," he said.

"You may be interested in knowing of one famous story. It tells of the Chinese princess in the first century B.C., who carried eggs of silkworm moths, hidden in her headdress, to Khotan. From there, it was said, the culture of silkworms spread to India and Persia."

As he was telling the story, my attention was drawn to a Maharaja seated two chairs away. His sleeves were pushed above his elbow and he was scooping his curry and rice with his *chappati.* *Chappatis* of bread are used in lieu of silverware. A rivulet of sauce ran down his arm to the elbow, which acted as a faucet. He was enjoying himself immensely. A fingerbowl was later brought to each of us.

These men, all royalty as are their wives, have known each other since their school days and verbally banter with each other. When we finished dinner, the men moved to one end of the room and we women went to the other end. I vowed that I would like to change that, as I became weary of listening to talk about clothes and jewels and people I didn't know and couldn't understand. We didn't stay late.

*   *   *

Today was a great change from our formal social gatherings. We traveled to Orissa State. It turned out to be a fascinating experience. It was market day for the Ghone Tribe. Another tribe, called the Bhils, also lives in Orissa.

The Ghones' society is different from other Indian cultures. The men hunt with bow and arrow, and their normal attire is a G-string.

The women at the market had dressed in their best wrap dresses, which cover them only from the waist down. The young ones wore combs of many colors in their hair. The more combs, the more popular they are. They eat meat and are plump and voluptuous, with great rounded busts and buttocks. They look more like the bodies in the statues than any other women that I've seen. The girls there are wonderful looking, and a rare sight in India. The girls live separated until they are married.

We were welcomed and given a bow and two arrowheads, each attached to a staff. The people had brought pots of clay in many shapes. They had knives, arrows, instruments and tools that had been made by the tribe. They traded rice and other utensils were bartered. We bought a number of pots and jugs made by the tribesmen.

*   *   *

Driving over the country in the Deccan, we have found a permanent monument to man's wastefulness. On the land lie gaping, snarled, and burned holes, eroded into fantastic shapes. The forests have been raped for teak and mahogany, which were taken to England for castles and manor houses, we were told. As far as one can see, there is nothing except red, hard earth ripped with crevasses into some of which a three-bedroom American home would fit.

The one advantage in a recent government program is that it has planted mango trees along the roadside. Broad stripes of white paint encircling the trees warn that they must be preserved so people can eat the fruit, and those walking the roads easily identify the trees.

During this year's drought, families in search of water and work fill the roads, carrying all their worldly possessions on their backs. The problem is enormous. There is little that we can do, except push ahead with plans to have individual wells sunk for common use. Mark has attended the formal opening of a canal project our government supported.

A large landowner, Mr. Pattna, and I had a long discussion this week about the people's willingness to accept everything as coming from their *karma*, whether it is good or bad. Instead of fighting, scratching and working for a more comfortable and prosperous life as we do in the United States, they simply adhere to ancient customs.

"I have offered them more money to raise the input and cultivate more acreage on my land. They need to spend more time in the fields. That would improve their lives; they would have more food, clothes and other benefits of work," Mr. Pattna said. "But they simply refuse to change their ways. They will only spend the same time as their fathers, brothers and sisters did."

"I find it very frustrating when we want to help them," I said. "There seems to be no problem with the educated people. Change must come from education of the masses."

CHAPTER 27
ON BEING A MOSLEM

Ramadan is here, the holiest season of the Moslem religion. A time of fasting and prayer, of purification and introspection, it falls in the ninth month of the Islamic calendar. Moslems believe the Koran was sent down at this time of year to direct their lives. During Ramadan, the gates of heaven open and the angel Gabriel asks grace for everyone.

The holy season is affecting all of our lives. Rafiq, a Moslem, is essential to our work, and he follows devoutly the laws set out in the Koran.

He and I have many opportunities to talk about his religion. It is still too hot to drive in the daytime, we must drive at night. I sit on the front seat while Mark, John, and the servants sit in the back—most often sleeping.

My job is to be on the watch for animals and be sure Rafiq stays awake, I tell myself. In the meantime, he explains the Moslem obedience to the Five Pillars of Islam. The first pillar is total submission to Allah (God). "Moslems believe that there is no God but Allah and Mohammed is His Prophet," Rafiq told me in our first conversation about the faith.

I had asked for a copy of the Koran translated into English but was told that it was against the Moslem tradition. However, Rafiq is fluent in Arabic as well as English, French, Hindi, and the major languages and dialects, so he serves as our translator on this topic as well as in other areas.

Rafiq prays, as he is required to, five times a day. Each time, the ritual of ablution comes first: washing from hands to elbows, from feet to knees, face and neck, and cleaning the mouth and teeth. After this comes the prescribed genuflection, kneeling and bowing to Mecca and prostrating himself. Through this prayer exercise, he repeats over and over the words, *"Allah akbar,"* God is great.

Rafiq is often irritable and exhausted from the amount of work and the lack of sleep. He is weak from hunger as he lives by the teachings of the Koran during these hot and humid days. Following the requirements is not easy. He drives fast to reach home or a place to observe the rituals at the right times. The aged, the ill and travelers are exempt from the strict Ramadan rules. Even though we are travelers, he won't accept the exemption.

Many hours are spent in the mosque praying, especially for the elderly men. The women pray outside the mosque. During daylight hours, Moslems abstain from smoking, food, drink and sex. The most difficult, for many, is the latter, according to Rafiq. Since the time of day or night is important to the ritual, the worshippers use a white thread as the test to determine when it is officially nighttime. If they can see the thread, it is day. When the sun has set and they can no longer see the string, they may begin eating. The meal continues through much of the night. Before the sun rises, they eat again.

"Men are often temperamental and fights break out," Rafiq told me. He is always happy to see Ramadan end.

I asked Rafiq to tell me about the Koran's teachings, and he described some of its content. "The Koran is a book of instructions on many subjects," he said. It covers topics from fornication and adultery to disobedience, alms, murder, corruption, dowries, persecution and fasting.

"It also talks about fighting, backsliding, backbiting, covetousness, gambling, infanticide, burying infants, heathenish, and inheritance laws. The Koran tells of prayer times and requirements, the scene of the judgement, the 'Day of the Burning,' prayers for the evil, Satan and raising the dead. One is told how to sleep, about the prohibition of wine and alcohol, oaths, dissension, the 'evil eye,' and about enemies and evil spirits."

The teachings cover many other aspects of life. For example, menstruation, wet-nursing, marital intercourse, motherhood, parental duties, orphans, eating in others' houses, ownership of horses, renegades, retalia-tion, repentance, slanderers, slaves, thievery, usury, cunning, transgres-sion, omens, diets and food laws, sexual abstinence and dishonor, unscrupulous business practices, vanity, eunuchs and even regulations for keeping concubines.

"The Koran teaches us that Mohammed must be believed," said Rafiq. "It talks of veiling women, about cattle fraud, niggardliness, idolatry, Allah's powers of imposing death, hypocrites, breaking bonds with kin, temptation, treatment of enemies, and the fates of sinners. Other topics are lewdness, those who disbelieve, ritual washing, head shaving, pregnant camels, rain, and perversity. It even teaches about plots and counter-plots, world unity, and mercy. This is only a small part of that which is covered in the Koran."

Islam had a difficult time getting started, and, but for the support of Mohammed's wife, history might be different. She had a great influence over her numerous kin, who accepted his teaching. The religion rose in the 7th Century, centered in the Arabian Desert, and moved progressively to Damascus, Baghdad, and Cairo and later to Istanbul. The leaders, known as Caliphs, are no longer from Mecca or Medina.

Every Moslem's dream is to make a pilgrimage to Mecca. There, the Black Stone sits in the Shrine of Ka'aba, surrounded by an enormous field. The Moslems believe in the Spirit Jenn that enters and controls their bod-ies until Allah snuffs it out. They are therefore fatalists. Life is not to be enjoyed. Instead, they believe life is a proving ground for the next world.

"I am especially interested in the life of the Moslem women," I told Rafiq. "How does the Koran treat them? I know that a man only need say three times to his wife, 'I divorce thee,' and they are divorced, but what happens to the wife then? How does she live, financially and emotionally? What happens in a world where women don't go out of the house and are covered from head to toe?"

"The Koran is mindful of women's needs," said Rafiq. "If a woman is divorced, she must be left with all the possessions accumulated during the marriage. She must be cared for as before, with dignity and respect. It is known that women over forty have not been taught to read and take for a fact what their husbands tell them. The husbands read, go to prayer, hear what the *Iman*, leader, says, and tell their wives."

Rafiq is a Sunni Moslem. Most of the Moslems are Shiites, who hold different ideas on the rights of assertion. Shiites are ready to martyr themselves by flagellation and death to prove their devotion and support for the Caliph.

I recall meeting a government official, a young Shiite, when he was in graduate school at a university in the U.S. He would become very excited when questioned about his religion as being reactive.

"One day we will take over the world," the young man declared emphatically.

"Do you think countries will stand by and allow that to happen?" I asked him.

"We will be very kind to the people we capture," he said.

I asked when he thought it would happen. "When the Bedouins come to the city."

"Well," I asked, "where are they now?"

"They are already there," he answered.

CHAPTER 28
LANGUAGES AND CONFLICTS

John was riding his bike today. I was reading in the living room when he came in, and his condition startled me. His face was red, with a nasty welt beginning to rise, and his clothes were dirty and disheveled.

"What happened?"

"Some men threw stones," he said. "I tried to turn my bike and get away fast, but they threw more, and then they ran away. They yelled something about English."

John is a quiet, peaceful boy. He has never been aggressive or prone to start a fight. He sounded frightened. As I took him in my arms, I said, "Bring ice, Das!"

I realized what might be behind the attack. "Good heavens! I know they are having a political battle on the native language, Hindustani," I told John. "Just stay close to home unless someone is with you. We will talk with the police. Take Gillie with you when you go outside. That will keep them away."

A wave of nationalism has swept the country recently, with many Indians saying the use of the English language must be discontinued. The Hindus want Hindustani spoken, also known as Hindi. By 1965, everyone must speak Hindi as the national language. Since there are now 14 major languages and 250 dialects in the country, it is a problem to sort out.

Zealots inflame partisan emotions that cause problems. The natives are passionate about their heritage. It is not unusual for a mob to gather demonstrating their beliefs. The incident that happened to John because he is unable to speak Hindi was just one small event, and we were fortunate that he was not seriously injured.

Recently, one of my Anglo-Indian friends told me about the time the radical element of the Hindus seized a Christian meeting place set up in Raipur. The stage was the focus of the auditorium and the cross was placed on the screen, as the central focal point of the Christian worship. There small groups of Christians worshipped. This building was burned down and the Christians left the town. We had not heard of the event before, so we had not been apprehensive of living here.

*   *   *

We have learned that we can drive no more than 50 miles, and often much less, before our interpreter has a different dialect to translate. Rafiq is constantly learning new dialects so that he can serve us better. We pick up a few word and phrases. Few Indians travel more than ten miles from their homes, or in unusual cases, fifty at the most—because of the heat, road conditions and the bandits called decoits.

Dennis is the member of our family who is learning to speak Hindi. He can't be with us on our travels, but we are amazed at his ability to learn languages. We usually hire a schoolteacher or principal as a translator when we go to areas where Rafiq, our interpreter, does not know the dialect.

Through long conversations with men who interpret for us in the hundreds of surrounding villages, we are becoming acquainted with the history of this country. Until this century, the entire Indian subcontinent was a mass of self-contained agrarian villages, as the greater part of it is today.

Each village has its own weaver, potter, oil-presser, barber, washer men, water carriers, scavengers, and other who are carpenters making plows. It has its own blacksmith for making plowshares and its own leather workers for skinning cattle, curing hides, and making thongs and sandals.

The function of each man is determined by his caste, for the village is an ancient Hindu polity that governs both duties and remuneration. Often the man is prohibited not only from aspiring to functions reserved for other castes, but even from aspiring to a role within his own caste different from the function to which he is born. No one competes, except among men born to the same hereditary function. Even if the villagers are converted to Christianity or Moslem or any other faith, the converts retain their Hindu castes and functions.

*   *   *

Despite the excitement over the Hindustani language, little has changed in our days here in Raipur. We have established our nomadic lifestyle, which revolves around events requiring adaptability and flexibility every day.

We miss the newspapers, and letters arrive irregularly. They arrive in the APO pouch, American Post Office, in New Delhi and are bundled and sent to Mark's office by Indian Express Mail. We keep in touch with the outside world by way of a one-hour program on the Voice of America from Shri Lanka whenever we can pick it up on our radio. It is not dependable, as we often have power shortages

Dennis writes letters from the school in New Delhi that show he is missing us. Goodness knows I miss him, Connie and Winnie.

Chapter 29
AN INDIAN LIFESTYLE

In these hot days, with no rain since the monsoon ended, our servants are constantly fighting the dust and grit that blows in. We have placed strips of rubber on each door in the hope of keeping dust out. Under Prem Chan's supervision, the house is kept clean.

The morning has a sweet fragrance, whether it is from the frangipanis in the garden or the incense the servants burn. Even the floor wax has a clean smell to it. We enjoy coming out in the morning to find the terrazzo floor shining in colors of variegated blues and grays.

We are using the household goods that I selected from a list at the Embassy, to fulfill our needs until our own household effects arrive by ship and by train from Bombay. Our sheets are ironed and an eau d' cologne sprayed on them. Our clothes are now hanging in our cupboards.

When we get up, we order a pot of coffee. I have spent some time teaching Lazarus how to make coffee for breakfast— strong, with hot milk and sugar. After breakfast, we are fortunate to be able to have a shower. If Mark had not inspected the house, we would not be so lucky. He found that instead of hot and cold water, mixed, we had a hot faucet and a cold faucet with no device to mix the two. One had to be ordered from Bombay, 500 miles away.

The water runs down a tile-slanted floor into an opening in the floor. It is wonderful to be able to wash the dust away. We are one of very few homes with running water. Most water in brought by pails and poured into a tub for a bath.

This morning, I dressed in a long Hawaiian muu-muu of soft cotton in yellow and chartreuse. I braided my waist-length black hair, tying a ribbon to the end. Then I emptied a couple of teaspoons of lanolin in the palms of my hands and rubbed it on my face, neck and arms. This was followed by sunscreen.

Olive oil is rubbed into my hair before washing. Usually my hair is piled on the top of my head in a bun. There are no hair stylists here. These grooming secrets are things that I have learned from my Indian friends.

*   *   *

John's interest in geography, history, science and art increases. His interest in learning math is a different story. I doubt that I am an inspiring teacher, although I follow instructions.

He has no playmates, when his friend Gatum is in school, no television or movies, and much of the novelty of India is waning. He has begun talking about his buddies in Florida.

Yesterday, John came to me, after spending the entire morning alone in his room, and said, "Mother, sing the song Granddaddy sings about the garden, the church song."

"I am not sure I recall the words, but I will try," I said.

"I come to the garden alone
While the dew is still on the roses,
And a voice I hear,
Falling on my ear,
The Son of God discloses,
And He walks with me,
And He talks with me,
And he tells me I am His own,

And the voice I hear as,
I tarry there, none other has ever known."

When I finished, John said, "I like that; Granddaddy always sang it when we sat on the front porch at night." He sat for awhile, and then touched my hand, slipped off the chair and ran to find Das, the young sweeper.

*   *   *

Lolita, my new Christian friend, has become my connection to the community. She wants to talk, and few women are interested in listening to her. I am glad to become her confidante. She knows what is taking place, what is being discussed at town meetings, how the money is being spent, what is being planned. Lolita is well educated, well known, and vivacious.

She is aware of what other countries offer citizens as she lived in Canada when her husband was attending McGill University. She wants a better life for Indians, which includes a supply of potable water, a sanitation department with sewers, streetlights, and especially laws that would get the cows off the streets.

When she goes to the council meetings and speaks of these needs, the men ask, "Doesn't your husband make you happy? Why are you trying to make trouble?" She has met the criticism and continues to persevere.

Her husband, Joseph, an electrical engineer, supports her in her pursuit. They are high class, Ksatriyas, Hindus by birth. An event in Joseph's family's life changed all their lives. Joseph's father became ill. None of the treatments used had healed him. One day a medical missionary came through the city, heard of his illness, stopped and offered his help. After the family talked with him, they decided to allow him to examine the father. When the doctor had a clear idea of a diagnosis, they gave permission for treatment.

The missionary doctor moved into the home, watched over him day and night, and saved his life. At some point in the recovery, the patient wanted to talk. He asked the doctor about his religion, and the doctor told him that he was a Christian. There were days of quiet talk and Bible reading with prayers. The patient became converted to Christianity and took the name of the missionary doctor for himself and his entire family. The family continues to use the name.

Joseph and Lolita have a son and a daughter. The boy is older than John, although smaller, and they have become friends. We all spend time together. I love her wonderful laugh. She sees mirth in life and her attitude has helped me to understand how she can laugh and enjoy life, despite what may be thought of as tragedy in this country.

*   *   *

This week, we traveled to the northeast part of the state, where we met a most remarkable woman. Mrs. Welthy Honsinger Fisher is eighty-five years old, and her late husband was a Methodist Bishop. I had made my way over hundreds of miles especially to find her, at the Literacy Village in Lucknow.

Literacy Village takes people just where they find them and trains them to do whatever they do, only in a better way. For example, a tailor may be taught to take measurements and read figures, and become more adept in his sewing. Young women are trained to teach. New ways of communicating are devised.

The Literacy Village teachers often use puppets to get the messages to people. I attended one puppet show on family planning. It began with the romance of Chanda and Birju, who were happily married, but in five years, had five children. The bride looked like an old woman. The puppet "children" cried, and one vomited up yellow liquid over the edge of the stage. Chanda shyly told Birju that she was going to have another baby. He was distraught. There was not enough food for his babies now. He tried to hang himself but was rescued by a village-level worker. The doctor who treated him gave him advice on family planning.

The Ford Foundation had granted money to continue this program. Mrs. Fisher went to Denmark in April to receive that country's highest award for a foreigner. I had read her book, *To Light a Candle*, before leaving home. We shared many ideas during the next few hours.

*   *   *

We have learned that some sects of worshippers perform unusual rituals in the name of devotion before their god. On our way to Bhubaneswar on the Bay of Bengal, we came upon such a man, who traveled by prostrating himself in a strange manner on the roadside.

He rose and fell again, like a tree in a forest—not bending his knees or back, just falling heavily. The Indian specialist in the jeep with us said that this act is done for penance to cleanse him for any misdeeds he might have done. The Indian men and boys near us acknowledged this *Sadhu*, by stopping and bowing their heads.

The man paid no attention. He rose by placing his feet forward up to his palms, working himself up like an inchworm. Then he would slide his hands forward and fall prostrate again. He wore a saffron robe and had white and red, black markings on his face, upper arm, and quads.

We were told that he was traveling to the Holy City of Hardwar. For hundreds of miles, he would eat the dust in this manner. He carried nothing with him. People gave him food and water, since he is considered to be holy because of his act. Those who go mad or fast to the death are also considered holy.

*   *   *

Today, we attended a ceremony here in Raipur, in which the President of India's central government spoke. Hearing him, I realized that all politicians are alike and believe that all politics is local. Mr. Kamaraj is from

Madras in the south of India and is called a kingmaker, we were told. He spoke his native Tamil. His words were translated to the Indians who had gathered there in Hindi, and then Rafiq translated it to Mark and me in English.

Arts and crafts that we are seeing here are quite remarkable. All the work is done by hand. The artist tediously sits bent over for hours, carving beautiful designs on copper, brass and wood. The fabrics are gorgeous, and one seldom finds two pieces of the hand-woven material alike.

Since the villages are self-contained, they depend on themselves to supply all their needs. In contrast with the huts, the temples and special buildings are made of beautifully carved marble, some inlaid with precious and semi-precious stone and gold. Delicately carved ivory screens cover the windows.

We have found the people here to be very gentle, very kind and almost too hospitable. There are exceptions to this, such as the riots that still occur sometimes because of language differences.

Chapter 30
FARMS, JUNGLES AND BUDDHIST STUPAS

For several weeks, Mark has been traveling through South India. He flew to Hyderbad and took a train to Madras. He was assigned a car and driver to travel across the south of India to take a hard look at the prospects for crops this year.

The driver is about to be sent packing. He ran into a bicycle, a little later he hit a cart sitting on the edge of the road. Then he lost their way, when signs were plentiful. Rafiq, who stayed in Raipur, is sorely missed, Mark says.

Mark is in Camp Tikkingahi in the Circuit House. The Minister of Agriculture for Madhya Pradesh wants him to assist with building an extension program patterned on ones in the U.S., so the various positions can continue to operate regardless of who the personalities involved are. The farmers are planting 61,000 acres of corn in Mark's districts. He has met with many of the agriculturists. The region has only had 20 to 40 percent of the normal rainfall and the rice paddies are failing. *Jowar*, a cereal crop, looks good and the *ragi*, another grain, seems to be progressing fairly well.

"We like the people here, they are making an all-out effort to move along. There is real hope where effort is being made," Mark told me when he returned home yesterday. "They still don't have the elementary knowledge of machinery. Dr. Gill is the specialist but can't always be present. They are sending pumping sets out of Bhopal without critical spare parts. Two pumps for deep wells were out of service in Tikkamgarh—both diesels with fuel injector pumps out of order. They always forget something of a crucial nature."

*   *   *

This morning, he told me, "I need to look at the project that is going on about an hour from here. Perhaps we can find an animal on the return trip, I see we are low on meat."

I thought perhaps John could stay with Gatum, Sonu's little boy, but when I sent a note over, Sonu was away. So John came with us.

We began our trip to see conditions and, on our way to Bhopal, we stopped in Sanchi, where some of the oldest and most interesting Buddhist structures are located thirty miles northeast of the city. It was a beautiful morning.

Although Sanchi is the site of probably the oldest surviving buildings in the Indian subcontinent, the main interests are the Buddhist *stupas*, situated upon Sanchi Hill, some 300 feet high on the left bank of the Betwa River. It has no real connection with Buddha. Emperor Asoka built the first stupas, or mounds that commemorated a sacred event here in the Third Century B.C. A stupa is normally a burial mound, but Buddhist artists raised this to a level worthy to accommodate the vestiges of saints. Eight of the 84,000 stupas that Asoka built are in Sanchi. The stupa consists of a base bearing a hemispherical dome representing the dome of heaven enclosing the earth. This is surmounted by a square railed unit, the world mountain, from which rises a mast to symbolize the cosmic axis.

The Sanchi site we visited is a huge sacred mound with an elaborate stone entranceway, gradually decayed after the Hindus came through the land. It was forgotten until a British officer discovered the ruins in 1818. Sir John Marshall restored the stupas to their present condition in the early 1900s. The scene was breathtaking. I had my camera set and took many pictures of the magnificent statues and intricate carvings on the pillars and fences. Buddhist carvings are sacred adornment without idolatry, and represent scenes in the 550 Jataka tales of Buddha's previous incarnation.

A guard at Sanchi told us there were many "cats"—leopards and tigers— as well as pigs in the hills ten miles away, and a wild boar was on the hill nearby. We did not believe him until we drove away. The boar, looking as big as a Raipur cow, appeared in the middle of the road as we rounded a hairpin turn. John thought he looked very mean, so we were glad we were in the jeep.

Back in Raipur, the rest of the week has been filled with catch-up chores. It was my birthday and none of our older children could come to celebrate. Also, Connie and Winnie were going to a prom in New Delhi, and I would miss seeing the girls in their pretty dresses. I was rather quiet.

The Elephant Gate circles Sanchi's ancient mound. The site is the finest specimen of almost all Buddhist architecture forms, with stupas, chaitya, temples and monasteries dating from 3rd Century BC.

CHAPTER 31
A STALKING TIGER

Today Mark came in saying we were going again to hunt the rampaging tiger that we had been unable to find for the villagers a few weeks ago. We left for the village. Mark had sent a message so the people were waiting for us. John and I were to stay in the District Forester's house during the hunt.

I went in and asked for a pail of water and towels, which the bearer brought to the bedroom. I sponged off and put on my Hawaiian dress, sleeveless and reaching to the floor. I walked out on the wide veranda, pulled a chair near the edge, and tucked my gown around my legs while I waited to see the moon rise over the banyan tree.

A cup of tea was brought when I said, "*chai,* please." I sipped it and relaxed. My hair had been unbraided and hung over my shoulders to my waist. I lifted it up and flipped it over the back of the chair. I could hear John talking with the bearer who was finishing his chores.

I closed my eyes and let my mind wander. "How do our sweet girls look tonight as they go out to the prom? What am I doing in the jungle of India anyway?"

Finally, John came out. He always has a sense about me and shows up when I need someone around. I told him to get some sleep. I was almost asleep.

Suddenly I sensed the presence of someone or something. I opened my eyes. The sound was ever so faint, like a cushion being tossed to hit a sofa. I was careful not to move my head right or left, only tilting it slightly forward so I could use peripheral vision. My hearing became more acute. I squinted my eyes to pierce the darkness. My nostrils seemed to flare. I smelled an odor, musty and vile, as the wind wafted it towards me.

Deep shadows covered most of the yard, only a small blotch of grey sand showed in the moonlight. My eyes continued to scan the darkness. Then I saw it by the tree—a silhouette of darker shadow. I stared and felt the creature must be staring; neither of us moved.

I knew that tigers have a strong sense of smell. I had been told that they attack from the front. We had discussed tiger hunting with the greatest hunters in the world since coming to India, as their records proved.

I listened, feeling my heart in my throat and temples. Finally the tiger turned and circled across the road. I watched it, slowly, gracefully sauntering through the clearing. I was within twenty-five yards of it at one point. When it was out of sight I eased my legs off the chair arms, raised myself to a standing position and quietly tiptoed to the door.

I knew that a carnivore moves silently. The secret of its success as a hunter lies in the animal instinct, watching where it places its front paws to make no sound. It places its back paws in the exact same spot as the front paws as it moves forward to take its next step.

I had left my sandals by my chair. I took three long steps on tiptoe to reach the inside where I could close the door. I knew that the cat could have pounced like a flash. I looked toward the charpoi at John sleeping there. I dared not make a sound. This was probably the man-eater that Mark, Rafiq, Prem Chan and the others were waiting for, with bait.

The oil lamp threw shadows on the wall. I tiptoed to get the gun, avoiding sleeping lizard-like creatures, called gekkos, strewn over the floor. Daylight will find these little gekkos so full of insects that they are sleeping like drunken sailors.

I was practically paralyzed with fear, but I knew I had to hold on to my emotions and be silent. I checked both barrels, then took two shells and went back to the rear door of the house.

The tiger was stalking me. I saw his shadow moving from dark to light. I watched him, and then eased to the front of the house. I didn't dare open the door so I sat on my charpoi thinking. I had checked the lock and the wooden latch inside both doors. I went to the door and placed my ear to the jam, listening. I heard nothing. The guard had gone off someplace, but I didn't want to think of him being alone, if he was. I moved quietly back to my bed, leaned the gun by the bed and eased onto the hemp webbing. I knew that I wouldn't sleep tonight, with the tiger on the prowl.

"You can just stay out there and we will stay in here!" I thought.

As daylight finally broke, I heard the vehicle speed up the road. I met Mark at the door. "Oh, darling!" I collapsed in his arms.

"What is it?" he asked.

By then, I began collecting myself. "Your tiger has been stalking us all night."

"Damn!" was all he could say.

For the dozenth time, we talked about tigers the next morning.

"Tigers learn quickly," Rafiq said. "You can call it instinct or self-preservation. It is unnatural for a villager to tie up their cattle for the night in the forest. Bait secured by a rope tied around its horns stands a better chance of dying. It is possible for an animal to get entangled in the undergrowth by its horns. Bait secured by its hind legs is also readily taken. The important thing to remember is that a tiger and a panther attack the throat of their victim. There should be nothing around the throat to prevent this method of attack."

I agreed that the big cats are smart. "That tiger knew that I was inside last night. I had some anxious times."

"Do you remember the three leopards we saw down near Dhar? How they were rather indifferent to us?" Rafiq recalled. "The one dug his claws into the tree as he stretched himself, disregarding our presence. The other two slept like tame cats until they saw the light— then they moved like lightning. Panthers are generally less careful than tigers. They take greater risks, for they are fast."

We drove home. At the door, Gillie came bounding up to us. Her nose was badly swollen. Mark looked at it and asked for antiseptic powder. "How did that happen?"

"She found a mongoose and attacked it," said Lazarus.

"She got the worst of the game," Mark commented. He counted sixty bites on her.

Gillie looked rather sheepish about her adventure.

CHAPTER 32
TIME AND LEGENDS

One thing that we have learned here is that news travels over the Indian "grapevine" with unbelievable speed. Discussions that we have in the "privacy" of our bedroom are known in the village. When we plan to be away, or to have guests, or other happenings of much less import, the plans are known.

Our sea freight arrived yesterday. We had waited three months since we moved here for this happy day. I had bought clothes for each of the children to last two years and a half, as well as those things Mark and I would need. There were socks, shirts, belts, and pajamas for the men— although we had not known that the word "pajama" is a Sanskrit word and all the lower caste men wear this apparel daily.

Our linens, silver, crystal, china, and many other items were part of the sea freight. When the freight reached the rail station here, a call came from the railway superintendent telling us that the crates had been opened, and only a few boxes remained inside.

It was heartbreaking to me. The children had chosen their individual things to bring with such care, and even the silver, crystal and china were to have belonged to them one day. Now, someone had stolen it all. The household effects that I had planned to use were gone. There was one belt and one of John's bedroom shoes left behind.

The official apologized, saying that the goods train had been put on a rail siding and stayed there until repairs could be made on the track. This was apparently when the theft occurred.

When Mark came home, all I could say was, "They have been stolen—all of our nice things."

"Don't cry, sweetheart, I will buy you more silver and crystal, sometime," he said, taking me in his arms.

At last, I said, "It is insured; we can replace it."

"Did you insure our sea freight?" he asked.

"No," I said. "I thought you would do that along with other official tasks." I was crushed. "Oh, Mark, all of my silver flatware, water tumblers, bread plates, crystal and china, all gone."

Looking at him, I knew he felt no better than I, so I decided never to mention it again.

*   *   *

Here in Raipur, our entertainment depends on our acquaintances, and us. Much of this enjoyment comes from reading stories and listening to friends we meet tell of their interests or what is happening to them.

An Anglo-Indian professor has been here visiting for the last few weeks. She has given several readings and she gave me a copy of the ancient story of Dantila. It is one of many treasures that I will always save.

Written in Sanskrit, 200 years B.C., it tells this legend:

"Somewhere in the world is a city called Vardhamana. A very prosperous merchant by the name of Dantila lived there. He exercised authority over the whole city. During his administration, he kept both the common people and the king very happy. What more can be said? A man as wise as that has hardly been heard of or seen, for:

"The man who seeks the good of the king is hated by the common people. And the man who seeks the welfare of the people is hated by the King."

In such conflicting circumstances, it is almost impossible to find such a man, loved by the king as well as the people.

In the course of time, the marriage of Dantila's daughter took place. Dantila invited the entire public and the king's officers. He entertained them sumptuously, gave them presents of clothing and, in this way, he honored them. Following the wedding the king, the queen and the entire court were invited to Dantila's house and he showed them great respect.

A servant by the name of Gorambha, who used to sweep the floors of the king's palace, came there too, but uninvited. He sat down on a seat meant for someone else. Dantila caught him by the neck and threw him out. The servant felt insulted and could not sleep all night for thinking, "How can I get Dantila into disfavor with the king and so get even with him? But then, what chances have I, an ordinary fellow, of harming such a powerful person as he is."

Several days later, early in the morning, when the king was not yet wide awake, Gorambha was sweeping the floor near the king's bed and said, "Good heavens! Dantila has become so brazen nowadays that he actually dares to embrace the queen!"

Then he said, "Master, I was gambling all night and didn't sleep at all. This morning I feel drowsy. I really don't know what I've been saying."

Jealous, the king thought to himself, "Yes! The servant Gorambha is allowed to go about freely in the palace and so is Dantila. It is quite possible that Gorambha has seen Dantila embracing my queen, for: 'What a man ponders over, sees during the day, he will utter in his dreams.'

"And there is no doubt about it when a woman is involved. She smiles at one man, with half-opened lips, throws a little remark at another, at the same time flirting with the third, her eyes half-closed, while in her heart she dreams of yet another man, the one she loves. Who can depend on the love of such a woman, with eyebrows like the bows of an archer? The man who thinks that a woman loves him is a fool. He falls into her trap—she'll treat him like a toy."

The king's thoughts were so troubled that from that day onward, he withdrew his favors from Dantila and forbade him ever to enter the palace. Dantila was astounded by this sudden change in the king's attitude and said to him, 'It is true what they say:

'Has anyone heard of:

A crow that is clean,
A gambler who is honest,
A snake that forgives,
A passionate woman who is calm,
An impotent man who is brave,
A drunkard with discrimination,
Or the true friendship of a king?'

"Even in my dreams, I have done no harm to anyone, not to the king himself, nor anyone in his family. Why then is the king so hostile towards me?"

Some time passed. One day, when Dantila wanted to pass through the gateway to the palace, the guards stopped him. Gorambha, who was sweeping the floor, saw this and he said with a smirk, "Ho! Guard. That fellow is the king's favorite. He can arrest or release people, just as he pleases. He threw me out. Be careful, you may suffer the same fate."

When Dantila heard this, he thought to himself, "It is surely Gorambha who has caused the trouble. Now I understand why they say: 'The king's servant, though he be of low caste, foolish or mean, is respected wherever he goes.'"

Dantila returned home in a very dejected mood. He thought it over, and that evening, he invited Gorambha to his house. He gave the sweeper a pair of garments and said kindly, "My dear friend, it was because I was angry that I threw you out that day, but because it was an impropriety for you to take the seat you took. It was reserved for a Brahmin, the Brahmin felt insulted, and that's why I had to throw you out. Forgive me."

When Gorambha saw the clothes, he was pleased. Full of joy, he said to Dantila, "Sir, now I forgive you. You have expressed your regrets and also honored me. Once again you shall see the favor of the king. In this way I shall prove to you my cleverness." With these words Gorambha went home happily.

Next morning, he went to the palace and started sweeping the floor. When he had made sure that the king was lying half-awake, he said, "The king is really indiscreet, he eats cucumbers in the bathroom!"

The king was taken aback to hear this and shouted,"You, Gorambha! What is that nonsense you are talking? It's only because you are my servant that I don't kill you. Have you ever seen me doing such a thing?"

"Master," said Gorambha, "I was gambling last night and didn't sleep at all. This morning I feel drowsy. I really don't know what I've been saying. But if I've said anything out of place, please forgive me."

When the king heard this, he thought to himself, "Never in my life have I eaten cucumbers in the bathroom. If this fool has said something ridiculous about me, surely what he said about Dantila was ridiculous too. It was wrong of me to insult Dantila. Besides, without him, the whole administrative system at the palace and in the city has become slack."

Grandparents and parents repeat this ancient story to young Indian children, who, once they are grown and married, will repeat it to their children in turn.

CHAPTER 33
OTHERS WHO ARE IN NEED

I am too busy these days to think of my lost valuables. We have had so many people coming for help with illnesses or injuries.

The first man came to our back door with a terribly infected foot, leaning on a branch of a tree as he walked. Wrapped around the foot was a dirty rag saturated in pus. I first had him soak his foot in warm soapy water, and then Das put Epsom salts into another pail for soaking. After that, I gave the man antibiotics. Lazarus explained and then wrote down in Hindi the instructions on how to take the medicine.

The man left, but he evidently passed the word to many others after he was healed. When news circulated that I had medicine on hand and I had treated some, others were not reluctant to come.

I cannot depend on getting a new supply of medicine from the States any time soon. The burden of disease and lack of health care here is too great to bear alone. I will do what I can with the limited knowledge and resources available.

Our servants are truly members of our household, and they have an assortment of duties that I have assigned them to perform. One task is helping to care for the sick or injured, since the experience we had with the first patient. Some of the Indians now call me "White Mother Doctor," Rafiq says. I feel honored, as to the Indians, the term, "mother," is one of great respect.

People who come for help are invited to sit beneath the huge, spreading tree and are given water to drink. I use a mop with soap to clean them, then soaks of Epsom salts in boiled water, as many are infected with sores. Others have matter running from the ears and eardrums that have ruptured. These I give the medicine that my American friends had given me. I follow the instructions on the form of a prescription written on each huge carton.

I have come to rely on the men who work for us, as our life could not go on without their help. We are always kind to them, and they are pleasant and obedient. We find them laughing at little things, which lightens our day. It takes one servant's entire time to boil enough water for the house. They keep the house and our clothes clean, and they are loyal. We are constantly concerned about maintaining hygiene. Vegetables must be soaked in *lugal* (iodine) for thirty minutes before cooking.

Prem Chan is the master and directs the other servants. He takes a personal responsibility for me by sleeping on a cot outside my door every night with a baseball bat by his side. A former paratrooper, who was imprisoned by the Japanese during World War II, he is well aware of ways to protect my life. When Mark is here, Prem sleeps on the veranda.

*   *   *

Mark is traveling much of the time. Whenever there is housing available, a jungle rest house, or a *dak* bungalow, John and I accompany him. These houses are great distances apart and must be reserved months in advance. The only occupants are the highest government officials. The houses are very well built with large rooms that can accommodate more than a couple of people.

On our last trip, we arrived about midnight at a bungalow, and in the light of our vehicle we spotted a man wearing a fine, brocade robe walking down the path. Our interpreter asked if he was staying there as we too had reservations. He answered curtly, "I don't look like a sweeper, do I?" Our man said under his voice, "He doesn't even act like a good sweeper."

With no hotels or even cities for hundreds of miles, these rest houses are the only places to stay.

*   *   *

We've been away from New Delhi for three months. It will soon be time for us to make a trip back there, as our gamma globulin shots are due. We are looking forward to spending some time with Connie, Dennis and Winnie.

I like our home here, although I miss the children. As for me, it is a wonderful feeling to rise in the early morning when the mist is still in the air. I love being up and out in this country before the day become hot, and the world of people begins stirring. The Moslems' morning prayers most often wake me, so I am usually out early, after a cup of coffee with Mark.

Today, Rafiq drove me to market. The fruits and vegetables, brought in from the farms in the early light of morning, were still fresh. We always get spices for the week, freshly ground and pungent. If the cook comes along, he barters, but today Rafiq did it.

After we finished our shopping, I said, "Let's drive to the lepers' place and see if they need anything that we have."

"Sure, Memsabji," said Rafiq. "You know some of them can ask for things for the others who can't speak."

As we arrived, we saw that they were all sitting in a circle on the dirt by the stone wall, with no trees nearby. They usually sleep here. The grotesque faces and bodies, sans eyebrows, noses, lips, toes and fingers, were pitiful reminders of their helplessness. Wrapped about their bodies they wore ragged shirts and *dhotis* (a cloth garment instead of pants).

The lower caste, the untouchables, are most often very kind to the lepers who themselves are now outcasts. Some come to shave them and help in other little ways. Certainly the help available is not enough.

I asked Rafiq to explain what my medicines could treat, and to find out if they could use it. As he talked, some responded with a half-grimace, half-smile. It was enough to show that they were grateful for attention. They wanted rice and fruit, Rafiq told me, and we left some of our supplies with them.

I asked Rafiq to tell them about some of the research being done in far-away cities and that someday they will be helped. We have become aware that cadavers are sold to laboratories abroad for experimentation in using ligaments to reconstruct missing thumbs, fingers and other parts. "Tell them only that surgeons are doing research on limbs to be able to reconstruct them," I said, knowing that it would be best not to mention the cadavers used in the research.

"Yes, Memsahib," Rafiq said.

I bowed to the group with my palms together, in respect for their severe infirmity, and we left.

*   *   *

Driving through the town yesterday, I saw a little mother scraping dust from a red brick embedded in the floor of a public building. She then raked the dust up in a little pile, put it in the palm of her hand and spat on it, then mixed it into a paste and plastered a sore on her child.

It is heartbreaking not to be helping all the people. It is estimated that half of India's elderly are deaf and blind.

I recall, as a child of about three during America's Depression, seeing my mother spend hours-sewing dresses for children whose mothers were unable to do so. She would prepare chicken and other foods, which she placed in a sealed jar so none of the nutrients escaped, and then we would take food to the poor. Often I could scarcely see them, lying in a bundle of dingy sheets in a darkened corner of a farm shack, and just as skinny as these women that I see in India. The Depression was terrible for the South, and the memories of what I observed when I was a child have never left me.

CHAPTER 34
A SPECIAL GUEST

Mark's secretary, Lal, brought us a postcard one day recently, postmarked Bilaspur. We know no one there. It is seventy or more miles from us. We have learned, though, that miles aren't important, as any travel consumes hours.

The card came from Father John Dela Hoye, an Anglican priest, who wrote to welcome us to our new home. He said he would come to visit us if it was agreeable. He wanted to stay over a Saturday and leave Sunday evening. We would be offered Communion. We wondered how he knew about us. I wrote a note back and the return mail said that he would be here in a fortnight as we had suggested.

This weekend, on the appointed day, we waited for a runner to let us know that he had arrived at the train station. Instead, Das came rushing in to say our guest had arrived by rickshaw. The priest came in. He had the broadest smile and I was just as pleased to see him. I apologized for not having met the train.

"I could get here more quickly by taking a rickshaw," he said. Tall, slender and English-looking although deeply tanned, he radiated warmth.

I learned he had come by third class car, very inexpensive transportation costing only a few pennies—and always packed to running over with people hanging on the sides, on the top and out the windows.

"You must be exhausted by the heat," I said. Lazarus brought him a glass of water and a glass of *nimbupani*, on a tray. "I'm sure you must be thirsty."

"Yes, I am a bit on the dry side." We sat quietly talking about his trip.

He explained that Bishop John of the Cathedral in New Delhi had notified him of our moving here. I had not expected this communication in the Christian community here, and was touched by Father John's thoughtfulness in light of his busy schedule. Christianity seems so remote, except in our hearts and minds, when we are surrounded by all the religious displays of Hinduism, Sikhism, and Jainism.

Father Dela Hoye told me of his life in India for over thirty years. His father had graduated from Oxford, come to India and served the British population as priest. His mother was Anglo-Indian. He spoke of the comfortable conditions before the end of the British reign and how difficult life had become afterwards. He himself had been sent to England for his education and graduated from Oxford before returning to India to serve as priest. He then married an Anglo-Indian girl as his father had done.

From what he said, I gathered that life has not been easy. He lives on the small stipend sent him from the Church of England. "The parishioners have some small offering, and they are generous and share what they have in the way of vegetables, rice and *pulses*— an Indian term for peas, beans and lentils. There is seldom a chicken or any meat."

I rang the bell for Das to bring us the lemonade-type drink, *nimbu,* and also gin and tonic. My guest greatly enjoyed that, he said, as he never has anything stronger than the wine for dinner.

         *   *   *

Mark had been traveling all week, but returned in the afternoon soon after Father Dela Hoye's arrival. There was a great deal of excitement among the men of the house as the jeep rolled up, dust flying behind. "It is Sahib, Memsahibji!" Prem Das exclaimed.

Mark entered and was introduced, soon excusing himself to head for the shower. India is a place that requires several showers and changes of clothes each day. When Mark returned, his drink was waiting for him. I left and the men talked a while as our meal was being prepared. A gentle and peaceful man, Father Dela Hoye is learned on any topic brought up.

This Sunday morning, seven of us, including ourselves and the James family— my friend Lolita, her husband and son—went to the center of the town where Fr. Dela Hoye had arranged for us to use a room above a store for a church service. It was a small, drab room that contained a few chairs and a table, which he converted into an altar.

Since Sunday has no religious significance to anyone except Christians, business in the village was going on below as usual. Horns on bicycles honked, and conversation rose in a steady hum as people went about their morning routines. Above all of this, our a capella singing could be described as robust, whatever else our limitations were. In this setting, we had morning prayers and entered into the communion service; three Indians, three Americans and an Anglo-Indian priest.

I sat listening to this dear old man, surely nearly seventy years of age. I was thinking about how he has given his life to help those who listen to him and follow his simple pattern of helping the needy. Those in need are so numerous that there is no way to imagine their problems are solvable except through God's grace. I believe Father John is an angel of mercy.

I remembered a day when I had been sitting in our garden in Delhi, and had heard a clicking sound of an automobile. It was the car of Bishop John, Rector of the Cathedral in New Delhi. The Bishop's Austin was thirty-five or forty years old, but shined and without a single rattle coming from it. His liveried chauffeur in spotless white opened the back door and the Bishop, in his black suit and white collar alighted. I recalled my talk with him when he had called at our home for tea shortly before we left for Raipur.

I told Father John Dela Hoye the story that the Bishop had told to me about his worst experience as a priest in New Delhi. It was during the time after the British had given India her independence. The sweeper caste had heard of the Bible's story of the loaves and fishes. They came to the Bishop thinking he could do likewise. He had nothing to give them, except the promise that Jesus had made to us of salvation.

Fr. Dela Hoye spent as much time as possible with our son John during his visit in our home and would always remember John later. He returned to Bilaspur carrying a few books, two loaves of bread, a bottle of whisky and one of brandy. I could imagine that he would nurse the drinks for many months.

CHAPTER 35
WILD GOOSE CHASE

"We are running low on meat," Mark said yesterday. Every eight to ten days we go on safari for meat for ourselves and our staff and their families. Rafiq brought good news today of geese having landed on a pond several miles away. He has checked the report out and the people seem reliable. We decided to leave about 4 a.m. to reach the pond by sunrise.

Early this morning, in the glow of the beams of light from the veranda, Das and Prem Chan packed the ammunition box and guns. We drank a cup of coffee and were ready to leave. We all got in the Jeep. John put on his jacket and sleepy as he was, crawled in the back seat, and Prem Chan and Mark joined him.

This was the coolest part of the day, but soon the light would begin to creep through the trees. The hills in the distance were blue with haze. As we traveled along the dirt road, it soon curved into a village, and then vanished into the hills.

We found ourselves behind a public bus. The driver squeezed the rubber bulb to sound the horn. It made a bullish obnoxious noise that resounded along the roadway and past the hill. There was no room to pass on this narrow road. The bus stopped. We stopped. A man in khaki uniform rode up beside the bus on his bicycle and dismounted.

"A constable rides each bus," Rafiq told us.

The constable stepped down from the bus and took the handlebars, and they heaved the bicycle onto the vehicle's roof. The constable got inside. The man stood in the door of the bus and shouted.

"*Chalo, chalo, chalo* (let's go, let's go, let's go)."

"Who is that passenger?" I asked Rafiq.

"A politician," Rafiq answered. "He acts like a politician."

People came running down the road, out of the huts and teashops and clambered aboard with sleep in their faces and eyes.

The bus started up and roared off, leaving us in a bath of dust. Finally, Rafiq veered into the first flattened ditch that he could find and passed without incident.

"Crazy man," Rafiq muttered.

The sun colored the Mahanadi River red and gold. Bullock carts, mounds of hay atop them, were lined up ahead of us, each waiting its turn to cross. When the bullocks plowed into the water, the water rose to their flanks. We turned left, leaving the dirt road and following the riverbank through the jungle, with no people in view.

We saw jungle birds, red, green, yellow and blue, that are larger than an American chicken. Doves, partridges, guineas, parakeets, mynah birds, peafowl and peahens were feeding. The peacocks are sacred to Hindus, and we are not allowed to shoot any, although they are so plentiful. At times we have counted hundreds of peafowl eating in a field, and they can devour a field of rice or wheat in no time. Farmers keep a constant watch from stands built on stilts, hoping to frighten birds and animals away from their crops.

We stopped on the riverbank to check the water's depth and determine the safety of fording it. A man came loping effortlessly along wearing a G-string and a cloth wrapped around his head. He paid no attention to us. Prem Chan yelled to him, and he stopped. Prem Chan communicated with him to explain that we wanted to cross the river. The man resumed running and did not slow up when he hit the water's edge, nor did he look back. The water came up to his knees. He continued running straight ahead until he reached the other bank and disappeared into the jungle. We decided the river looked harmless.

Rafiq headed the Jeep into the water. The river rose slowly over the tires and then the vehicle took a big drop into deeper water that covered the hood. Time and moving water had shifted logs and branches that were now floating about us. We were in the mud and water, and it was seeping into the cab. Steam was boiling off the engine.

"Get out," Mark called. He, Rafiq and I acted in unison. I opened the door. It took all the strength that I could muster.

"The guns!" Mark shouted, but Prem Chan had managed to get out with the two guns. I motioned for him to hand them to me. I held them over my head. Mark took John on his shoulders, and we headed for the bank. Upon reaching it we spread our guns, shells and jackets to dry.

Mark went back into the river to the jeep. "I will be back for you as soon as possible."

Rafiq had sent Prem Chan off to get help. Time passed, and finally he returned with a team of bullocks yoked together, driven by a small man. The rope lines from the animals were attached to the bumper of the jeep. Using his whip, the man yelled "*Chelo, chelo!*" to the dumb-looking animals whose huge heads dropped as though they might go to sleep and didn't "go" as was commanded.

Finally, the bullocks waded into the water, followed by their master and the other men. The team lurched forward, leaning on the lines. With a snap, both ropes broke. They were no competition for the weight of the jeep.

The sun was rising higher in the sky, and it was getting hotter by the minute. Mark's drooping shoulders showed his disappointment. He dug out his pipe and lit it. The pipe has always been his comforter.

John and I moved back beneath the trees. Minutes stretched into hours. We were thirsty and hungry. We saw that Mark had a jack in his hand, and he reached in again and next brought out the tarpaulin. I thought how foolish we were to come unprepared, no ropes, no water, and no food. "If we ever get out, I'll have learned a lesson," I thought to myself.

We have been told that tigers, leopards, bears and other animals roam this jungle. When we heard the roar of a tiger after being here many hours, we were frightened, and I told John to fire a gun once into the air. He did, and after a flurry of noise, the jungle quieted down, but our fears remained. We knew we couldn't get out of here fast enough.

John and I watched intently to see what was going on. The sun was white hot now, and there were no clouds, just a bleached, milky colored sky. We could see that they were placing the tarpaulin underneath the front wheels, then they all pushed the jeep the length of the tarpaulin, repeating this over and until the water was below the engine. Rafiq and Mark went to work drying the wires. Mark waved his fist up in the air when it looked promising that they'd soon be out.

Indeed, after sputtering and popping the engine started, and they drove up the incline of the riverbank. We were joyful. The sun was setting fast and darkness was upon us. Rafiq carefully drove over bumps and hills getting out. In the distance we could see a dim light. We headed for it in the deeply trenched road.

Men were sitting on the porch, and Rafiq asked for water. They were pleasant and hospitable. One man called his wife, and she began to boil water for tea. The cups were filled with rich buffalo milk and sugar and tasted like manna from heaven. Tears stood in John's eyes. We all enjoyed the refreshment.

The men were inquisitive about what was going on in the country. They talked about their needs. The village has no school and no doctors. It is a truly depressed setting, yet they were appreciative for our visit and said, "God sent you to us."

Mark promised to inquire about the situation and whether anything could be done for their village.

When we arrived home, it was about midnight. Lights were burning. Our servants were all awake. They said they had been waiting for sunrise to assemble a hunting party to go find us. It was a good reunion.

We were starved and ready for the tea and sandwiches Lazarus brought us. I told him to defrost our last haunch for Sunday dinner. There will be no goose this weekend. But one never gives up hope.

The monsoon came and rivers poured over their banks. When we could not ford a river, we often relied on a floating barge, driving our jeep aboard with rough planks. The barge would be pushed across using poles, unless an old engine was available.

CHAPTER 36
THE WASHERMAN IS IN TROUBLE

Our home has many conveniences that include a place for the *dhobi* to work. We have tubs underneath a water faucet, a flat stone on which the clothes are beaten, and a line that clothes are swung over. All are part of the garden area, behind the servants' quarters. The dhobi works there every day to keep the clothes clean, as the dust and heat require at least two changes daily for all of us. The dhobi normally squats while removing the dirt and rinsing the clothes, then rises to hang.

Mark was sitting on the veranda yesterday with a drink when he heard a slapping noise coming from the back of the house. "Ram, what is that sound?"

"Dhobi, Sahib, sir," Ram answered. Mark sat his drink down, jumped out of his chair and went through to the veranda and into the back garden. He found his shirts being slammed across a flat stone.

Mark grabbed the dhobi by his shirt and lifted him up. "My best shirts, you are ruining my best shirts!"

"Rafiq, tell this worthless man what I said. I had you explain to him before about the care of my shirts. He pays no attention." Mark ushered the dhobi to the Chokadar, then out the gate.

Mark and Rafiq walked away, leaving the dirty clothes in the tubs, and came inside. I was waiting in the kitchen where I had gone when I hear the ruckus. Mark's temper had not abated.

"It is hard enough to get shirts! Those are my Italian ones."

"I will wash the Italian ones," I offered.

"No, you will not. We pay good money for his service."

I said to Rafiq, "Here, come with me. I want to send some notes out to friends to help search for a dhobi."

"Let's have a nice cup of tea, darling," I suggested to Mark.

"I don't want tea, I want a drink. Das, whiskey."

Later, I talked with Rafiq. "I know word will get around to all the dhobis. I think we might have trouble keeping someone permanently. What do you think?"

"I would not be surprised," he said. "There is the most pride imaginable in each caste, and the dhobi caste is very powerful. You talk to them, Memsabji, not Sahib."

My friend Sonu came to our rescue, as her head servant sent their household's dhobi to fill our need. Through Rafiq, I explained carefully what must be done to give proper care for the shirts.

*   *   *

My friend Lolita came to see me today. I was delighted to have her here so I can discuss the dhobi situation besides our usual chat.

"My dear, what are you going to do about your skin in this heat?" Lolita asked me.

"I brought a bottle of lanolin. That's what I use in Florida," I said.

"Our skin is one thing we Indian women do not seem to take enough care of. I learned that with a very little bit of money and two hours a week I can get very good results. Would you like to know what I do?"

"Oh, yes, tell me," I said.

"The rice flour treatment gets rid of facial wrinkles due to overstrain and weariness. Prepare a paste from rice flour and milk and apply to your clean face and leave it on for an hour. Wash it off with lukewarm water and splash with cold. You can tell the difference immediately."

"Wonderful," I told her happily. "I can use all the help I can get."

She gave me a recipe for a paste made from two or three almonds ground with water, applied and left for about 15 minutes before washing, to make the complexion fairer and smoother. Oatmeal and a little honey added to an egg white makes a good facial mask, according to Lolita, and an egg white with a few drops of lime juice is also helpful.

"You are full of ideas," I said. "Where did you learn all this?"

"Mainly by word of mouth. I read the columns of a writer named Veena Sharma, when I can get the paper. She has never led me astray.

Lolita also told me of the famous "milk bath" method she uses. Taking a piece of muslin, put into it a heaping cup of powdered skim milk, one cup of ordinary oatmeal and a cup of laundry starch. Tie into a bag. Fill your tub with warm water and swish the bag back and forth in it. When the water is milky white, lie down in the liquid and relax. Scrub yourself with the muslin bag about 20 minutes. Dry yourself well.

*   *   *

My Indian friends requested that I hold some classes on nutritious meals. They were eager to participate and take the information back to their households and servants. We held the classes last week. I taught them to make a vegetable stew using corn, instead of roasting corn until it became blackened, and other dishes that could be cooked in one pot.

Along with cooking and healthy meals, I also got around to talking about family planning and explaining what was needed to reduce the number of children.

The women, who seemed glad to have been at the classes, showed their appreciation when one of the ladies, Sanjamana, brought me a sari. It had been bought in Lucknow, and like all saris, it is six yards long. It is tissue-thin and soft, in a delicate blue. Beautiful embroidered flowers of the same blue are sprinkled over the material. The work is known as Chicon work, a technique handed down from father to son for as long as anyone can remember.

I have had an underskirt and a blouse, called a *choli*, made. I have added the sari to my wardrobe and wear it on all social occasions when Indians are present.

*   *   *

We have been invited to the home of the Chairman of the Board of Regents at Rajkumar College, where the sons of the Rajas attend school. In return, Mark and I wanted to entertain the Rajas and their wives who had arrived for their sons' graduation exercises. I began to plan a dinner for ten Rajput Maharajas and their wives, called Maharanis. We spent three days in preparation for the evening, which finally came last night.

Although we had no Indian recipes on the menu, I could use no meat, eggs or any food that had been a living creature. I used a hearty supply of pastas, cheeses, and vegetables, cooked and in salads, breads, jams and fruit with clotted cream. With the coffee and tea, we served nuts and shortbread with chocolate frosting.

The guests ate heartily, especially enjoying the coffee. Afterwards, we offered brandy and liqueur. They all passed, one saying, "We had all of these things during the time of the Raj (when the British were there). That time has passed and we must love what we have."

A lively discussion followed. They were interested in all phases of the U.S. agricultural program, and talked about their eagerness to see the irrigation program get under way.

After dinner, the women went to one end of the room and the men to the other, as had been the case in every event we had attended. This time, I was determined to change the pattern.

"How would you like for me to teach you the Mexican Hat Dance?" I asked.

"Yes, do," they all exclaimed.

I sent for the big sombrero that we had brought for sun protection. It was tossed on the floor, we formed a circle and began clapping and dancing around in a circle. I had only seen the hat dance done in the movies, but it was a smashing hit, nevertheless.

Then one Maharaja said, "Let's all do things that we do best." Some stood on their heads, one had a bicycle brought in and he balanced on the handlebars, and the women danced.

I sang a love song to end the evening.

"I love you truly, truly, dear,
Life with its sorrow, life with its tears,
Fades into dream land when you are near."

The Maharajas and their wives loved this old song, with its romantic theme that seemed to span cultural differences.

CHAPTER 37
TRAVELING THE COUNTRYSIDE

I have learned that you cannot depend on the clock for Indians' adherence to a timetable. They believe that things that happened before will happen again, or things that have happened before will never happen. When we want to know what date an event happened—when a tiger's pugmarks were seen, for instance—or set a date for a planned meeting, no one can tell you a date or day. This has been exasperating. Now, when we plan a trip, our staff knows the hour set is firm. After Mark has spoken to them once, thereafter they go by our time.

For the past few weeks, we have been visiting innumerable villages throughout Madhya Pradesh. The scene is always the same, children up to two or three years old running around naked, filthy, and skinny, often with protruding stomachs. The thin young mothers just out of puberty are caring for their babies. Dried mud and debris cover the ground. A goat or two may be climbing on rock piles, on the roofs or any small obstacles in the village, as goats like to climb on anything.

My friend Margaret in New Delhi told me before I ever went to a village that I must not think of adopting the starving children that I would see.

"Don't do it," she said. "It has been tried unsuccessfully. The cultures are too diverse. There is a chasm that can't be breached now. You will be giving your training and energy, and that will require the best of what you can do."

The purpose of the Agency for International Development's program here is to give the people the means of helping themselves. It starts with instructing the district administrator and Mark's counterpart, Dr. Kondapika, in the use of improved methods of farming. They, in turn, designate those who demonstrate the methods to the farmers through universities and other means.

Our program is to furnish the training and supply good seed, fertilizer and irrigation by building canals and deep wells for potable water. Emphasis is on the staple crops, rice, wheat, bulgar, *ragi* and other cereals desperately needed to feed the growing population.

The World Health Organization works on eradicating disease and promoting birth control, as the families are large and weak.

*   *   *

Our travels take us through the countryside over narrow roads, hard packed, and rough trails, where even the hardiest jeep must be operated in low gear. In each village the same scenario plays out. As soon as we come in sight, the women cover their heads and faces with the ends of their saris until we pass. They squat to rake leaves and break twigs to cook with, and they pull roots from the earth to make a concoction to drink.

The woman's work is physically harder than anyone else's. She always has a baby on her hip or at her breast. She carries a basket or perhaps a brass container on her head, for food or water. While it is still dark, before the sun has risen, she can be found gathered at the well with other women, exchanging gossip about families and the village.

The young children gather about the women and take turns splashing themselves in the water that has been drawn. They use a finger to brush their teeth. There is much laughter and play among the children as the mothers scrub their copper or brass pots with sand and ash. When they finish, they fill the pots with water and help each other raise the containers to their heads, where they set the container on a round ring and leave for their huts of straw and mud.

If there is a river or a tank or pond nearby, it is used for every purpose. The buffaloes will lie contentedly while the children rub the animals' bodies in the water. Each day the animals are bathed alongside the yelling, laughing children, while men and women squat in the water and wash themselves and their clothes that they are wearing. In this way they create privacy for their bodies. After completing their baths alongside the animals, they take up an extra piece of clothing they have brought along and beat it over soapstones that are found on the waters' edge.

The sun rises in the sky until it is white hot, bleaching and drying the landscape throughout the months following the monsoon. The tanks become nothing more than shallow, slimy spots of green liquid, which turn muddy with the entrance of the first animal and grow progressively muddier as the days wear on. In the evening, all return for the same ritual.

During the day, children and women run along with hands uplifted within inches of the animal to catch the droppings, so the manure won't be wasted. To see a beautiful little girl holding her small hands in this manner to be filled with dung makes us angry and sad. The child knows nothing more than that she is helping her family.

When the dung is made into cakes and dried, it is used for fires. While wet, it is smeared on the floor of the huts, soon becoming smooth and hardening to seal the floor from water.

The children have black tar soot called *kohl* smeared beneath the eyes to keep the sun's glare from harming the eyes, as well as to help keep flies and insects away.

The children have much freedom to run about and they do not cry, yell, or beg. They laugh. Seldom corrected, they run naked, with only a string around their necks holding a medal to ward off evil sprits and bring good health. Their mothers do not yell at them, as far as I have ever heard while visiting the villages or passing through at a snail's pace. I feel that if there were abuse there would be signs.

Beside a roadway stood a Sadhu, or priest, who bestowed blessings on all who passed his way. He lived on the sparse coins tossed by travelers at his feet.

Chapter 38
VILLAGE SCENES

"Rafiq, stop and let's stretch our legs. We've been bouncing along for several hours now," Mark said, as we entered a small village many miles from Raipur this afternoon.

"I'm thirsty," John declared, his face red. We were all suffering from the heat.

We had a container with water and cloths to saturate for mopping our brows. The coolest water was in a clay pot, held by a loosely woven rattan net. This air-cools the water as it evaporates through the pot. We all took our cups and had a few sips. It is not wise to drink heavily.

The village was like the thousands of others we had driven through; mud walls within which people lived, sharing the dwelling with a goat, perhaps, and with a cow sometimes tethered outside. The roofs were thatched; some were covered with metal strips, if people were lucky enough to find odd pieces.

The streets were narrow with no windows facing them. "Why no windows?" I asked.

"They are accustomed to having their homes pilfered of their belongings," Rafiq explained.

Occasionally we saw a whitewashed hut, a sign of the residence of a *Burra sahib*, an important person. Dogs, scrawny and hungry looking, lay around under the shade of the *neem* trees, as did the cows of the same underbred variety.

This village had three wells where people drew water: the caste-Hindu well, standing in an open space, the Moslem well, in a separate area, and the outcaste, or untouchables, well behind the mud huts, near the village edge and near the tanning pit. Tanners and cobblers are occupations of the lowest caste, since cows are considered sacred, and handling them sinful.

Children here were shy and scampered nearer their mothers, some hiding behind the mother's dress. Their hair was often filthy and hung in matted strands. I longed to have tubs of soapy water and wash every one that I saw. They were smiling, with big black eyes, asking questions. I wanted to give them food and cleanliness.

"Memsahibji, the mothers are trying to scratch enough to eat and survive, appearances don't mean much to them," said Rafiq, practically. "They don't have the time to wash and clean, as the children are playing in the dirt." These were the children of the untouchables; two were holding a nubbin of corn, nibbling on it.

The low minarets of a small white mosque stood near the center of the village close to the Brahmin houses and the *baniya's* shop, where the moneylender operates.

*   *   *

We have learned that the "social security" of India is the birth of sons, to care for the parents in their old age.

When girls are born, the search for a husband among friends of the family or through a third party begins very early. At three to five years old, the little girls are selected for the small boys who will become their husbands. The first marriage takes place at this time, with a ceremony that is performed by placing a ring on the toe next to the big toe of each foot. It is believed that this toe has some connection with the reproductive powers of the girl and leads directly to the uterus.

Girls live with their parents until they reach the age of puberty and have begun their menstrual cycle. Then another, grander ceremony is performed.

The powerful figure of the household is the young husband's mother. She is the determining figure in all activities, including the sexual relations of the young couple. Since the family is joined and all work together for the common existence, the mother becomes the ruler and guide as long as her husband lives. Often there is much unhappiness, and the treatment by the mother-in-law can be harsh, but the son and daughter-in-law are helpless to do anything. Leaving the family roof is too risky.

The mother-in-law even decides when the husband may join his wife's bed. The men sleep in one building and the women in another. If the wife is permitted to have her husband with her that evening, she places the food on his plate in a certain way to indicate that she will be waiting in her bed, placed where there is as much privacy as possible. He can slip into her bed during the night.

Always at mealtime, the men are fed first, then the sons, and then the women and daughters are fed last. Women seemingly have no privileges since they are never allowed to come out if anyone comes into the village to talk with the people. The wife is always sitting behind the mud wall, yet in fact, she is the ruler of the home and disciplines the children.

Women work in the fields, planting and gathering rice, while the men sit after they have completed the plowing with their bullocks. The woman scythes the fodder and ties it into sheaves. If she is working for a cultivator rather than on land belonging to the family unit, she will get one sheaf of rice for every ten she has cut during the day. The rice will be beaten off the stalk for the families' consumption, and the fodder will go to the ever-hungry bullock. The average daily intake of rice for the villager is determined by its availability.

*   *   *

One of the areas we visited yesterday is deep in the jungle. There are no roads. Not even a track for any vehicles. It is so remote that wheels have never been seen here, although airplanes fly overhead. Mark was to inspect this area for a project. It was beginning to get dark and I was waiting in the jeep for Mark.

A guard had been assigned to protect me, and he was squatting on his heels, smoking *bedis*.

A man approached, from a path out of the jungle. He spoke to the guard, and I could understand a few words: "American Memsahibji." The man walked up to the door and nodded with great respect. He asked in English if he could speak to me. He was dressed in the typical Indian pajamas. He wore *chappads*, the sandals most men wear, and his hair was combed. In my estimation, he looked like a decent man.

"We learned that your president, Sahibji Kennedy, was shot," he said. "I am sorry."

"Thank you," I replied.

"You do not ask me how and why it happened," he said.

"No, because there has been an arrest; then the man was killed who was believed to be the criminal."

"But they shot the wrong man," the Indian said very positively. "The president was shot by Mr. Johnson's own man. Yes, I know this to be a fact. Mr. Johnson had it done," he insisted.

"But we don't do things like this in my country," I told him.

"This is well known by those of us who study these things," he declared.

At this time, Mark returned to the car and the Indian man left. I never mentioned this to Mark or anyone, as life is tedious enough here. I don't want to start a rumor.

*   *   *

When we returned to Raipur this week, we were pleased to catch up on good news about our family, but very upset and sad about one piece of bad news from Delhi. A rabid puppy has bitten Winnie. She played with some puppies at the large house next to the hostel. She has taken the series of vaccine shots, poor dear, and missed a number of classes because of it. We were out in the country and did not know about it for a week after she began the shots.

She has an active schedule. She is busy with her course work as well as on the school newspaper.

CHAPTER 39
VISIT TO A ROYAL PALACE

Four months have passed since we came to live in Raipur. The organization of Mark's work is finished and the project is in operation. The house is organized; the servants are into a routine.

We decided that we could use a fun weekend away from work. This was a good time to accept the Maharaja and Maharani's invitation at last. They had asked for a week's notice, so a message went out to them to expect us. We debated on what to take as a token gift and settled on a loaf of bread, Kraft's processed cheese, a jar of Skippy peanut butter, crackers and a box of chocolates. I took an assortment of clothes, not knowing what to expect to wear in a jungle palace.

Our route took us to the Mahanadi River. Generally at this time of year, it is a mile wide. When we arrived we found dozens of carts and wagons, drawn by bullocks and heaped with hay, ahead of us. Finally it was our turn to ford the river. The jeep went deep into the water as it rose to the fenders; steam poured from the engine. We held on as we chugged through, all four wheels working to pull us out.

We had traveled only seventy miles from the nearest electric light bulb, but years from a modern society. Our little group wound its way across the bumps and washed-out shoulders of the road, as we were forced to give way to the assortment of traffic. A procession of elephants waddled down the middle of the road. The *mahout* (driver) managed to get his animals to the edge so we could pass.

Finally, we entered the jungle where monkeys sat grooming their families. Others hung from branches like gourds from a vine. Light penetrated the thick over-growth, giving radiant colors to birds that flew into view. Then, the open plains lay in front of us again. Peacocks and peahens by the thousands foraged the fields. Egrets rose on the wing as we drove into the open; untold numbers whitened the sky as they ascended ahead of us. For many baking hot hours, we drove over rough roads and through jungles.

In time, we began to see a remarkable change in our surroundings. The fields were fenced. "Look, there are hearty groves of bananas and oranges here," Mark remarked. Houses were well kept and whitewashed, but most noticeably different, there were fewer people. The places showed, clearly and outstandingly, pride of ownership in the property.

We arrived at the compound gate. The palace came into view, its gilded dome shining in the sun, the gleaming elegance an enormous contrast to all that we had seen before entering this land. Wings jutted from either side of the main building. A pink wing sat to the left and rear. I wondered about it. "I think the women live there," Rafiq offered.

We must have looked a sight—weary, sweaty, grimy travelers, with rolls of equipment loaded on the roof of the vehicle. We must always take automobile supplies, parts and gasoline on each trip. Fleet-footed servants in white shirts and khaki shorts descended upon us. We stood for a moment observing the dismantling of the vehicle, when a handsome young man appeared. Rafiq announced, "Sahibji and Memsahibji Stepworth from the United States."

"Welcome, welcome, we are delighted to have you here at last," said the Maharaja, named Vishnuraj. He was the tallest Indian I had met, with all the looks that care and good breeding could bestow. He had incredibly beautiful features, and appeared happy and relaxed, exuding warmth and simplicity of good manners.

"Come, let us have a cool drink. You must be very tired," said our host. He motioned us to a group of chairs in the shade on the veranda curving around the front of the building. The floor was of marble.

We talked of our experiences after arriving in India. He wanted to hear about our home in Florida, a prosperous town reputed to be the wealthiest per capita in the United States. The availability of study at Florida State University and other nearby universities is a factor, and ownership of stock in the world-known bottled drink, Coca-Cola, is another. Productive farming, imaginative and creative, hard working people owning other investments also contribute.

The Maharaja was eager to hear everything. The Maharani did not appear until later, at teatime.

We retired to our suite to rest and bathe before tea. The servants had hung the contents of our luggage in closets. Our room had the first mattress I'd seen on an Indian bed since Udaipur. The furniture was massive, and oriental rugs covered the gleaming teak floors. I walked from the living room to the bedroom and into the bath of Italian blue tile. In one corner was an enormous porcelain vessel that must hold thirty gallons of water; then I realized that no water is furnished through pipes, and all must be ladled out with a silver container.

We returned to the veranda. In the doorway paused the Maharani, a delicate young woman swathed in a silk sari, with braided jet-black hair falling down her back. Her attractiveness was not only in facial features, but also a quiet inner beauty showing through. A red line painted in the part of her hair and a tiny red dot on her forehead between her eyebrows showed she is a married Hindu.

The Maharani, Shashi, said, "Things are very different since the late Maharaja turned over his domain to the government. We only kept enough to support our servants, his servants, and us."

After tea, when a lull in the conversation came, she suggested a walk. That became a ritual for us each morning and afternoon. Our path took us through the garden past calla lilies, flaming red and golden marigolds, which are among a few flowers that can withstand the heat and drought. A gate opened in a wall two feet thick that surrounded the palace. The mountain rose in front of us, as we walked the path lined with berry bushes. Three servants led the way, five more came behind us carrying sticks. When she saw me observing them, the Maharani said, "We have wild animals foraging for food."

I asked if she were not lonely here. "I have so much to do, I really don't have the time to be lonely," she said. "I direct the activities of the palace instead of turning it over to the servants. I write, care for my children and my husband, then there is yoga to do daily. I read a great deal; you must come into our library." She always referred to Vishnuraj as "my husband" and explained to me that it is forbidden for a wife to use her husband's name in conversation.

"What did you mean when you said, 'Things are different now,' if you care to tell me?" I asked.

"My father-in-law was a very diligent and industrious man. He had fine machinery and generators for power. He kept every thing in working order. It is a terrible thing to see what has happened to these things. The government sent a very lackadaisical fellow here to direct the property," she said.

"We had lights, now there are none, and buildings are falling down. It has been very bad for all of us. It comes from bad administration and corruption. My husband cannot maintain our land and interest and fight with those people. We are hoping that somehow your husband can give us ideas and that together, your ideas can be implemented."

I could understand their need, I told her. I do hope we can help. It was like a haven, walking through the sweet smelling cool of the evening shade. The green trees and heavy underbrush were peaceful in contrast to the dust we'd traveled through.

At dinner, we talked about the past. When his father lived, he gave yearly gifts to the people, the Maharaja told us. To determine the amount, the father would be weighed on the great scales, and the scales balanced with silver to match his weight. "We will show you through the palace tomorrow evening before dark. The throne room is used, but not nearly as often as in the past," he said.

"You must join us in a hunt. I will have my people arrange for a shoot; wouldn't you like that?" said Vishnuraj, whose name means "king of the world."

"What will we hunt?" Mark wondered.

"Tigers. There are too many here now. We do not kill as many as we did in the old days. Also, gun shells are expensive. Do you know that a shell for your .38 costs sixteen rupees and fifty pisa ($4.10)? At those prices it is a very rare thing that we shoot any more. The servants use a net to catch the partridges, other birds are caught in traps."

He added, "We cannot allow an injured tiger to escape. That is the one rule that must be followed. If not found and destroyed, it will turn on people."

When we went to bed that night, I told Mark that it gave me goose bumps to think we would be hunting a tiger. Knowing that the tiger can climb a tree, can take a grown bullock and toss it over his shoulder and then jump a fence makes me apprehensive.

"Let's get some sleep, we'll need to be rested tomorrow," said Mark.

*   *   *

In the morning, following a pot of tea steeped with rich milk and sugar, I was ready for breakfast. I took a bath in water that had been drawn for me in the beautiful bathtub with gold faucets. I found my way to the veranda. A number of books, including one of Rudyard Kipling's, were in the living room. Vishnuraj had told me that Kipling had lived near their place.

A servant found me and asked me to come upstairs to the Maharani's suite. We ascended the marble stairs. To the left was a room were gymnastic equipment, barbells, bicycle, and treads. I commented on this to Shashi when we were seated in the library.

"We use these for our yoga extensions. It is very difficult to accomplish what we must without being very fit," she said.

I did not understand this and said so.

"There are stages of our life, we believe. During the early years we accomplish all the sex acts as carved on the temple walls," she explained. "I get very tired unless I am in fit shape. We will go to the temple and then you will understand what I am saying."

Dinner that evening was a very special meal. We had water with it, as Hindus do not drink wine. A dish served just for our family was a curried quail breast, with quail eggs, rice succulent gravy floating with cashews, bits of ginger root and spices. When we commented on the curry flavor, she said that it could contain up to twenty ingredients. Finally, we had our favorite dessert, *Gulab Jamuns.**

We lingered over the other courses and washed our fingers in gold fingerbowls where a slice of *nimbu*, or fresh lemon, floated. Tea was served in the sitting room. We learned that it is Indians' habit to go to bed directly after the meal.

*   *   *

The next morning, guns and ammunition had been loaded in the Land Rover by the time we were dressed. I had been offered the late Maharani's gun, a light, beautifully balanced rifle. Mounds of equipment for cooking and camping were loaded. A rope net swag was attached to the front, waiting to carry a kill.

Within minutes, we were in the jungle surrounding the palace. The property is the size of a large part of a state, so there is plenty of area in which to hunt. We were soon parked and followed the Maharaja and his lead hunter, or *shikar*, to the place where the mashan had been built in a great spreading tree. Mark and I climbed up and sat behind a wall of leaves and branches that allowed us to see over into the jungle. We were told we must not speak once the beat began. My heart was pounding wildly. I pressed Mark's fingers, then released them.

John went with the Maharaja and Maharani into another tree. Mark and I sat with our guns at the ready. The beaters were waiting for the signal to begin. Soon, we heard them in the distance pounding their drums, ringing bells and hitting sticks together. As the first evidence that the jungle had become alive, birds began to fly through the trees in swarms. All this commotion was because animals were rushing through—monkeys, antelope, deer and a bear. No tigers were seen. The beaters had moved too fast which allowed the tigers to escape them.

Our host was very apologetic. "Follow me, there is another mashan nearby, we will walk up the mountain side."

The Maharani and I walked along, talking casually. She was wearing a sari, while I was in slacks. Almost immediately we heard a loud noise that sounded like a truck bolting down the mountainside in our direction. Orders were given to take cover. She quickly climbed a tree. I jumped, grabbed a tree limb, pulled myself up and threw my leg over the limb, just as she said, "Shoot, Mary!"

I caught a glimpse of an enormous animal, leveled my aim and pulled the trigger. A wild boar slid down the mountain, through the bushes and landed beneath the tree where we sat. A loud chorus of "Hurrah" rose from everyone.

I looked at Mark, and he was not happy. I didn't find out until later that a ray of sunshine had hit his gun's scope and caused the animal to turn in our direction. The Southern male does not want to be seen as inept, most certainly at such a masculine pursuit as shooting.

*   *   *

The next day, our hosts took us to the temple of Bhoramdeo, an 11th century Siva temple. It took us forty-five minutes to reach a small lake surrounded by a dike. The walkway was cleared, so our trek became easy. In the grey distance, a stone wall came into view, with the temple standing inside, quiet except for the calls of birds; parakeets, minar birds, yellow finch and others, gold and blue, red and green, flitting from columns to branches. Unlike most of the Khajuraho temples, which have suffered destruction during battles, this one is in perfect condition and still used today. We followed our hosts to the temple entrance, with a curved façade held up by slender columns.

The decoration was exquisite. Carvings covered virtually every external surface of the temple. Here, deities, mostly life-size, were shown indulging in a vast range of sexual acrobatics. The eroticism is presented in such surroundings and in a manner to be honored as sacred.

Shashi walked with me, explaining the delicate, explicit carvings, while the Maharaja took Mark with him. Shashi told me that she and her husband make a pilgrimage each year, to study the sacred carvings, which become expressions of love for the couple in their marriage. "They help to keep our marriage bond and our love life active," she said.

I could see that this was not a frivolous concept. I asked if others came to see the carvings as well, and she told me many couples do, although it is thought to be private, or at least I gathered that.

We went outside. Plaques similar to simple tombstones were placed upright in the soil and surrounded the temple. On some were the palms of ladies' hands facing outward; these indicated wives who performed suttee on the husband's funeral pyre. I noted that Shashi had taken a coconut and wrapped it in a hundred-rupee note. I asked her why she did this and was told that prayers will be said for another child for the couple.

While we were touring the temple, outside two men were dividing the meat from the boar killed on our hunt. There were six rows of plates, made of huge leaves of the peepul tree, held together by spikes of grass. I asked why the plates were separate.

"That separation is because of the religious differences in the tribe," said the Maharaja. "Each religion has a different custom." The men moved along the rows dividing the meat equally and we commented on their accuracy. Vishu's comment was, "Yes, they are very honest men."

*   *   *

The following day we drove for an hour, as the Maharaja pointed to the problems of his land with one hand and drove with the other. The narrow single-lane dirt road was cut six feet deep through hills with stones lying on either side. He stopped the jeep and talked with Mark, who listened to the problems being encountered on the land.

I had lost interest in the conversation momentarily and turned my head to look at the top of a mound that rose several feet over the top of the jeep. The sheer wall was near enough to be touched. Then came a faint tapping noise on the roof of the vehicle. I looked at Mark to see what he was doing. He opened the door and is standing outside the door looking over the roof.

"Shhh," I hissed, as I caught sight of a leopard no farther away than eight or ten feet.

The Maharaja took the gun from the frame above the door and brought it across me to Mark. With his eye on the leopard, Mark reached for the gun, as the Maharaja extended his arm with the gun's scope end first. The gun struck Mark above the eye. Blood spurted and Mark grabbed his eye. I slipped out of the vehicle, took the rifle, steadied it on the roof and squeezed the trigger. The animal dropped. Fortunately, Mark was not badly injured; the cut was above the lid. Poor thing, it was not his day and I could see he was seething inside.

It was a beautiful cat, eight feet long from tip to tip. In all likelihood, it would have attacked us. Yet I didn't feel elated about killing the creature or the boar I had shot the day before.

Later, at the palace, the Maharaja's men began the job of skinning the leopard. They took the animal's genitals, for the oil which is smeared on their genitals and massaged for potency.

When we were at last in bed together, I snuggled to Mark's back.

"Sweetheart," I said, as I gently caressed his shoulders with my hand.

"Can we talk about what we saw at the temple?" I asked.

"No, I will not talk about what we saw now, or ever. It was a disgusting display that I am not willing to talk about," he replied.

"Or use in our love making?"
"No, forget it!"

*   *   *

We have returned to our home after our visit with royalty at the palace. Our servants have begun processing the leopard for the taxidermist, a job that takes time. They rub the skin clean of fat with bricks and salt, remove the bones from the skin, leaving the skin intact and boil the bones in a pot in the back yard. Teeth, bones and skin will all be carefully wrapped and shipped off to Van Engen in Mysore State. It will take a year to get the skin but it is well worth the wait.

Yesterday I went to tell my friend Sonu about the leopard skin and found her looking very thin, with dark circles around her eyes. She was not smiling and laughing, as she usually does. I asked if she felt well and she said she did. I said no more and sat listening to her talking slowly, unenthusiastically. She asked a few questions about my stepdaughter. She seemed to be looking far into the future.

I suggested that she and her husband come for dinner when Mark returned. She politely refused but asked that we come there to dinner with them. We have had rather brief meetings—a cup of tea or a cocktail—but have not ventured into each other's lives. I accepted the invitation. When we arrived at 8:30 p.m., it appeared that her husband had already had something to drink. After a drink for me and two for Mark, dinner followed.

We returned to the living room, where R.C. started the record player and asked me to dance. We began with a slow waltz, and he embraced me warmly. I tried to move back, but he drew me even closer, even putting his leg between mine. It was clear he was sexually aroused. When I laughed and whispered that he was holding me too tight, he kissed my neck and turned me loose, as the music ended. I suggested that we must go, against our hosts' persuasion that we stay. I rose and Mark followed. We left. I didn't mention this, as they are our only neighbors and friends in this place.

The Raj Mahal, Royal Palace and home of our friends, the Maharaja and Maharani of Kiwarda. We traveled through 70 miles of jungle to reach the Maharaja's 11-square-mile property. The palace entrance is white marble trimmed with gold, and the Throne Room is elaborately decorated in brocade, gold, silver and paintings.

CHAPTER 40
PROBLEMS ARISE

This is November, and we have been in India seven months. We have been so busy and the weather has been so miserable that Mark is showing signs of wear. His co-workers are often arrogant, not cooperative. He really needs another professional to off-load some of his concerns on.

He has begun to be more withdrawn. It is difficult to get him involved in conversation. He often puts his hand to his ear that had been injured by bomb blasts during the war. He sits deep in his chair, staring into space, as he has a few drinks. I worry about him and try to ply him with any other beverages.

Last night, I reminded him that we are having the Rector visit us again this coming weekend. "Won't that be pleasant? He knows so much about India. He is a dear man to come all this way on the fourth-rate railroad car."

Mark did not seem especially happy that he was coming.

"He is so unobtrusive, and yet enters into conversation with enthusiasm," I said.

"Mary, you are the social person," he said. "People come here because of you, not me."

I was startled. "How can you think that? You are listened to with great interest. The men want to learn from you and come to know you. It is not me they want to see. I am here to give something to you and all the family, to help accomplish our work."

Mark's reply was brief but his mood did not improve. I thought, "You are working too hard."

Aloud, I said, "You need a game of golf and a good Chinese meal at the Hotel Oberio in New Delhi. Let's plan a trip there as soon as possible."

"I think it is time I go to another region, or take on the country," he said. "I have accomplished about as much as can be done here. I can still visit here and see that the program is doing well."

*   *   *

One thing that depresses Mark, I feel, is the slow rate of progress in changes that can improve the people's well being.

Madhya Pradesh, where we are living, is one of the poorest states in India. Eighty-eight percent of its population is rural, a larger percentage than that of any other state. About twenty percent of its population is tribal—again, a larger percentage of that of any other state. Its per capita annual income is lower than that of any other area—201 rupees (12 ½ cents, U.S.) as compared to 252 rupees for the country as a whole.

Chattiagarh, where our town, Raipur, is located, is an undeveloped province. Cultural standards and educational standards are low, many of our people are underfed, diseased, and badly housed. Our towns are unhealthy, our villages are unhealthier still, hardly fit to live in. The need for planning in every department is desperate, but none more so than in industrialization.

We have read about the first five-year plan the government developed about eleven years ago to improve the economy. Plants were to be built, minerals to be explored. The country held discussions with the governments of United States, Great Britain, West Germany—and also the Soviet Union, which at the time had no significant program for economic aid to India.

By 1956, when the second five-year plan came, India had a vision of building three new steel plants. One was to be built by a West German combine. A consortium of Great Britain would build another, with equipment suppliers and a loan from the British government. The third agreement was with the Soviet Union, which caused great excitement. The Indians had considerable experience in working with the British, and some experience with Germans, but the Soviets were strangers.

The three governments' engineers were all to start building their steel plants in India about the same time, and their achievements would naturally be compared. Since independence, the Indian government had conducted studies of prospective sites. All the states had been maneuvering for the industrial prize.

Fields rich in coking coal were to be found only in Bihar and in West Bengal, and iron ore close to the supplies of coal was found in Bihar, West Bengal and Orissa State. These three states, sometimes referred to collectively as the Ruhr of India, clearly would be most suitable for steel production. And, indeed, the German plant was eventually situated in Orissa, and the British plant, in West Bengal. The site proposed for the Soviet plant was in Madhya Pradesh.

Government studies had shown that of all the non-Ruhr states with iron ore reserves, Madhya Pradesh was the most suitable for a steel plant. It was adjacent to Bihar, and since both states were on the Southeastern Railway, Bihar coal could be transported to Madhya Pradesh.

In our state, the area adjoining Bihar had been singled out as the best site for a steel plant. Bihar was at this time little more than scrub plants, duck ponds and rice paddy fields. Its contact with the modern world was confined to an occasional visit from a revenue collector or a health inspector. In fact, Bihar was all but indistinguishable from thousands of other rural locations throughout India.

However, the site, near the Tandulla and the Seonath rivers, had an abundant water supply. It had reserves of iron ore and deposits of manganese, limestone and dolomite, and it was near Madhya Pradesh's own vein of coal.

But the Soviet engineers, after making their own studies and touring locations, chose Bhilai, another village in Madhya Predesh. Together, the Russians and the Indians began planning for the day when Madhya Pradesh—particularly Durg, the district within which Bhilai lies, and Chattiagarh, the district in which Raipur lies—would begin to define a new India.

Yet, when we arrived in Raipur and visited Bhilai, we were told that not a single product had been manufactured at the new plant. However many difficulties in obtaining materials and shipping from Russia to India might account for some problems, still it was an extremely long time to delay production.

Chapter 41
A MOST REMARKABLE BEAST

Our friend, the Maharaja, has planned a hunt that I am looking forward to, as we will ride elephants. I have ridden an elephant on several excursions with pleasure. They kept your body swaying with each step they took. It is great fun to ride one.

Here in Raipur, it's not unusual to see an elephant family swinging along down the road. They are work animals and a familiar sight in the jungle.

Among the mightiest creatures on earth is the Indian elephant. A sage told us several stories and legends that are familiar to the people here.

The elephant plays many roles in life. Standing only three feet high at birth, when he is small he follows his mother, who is the leader, and is protected by the family made up of females. He is playful with them and likes people. The male pays little or no attention to the young one, but the female elephants hover over the baby when a threat of wild animals is perceived.

When a *Mahout*, or trainer and lifelong caretaker, is assigned, the first word the young elephant is taught is "*Beht*," which means "Sit down," and then, "*Oot*" for "Get up."

When he gets older, standing eight to twelve feet tall and weighing as much as fifty men, he becomes a worker, carrying out the orders of his mahout.

A very special relationship grows between elephant and master. The mahout treats him very kindly and speaks in a gentle voice. It is only very seldom that the elephant must be goaded with an iron spike.

When the elephant is being steered through the jungle and comes across a tree that has fallen or tough grass that must be trampled to make a pathway, then his mahout sings a song, in a chanting, singsong way: "*Salai, dalai, dab. Dalai, dalai, dab.*" At each "*dab,*" the elephant makes an extra effort to flatten the obstacle or move it out of his path.

The mahout strokes his elephant so that when people touch him, he will not be upset. He washes him frequently. The elephant sprays water on his back while submerged in the pond or river, and the mahout scrubs him. They both come out of the water clean since the mahout has taken his share of the spray.

This is a legend told to us by the elephant keeper at the Maharaja's estate:

"One day, five blind men came down the road, led by a sighted man. He asked the blind travelers to tell him what they had come upon.

One put his hand up and felt a long switch with a bit of hair on the end. "I have found a fly swatter," he cried.

"How strange," said another, when he felt something firm and large. "I have found a tank." .

"I have found a hose," said the third, as he grasped the long snout.

"I have a fan," said the man who felt the ear.

"There is a stump by my feet," the fifth man said. They felt lost and knew not which way to turn.

A wise man came along and found each touching a different part of his sacred animal. He offered to give them a ride in his seat, called a howdah.

As they rode, he told them what they had experienced. "Your fly swatter is the tail of the elephant, the large tank is the body, the hose is the trunk, the fan is the ear and the stump is one of the animal's legs."

"By sitting on top and riding him, you find that all things work together to serve us," the wise man said.

*   *   *

We returned from a trip this week, and a big Harley-Davidson motorcycle was in front of our house.

"That is American," Rafiq said. John allowed, "Looks like it."

A huge young man, 30ish, came to the door when he heard us talking. He could have been a lineman for a NFL team. With a great grin, he introduced himself as Harry Jackson. Following introductions all around, we went indoors. Lazarus, who had brought the tea tray out for our visitor, returned with two extra cups for John and me.

"My husband is at his office doing paperwork today, so I have the use of the vehicle and interpreter," I told the young man. "Perhaps you can meet him later."

He said he would like that. "I'm an old India hand. My wife and I have been in India 10 years. We have three children born here," Harry said. "I am an Evangelical Reform minister. But since proselytizing is prohibited, I have a fertilizer business."

"How interesting," I said. "You will have to tell us how that works."

"You've seen the vultures at the carcass of an animal?" he said. "We come after the vultures have done their duty—they clean the carcass in thirty minutes. My people take the carcass away. We take the bones and process them."

The material is bagged and is used for fertilizer. He felt there could be a possible interest in this project in conjunction with our agricultural program.

Later, we talked about the religious situation in India. We have been told that Christians in this country are unhappy about the prohibition against missionary work. Christian missionaries throughout India have condemned the possibility of a bill that is being considered to ban missionaries coming here. Mother Teresa, who runs homes for the destitute in Calcutta and other cities, wrote to the Prime Minister appealing to him not to accept the bill.

"There were about six thousand missionaries in India at one time. Christians make up about two percent of the population and are growing faster than any other religion," Harry said. "They are concentrated in the poverty-bound states of Tamil Nadu, in backward tribal districts here in Madhya Pradesh, Orissa and Bihar and in frontier tribal states."

I invited Harry to stay for dinner, and I rang the little bell that I keep on the coffee table and on other tables about the house. A tinkling bell is much preferred to call when one needs the servants.

When Das came, I sent him to get Lazarus, the cook. He ran with his bare feet softly padding on the floor. In a moment, Lazarus appeared.

I told him, "Please prepare the potato stew, and we'll have some cold venison slices, *puris* (fried bread), a salad of cucumber, tomato, onions, with yogurt and a touch of lemon juice. Oranges and bananas for dessert, please."

"Yes, Memsabji."

Mark came home at 5 o'clock, so he and Harry had a chance to meet and exchange ideas.

*   *   *

German priests came and spent a day and an evening with us this week. I am very pleased that all the Christian community feels welcome at our home. It is not unusual to have them visit monthly. It is at times like this that I am thankful for our supply of meat in the freezer and it's great to see them enjoy meat as they seldom have any. The housing officer was wise to realize that we would have visitors and would need not only a refrigerator, but also a freezer.

I was reminded of the problems that we encountered with the freezer and refrigerator recently, when I looked in the refrigerator and found that it was not cold. We had the appliances sitting on the back veranda. When Mark returned home, I told him, "The machines are working very hard but nothing is happening. Do you suppose we need refrigerant?"

"Those are new; I can't believe that is the problem," Mark said.

Rafiq came in and we told him about it. "Sahib, every Indian that I know who owns a refrigerator keeps them in their coolest room, the sitting room."

"We won't be keeping ours in the living room," Mark replied. "But I remember from my college classes, that the air must be cooler around the refrigerator than inside. I'm glad you reminded me," he added.

"We can take the example of reserving water that we find here. Water evaporates fast in this country since it is so hot. That is why the ponds have a dike of mud around them. The mud dries like cement and the water stays in for the use of people and animals as long as possible."

"That's a great idea!" I said.

"Let's build a mud dike around the freezer and refrigerator, leaving a space in front, so one can reach the door and remove food. We don't want to get electrocuted. We will fill it with water, set the fans directing the air onto the water." Mark offered.

Mark, Rafiq and Prem Chan got busy building the dike, pressing the mud firmly. It was dry enough by midnight to fill with water. Mark went to check on it in the early morning. He came in wearing a big grin. "It worked! It is freezing." He said, "Thank heavens! We haven't been tested, as we would be with no place to keep the meat safe."

*   *   *

Good news came today by way of a fold-over letter from the children at the American International School. Dennis has been tapped for the National Honor Society. We are proud of him. We are invited to the Society dinner in New Delhi. Mark has had little time to spend with Dennis, and I am hoping he will be there to attend.

Connie is named to the honor roll every month. She competed for a class award for an article and won; it was printed in the school magazine, *Taj Times*. One of the disappointments for her is that there is no time to travel in the country. Her schoolwork is demanding. Her friends are American and English, as there are few Indian students attending the school. Winnie has several friends and spends any spare time with them.

A family of elephants, each ridden by its lifelong caretaker, lumbers along the road to Agra. Seen frequently on our travels, the elephants are diligent workers and each is devotedly cared for by the mahout who is its sole trainer.

CHAPTER 42
AN ABUNDANCE OF FESTIVALS

It is December now, and we are in the midst of a wonderful holiday. It is the major celebration of the Hindu New Year, called Diwali, or "festival of lights." Hindus dedicate this festival to the god Kali.

For everyone, Hindu or not, it is a lovely holiday. Legend has it that on this night, Kali fights a battle with evil, so her humans build fires and light the world for her. Lights are everywhere, on the eaves of buildings, the steps, palace walls, and turrets of government buildings, shops, and temples, down paths, at crossroads, under trees and on cowsheds and huts. Thousands upon thousands of tiny, twinkling lights shine out, from wicks burning in tiny clay pots to leaf-or boat-shaped earthenware lamps to reflect in ponds and reservoirs, fountains, and pools of water.

Neighbors, even those whom we have not met, have brought gifts to us. We have been invited to homes for special foods. At the home of the director of the District Electric Power Works, we saw an elaborate picture on the ground, in front of the porch steps, that had been painted for the occasion. Rice paste in various colors was the medium. When the rice paste dries, it leaves a soft misty texture to the painting. This method of art is passed from mother to daughter.

In the villages, the mud huts are cleaned and painted with the rice paste. Color is added and mixed to paint shapes and designs. The Indians are famous for this lovely art. The towns, villages, and cities have been cleaned, and a festival feeling is in the air.

This is the time of year that the books are closed, new accounts opened and business begins all anew. We returned from several of the parties and met with Dr. Lal, our neighbor, who practices aruvedic medicine, an ancient science using plants and herbs. He had escaped from Burma, where he had practiced until the dictator took over the country. He is staying with a Brahmin friend of his, whom we had met briefly before.

We had thought this would be a pleasant social evening. We found that it was serious business for the two Indian gentlemen. Mark and I considered that we could hold our own against other bridge players. They made us feel rusty and we played badly. There had been no opportunity to play for months. Our neighbor told us that whoever loses is assured a prosperous year. That was apparently our undoing. Afterward, we spent several evenings reviewing our bridge book.

*　　　　　*　　　　　*

We see statues of the many Hindu gods everywhere we go.

"How many gods are there?" I asked Shri Nadu, a former professor who visited our home this week.

"It is as difficult to learn all their names as it is the religion they represent," he said. "I find that different people might answer questions on gods or religion in different ways, and all their answers would be true to themselves. The true seekers of enlightenment can only appreciate the gods' manifestations by meditating and through stillness; reading the ancient books comes next."

Pictures of Krishna hang in frames in houses, stores, and buses. He is always young, blue skinned and playing a pipe. He is the second person of the Hindu Trinity, being incarnate of Vishnu, the Preserver.

Animals seem important to all the Indian gods. Sarawati rode a swan, carrying a guitar-like instrument called a vina. Siva rode the bull Nanda, which we first saw at the site of the water temples in Southern India. It is an enormous statue of the bull. It is said that Vishnu rode Guruda, the eagle. The Great Goddess Kali or Durga or Parvati, as she has other names) is always shown accompanied by a lion or a buffalo.

Festivals play a great part in the life of every Indian, from the highest to the lowliest. An Indian employee of the American Embassy once researched the holidays and festival days, determining that the number of days an Indian Civil Servant need work is 120 days a year. In the U.S., we would not hold that job very long nor be profitable in it.

However, there is little wonder that they give so much attention to the holidays, with attractions for young and old to enjoy. The people dress up for the events, garland their oxen, and decorate their bullock carts, their homes and temples. They find nothing incongruous in such extravagant displays.

Most festivals revolve around the legends of the past. One of the most important and impressive holidays is Durgapuja, which celebrates the ten days of fighting between Ravana, the king who abducted Sita, and Durga, goddess of war. During this period the goddess Durga, in her aspect of Kali, the goddess of destruction, is worshipped with offerings of flowers, fruit, and food. Since most of the princely families belong to the Khatriya, or the warrior caste, Durgapuji holds a special importance for them.

In the old ruined capital, called Gosanimare, was a Durga Temple. A Maharani who visited our Raipur home told us of a legend about one of her own ancestors, who had mortally offended the goddess Durga. Long ago, her ancestor hid in the temple one night to spy on the goddess, who was said to take on a human form and secretly dance in the temple. But Durga discovered him and flew into a rage. As a punishment, she cursed him and all his descendants, forbidding them to set foot in her temple again. She left him a silver anklet as a reminder and a warning.

In our travels through Durg, we came upon a temple that was reputed to be the one that had been the object of this story. We had taken a photograph of the temple, before we learned that pictures are forbidden, according to tradition. (The picture is found here).

At a temple of Hindu goddess Durga in the remote Deccan, a holy Sadhu stands silently at attention. The wall carvings are dark in color, from the long tradition of worshippers applying ghee (oil from butter) to the stones before entering the temple.

CHAPTER 43
MEDITATION AND MYTHOLOGY

My friend Sonu, a Hindu, has been on a retreat to an *ashram,* a place where individuals can go for awhile to live a quiet, strict and austere life. The inmates look up to their Guru, or preceptor. They attend lectures and spend time meditating. The ashram is organized so that if people cannot pay, they work while there. One takes care of one's assigned duties. The ashram features calmness of atmosphere, unity of endeavor, hard work and spiritual purposefulness.

The upper castes often practice asceticism, withdrawing from society for two reasons— to seek freedom from the demands of the world by relinquishing natural pleasures, or to promote austerities and meditation in order to acquire mysterious, magical powers. Some ascetics also practice unconventional practices such as nudism.

The ascetics do not always remain isolated; they may leave the forests or mountains and return to challenge the existing patterns of society. Some advocate a sequence dividing a man's life into four stages: first a student, then a family man, then a hermit and finally an ascetic.

Sonu talks with me about Hinduism and has many books that interest me. One tells the legend of the progenitor and lawgiver of the human race, called Manu Svayambhe (Self-born). According to Hindu legend, Manu was born directly of the god Brahma and was a hermaphrodite.

From the female half of the ruler's body, he bore two sons and three daughters. One son, Prithu, became the first consecrated king of the earth and gave the earth its name, Prithui. He cleared the forests, cultivated the land and introduced cattle breeding, commerce, and other activities associated with a settled life.

Manu was the most famous king of all. It was when he ruled over the earth that the great flood occurred, when everything was submerged and only Manu and his family survived. The god Vishnu warned Manu of the flood, and Manu built a boat to carry his family and the seven sages of antiquity.

Vishnu took the form of a large fish to which the boat was fastened, and the fish swam through the flood and lodged the boat on a mountain peak. Here, Manu, his family and the seven sages remained until the water subsided and they could safely return. After the flood, the human race sprang from Manu and his nine sons, the eldest of whom was a hermaphrodite—hence known by a dual name, Ila and Ila'. From this son arose the two main lines of royal descent.

*   *   *

Sonu has also helped us understand the all-important influence of the caste system, which was secured by being hereditary. This continuity depends on the vast network of sub-castes, which are intimately connected with various occupations. Marriage within related groups is strictly regulated, and the system places an automatic check on individuals moving up in the castes.

The doctrine of Karma (action) is the logic of the theory that souls are born to happiness or sorrow depending upon their conduct during their previous lifetime. The doctrine of Karma became the broader concept of Dharma, which is the philosophical justification for the castes. One's birth into a high or low caste depends upon one's action in a previous life.

The unit of society is the family, which is patriarchal. Women remain the gentle figure in the background. A widow performs a symbolic self-immolation—breaking her glass bead bracelet—at the death of her husband. The act may have been related to the practice of *sati* (suttee) in earlier centuries, when the woman actually burned herself on her husband's funeral pyre. The practice has long been outlawed, although it may still occur in remote, isolated areas.

The association of fire with purification may have led to the custom of cremation, which has been the usual practice in India for centuries. Cremation has made Indian history difficult to assess.

One day, as we were discussing India's ancient past, Rafiq said to me, "The Egyptians and the Greek buried their history in their graves. We burn and destroy our own."

CHAPTER 44
BRIGHT IDEAS

We have just had a visitor, a law professor and geographer from Nepal, who brought a light into our home with his optimism and positive attitude. Tilak was happy to be speaking English and learning about the U.S. He talked about his youth.

And he read to us this story that he had written for his brothers and sisters about their great-grandparents: "Dear Brothers and Sisters, you all might have wondered how come we get so many bright ideas. To tell the truth, it is our family trait. At least, this is what our great-grandfather told us when we were still young children. Those days my great-grandfather was already in his nineties but still could walk around, ride ponies and tell us stories. He told us the following story.

"One fine morning, my great-grandfather was passing through a road minding his own business and looking around the beautiful valleys and hills and the royal palace. The palace was, as palaces come, a very large, well-made building surrounded by a thick, high wall. There were a number of small side doors in the wall, always locked and guarded. Of course, the large main gate, through which people were admitted, was always guarded by at least a hundred well-armed soldiers.

"The road upon which my great-grandfather was passing through skirts around the wall for a short stretch. As he was passing, he had the bright idea of robbing the palace. The idea came so spontaneously and strongly that as if he could hear the wall calling him. 'Psst, come here tonight, psst, come here tonight!' So he went home, brought out and cleaned his coat of mail, and sharpened his *khukri*.

"As the night came, he put on his coat of mail, tied his *khukri* at his waist, took a piece of rope and a bag; and marched toward the main gate. On the way he had another bright idea, that instead of frontal assault perhaps he should break through one of the side doors. So he tried his luck with the side door he came across. Surprisingly, the door was not locked. Cautiously he went inside. Again surprisingly it was not guarded either.

"He thought, 'So far, well and good, now what?' He thought that perhaps he should take home something interesting like the marble statue. Then he had another bright idea that perhaps he should take home a bag of gold or some expensive jewelry. Then, to his surprise he saw a beautiful young lady holding a bundle in her hand.

"She also was utterly surprised to see him. For a long moment both of them just stared at each other. Before she could scream and alert the guards, my great-grandfather grabbed and gagged her. He realized that the girl was wearing all kinds of fine jewelry. Matter of fact, she was covered from head to toe with most expensive ornaments. He started to pull off a few of the jewels and pocket them. Then he had another bright idea, why not carry off the whole girl and bother to take all the ornaments later. So he slung her and her bundle over his shoulder.

"She started to protest and kick him; and then my great-grandfather realized that she was the princess he saw in the market a few days before. He thought. 'No wonder she had so many jewels on her.' Gods must be smiling at him that day. He carried her on his shoulder and thought maybe that was enough for the day or rather the night. My great-grandfather was not a greedy man. Then he saw a beautiful, strong, well-groomed and saddled horse nearby. You know, horses are one of the weaknesses of my great-grandfather. He would never let go such a beautiful horse. He tried to carry the horse on his other shoulder, but he could not.

"Then he had another bright idea. 'Why not just drag the horse by the bridle?' After a mile of walking, he had another bright idea. Perhaps the coat of mail that he was wearing was pinching the princess. So he put her down and let her walk, but kept holding her hand so that she would not escape. She did not protest too much and let him pull her along. Then he had another bright idea. Why not ride the horse? So he rode, with the princess in front of him and her bundle behind. That is how the saying, 'Don't drag the horse when you can ride,' began. The horse was strong and easily carried both of them.

"They rode along and pretty soon the sun started to rise. My great-grandfather decided to take a look at what he had gotten. The princess was very beautiful and of good breeding. He opened the bundle to see what was inside. It carried her clothes and belongings. Luckily he also found a nice hood of his size which he wore over his coat of mail. He was also lucky to find another hood of her size, which he put on her to hide the jewelry she wore.

"Then he took the gag off her. She did not scream but looked very angry. He also noticed a nice dimple on her. It was a beautiful and deep dimple and was on a beautiful face with bright eyes. There was the beautiful body with narrow waist to go with the beautiful dimple. Luckily, he also found some food and drinks in the bundle. They sat down and ate the breakfast. Then they rode again. Luckily, there was enough food to make lunch also.

"Almost by sunset, they arrived at the house of my great-grandfather. He cooked some food for supper. She refused to eat. He thought perhaps she did not like his cooking. He was a good cook but no way comparable to the chefs of the royal palace. Then he had another bright idea. 'Why not let her cook?' That way, not only she gets to eat whatever she wants to but he also would get to eat tasty food. Ever since, he has been eating very good food. Even his parents, that are my great-great-grandparents, were very pleased with her skill. It was early spring and weather was cold. My great-grandfather used to live alone and did not have enough blankets for two. Then he got another bright idea….

"My great-grandmother, who was listening to this story, cut in, 'Children, aren't you tired of Grandpa's bright ideas? Let me tell you some of my bright ideas as well.'

"My great-grandmother was also in her nineties but still could walk around and cook us soup. Her eyes were still bright and the dimple still could be seen through the wrinkles. When she was young, she also used to get lots of bright ideas. And then she told the following story:

"When she was still a young lady, she said, she had a big problem with her father, his majesty the king. You know, she was the princess, only child of the king. She thought and thought and got a bright idea. 'Why not go fishing?' And with some of her retinue, she went around in markets and other public places. We interjected, 'Fishing in a market? Not even a fish market?' Of course, she was a princess and her fishing meant much more than what it sounds.

"My great-grandfather expressed his resentment of being considered as a fish, albeit a big one. The market was the place where my great-grandmother saw my great-grandfather. He was a dashing young man working as an apprentice in one of the businesses there. She sent her retinue to spy on him. When she decided that he was the fish she was looking for, she arranged to have him go along the road that fine morning to his business. So it was true that he was minding his own business that morning. As he approached the palace and proceeded along the wall, she whispered to him through a crack in the wall. 'Psst, come here tonight, psst, come here tonight. I will have the door unlocked, and the guards sent away, and a horse will be ready.'

"Then she collected some of her clothes, a hood for herself, a hood for him, and enough food and drink to last all the way to his house. But later, she was surprised to see him wearing his coat of mail, which, of course, was not needed at all. She was so mad at him for not letting her tell him that there was a horse ready.

"Later, in his house, she realized that she should have brought some blankets as well. But she had another bright idea. When he went out to chop firewood, she made some hot spicy chicken soup. My great-grandfather cut in, 'Hey, that was my idea.'

"He would ask her, 'How good was the soup, Grandma?' She would give each of us a bowl of soup and say 'this good.' Her soup was always delicious.

"We children got this bright idea early that every time we sat down and listened to their bright ideas, we got to eat her delicious soup. We heard this story many times, but neither the story nor the soup ever lost its originality or taste. Somehow the soup without the story or the story without the soup would not have tasted that good.

"We would request to continue the story. With the bowl of soup in our hand, the story tasted even better. When the king found that somebody stole his daughter, they told us, he got real mad. Hot pepper came out of his eyes and ears, and he ordered servants to find the thief and chop his head off. His soldiers went around all over seeking the thief. We would act scared and ask. 'Aren't you scared, Grandpa?' He said he was not scared because they had another bright idea. They put a signboard outside stating: 'Here resides Her Highness, the princess, and His Highness, the son-in-law of His Majesty, the king. All the faithful employees of His Majesty should present a gold coin before requesting an audience of Her or His Highness.' That worked well and nobody came to bother them.

"Grandma would pour in some more soup and we would again be all ears for more stories. We would ask, 'Grandma, why do you have problems with the king?' The king wanted to give her away to the king in a faraway country, she said. Of course, she did not like the idea and protested in vain. That was why she went out fishing. After she left the palace, the king was very mad, hollered and thundered, fumed and fretted for a whole month. She was the only child he had, and he missed her terribly. Then he had a change of heart and decided to be civilized.

"So civilization was promulgated in our country by the king, exactly one month after she left the palace. At the beginning nobody liked the idea of being civilized. Everybody cried, 'Oh, no!' But the king was very firm and would say, 'Oh, yes.' Of course, a king is a king and had his way. That is what happens in a barbarian country. The king gets to do whatever he wants to do. He wanted to be civilized and that was that, she said.

"My great-grandfather interjected, 'Mad king, bad decision.' Or, have your way, 'Bad King, mad decision.' My great-grandmother would ignore him and continue the story. 'Actually, after the royal promulgation of civilization, nothing much changed—only a minor change here and there. We had to adopt the metric system. The death sentence was abolished. Free schools and hospitals, shelters for the homeless were made. Boot camps were established to train the battalions of social workers who would go out and fight against strife, poverty, disease and injustice. When needed, they would be para-dropped into the foreign countries. Violence and nudity were taken off the streets. The "earth day"' was made a major national holiday. Ashok's pillars were erected in many places.'

"So, my dear brothers and sisters, I tell you bright ideas run in our family. *(Signed)* Tilak."

Tilak has been a part of our family since that hot day when he first drank iced tea and wrote this letter to his family. (He went on in later years to acquire a Ph.D and work in studies of earth/space imagery.)

*   *   *

Today, Tilak brought a Buddhist professor friend to have tea with us. Buddhism is one subject that I had not become knowledgeable about. Dr. S. Bonia gave a lecture on the subject to an interested audience. I used shorthand to record his words just as he spoke them, changing none of his grammar or sentence structure. It is one more fragment of knowledge in this vast society. Dr. Bonia told us:

"Buddha taught to throw away all the mental chains and to critically examine everything and any concepts. People asked him, 'Are you a god?' Buddha replied, 'No.' 'Are you an angel?' 'No.' 'Then what are you?'

"Buddha replied, 'I am enlightened, I am Buddha.' 'What is the enlightenment?' He replied, 'It cannot be taught, as a sleeping person would not know the state of being awake. When you get enlightened, then you would know for yourself. I can only show you a way, cannot make you enlightened.'

"He asked 'on what basis?' about every thing. His way of finding truth is strictly empirical, and he achieved *nirvana (*salvation) following it.

"Hindus believe he is an incarnation of Lord Vishnu, the preserver. Buddha was born Sidhart Gautam, a prince, in Nepal, around 60 B.C., married, had a child and lived a luxurious life. But he was acutely aware of the worldly suffering. It troubled him and finally he decided to search for the cure leaving everything behind. He tried many ways. He tried asceticism and almost died of hunger. He went to many schools and many masters, but he failed to find the answer. One day he was meditating under a fig tree, then suddenly he became enlightened. Thus arose the Buddha.

"He taught to hold to the truth and not to be swayed by emotion. One day a pupil greeted him as the wisest person of all time. Buddha asked, 'I assume you know about all the people before me.' They replied, 'No, Buddha.' 'Then how do you know I am the most wise man?'

"Buddha asked for personal effort, not to believe him. He declared, 'Be a lamp unto yourself.' He asked us not to be led by an authority, tradition, book, or miracles; but to 'know for you.' To the people claiming to be able to perform miracles, Buddha requested, 'Please lay an egg.' He insisted on the way of knowledge. Miracles or rituals are interesting to observe but do not add to your knowledge. What you know for sure, however insignificant it may be, is better than not-understood miracles, however spectacular it may be.

"Buddha is focused on his main theme of world suffering. 'I do not say world is eternal, nor I say world is not eternal. I do not say soul and body is same, nor do I say soul and body are different. In any event the suffering exists.' Solution for the suffering has nothing to do with any of these metaphysical views. If a person is struck with an arrow, the first thing to do is to pull out the arrow. That is the direct cure for the suffering. Not to sit down and insist that I will not pull this arrow out until I know what kind of arrow shaft it is, or how the bow is made, or whether the person who shot the arrow is fat or tall.

"Buddha asks to follow the truth that can be directly observed and the truth which can be logically deduced. 'I do not teach whether soul exists or does or does not exist. For human being it is not possible to know for sure the existence or nonexistence of soul. Why do people like to believe in existence of soul? Because it helps lay down the fear of death, and helps vanity of being immortal. Here, we can recognize and do something about the fear and the vanity. Therefore, instead of profitless speculation about existence of soul, we should try as a first order of business to control the fear of death and the vanity of being immortal.'

"Buddha is scientific. How to face death? 'Do so as if you are about to enter a room where nobody has gone in or come out. We know nothing about the room of which we will enter. Should we be fearful, happy, cautious, full of expectation?' If there no information exists about the room, then we cannot have any frame of mind. If we assume any of the frames of mind, then it does not reflect what is in the room. Rather it reflects the person's past experiences."

"Buddha's approach to problems of life summarized as the four 'Noble truths' is like that of a therapist," Dr Bonia explained to us. "As long as everything is running smoothly we would not notice any problems or suffering. When things do not go smoothly, as a wheel out of joint, then we feel suffering. The reason for such disjointedness is the drive for private fulfillment or personal craving. Overcoming the egoistic drive for separate existence can cure this disease. The way to the overcoming of self-seeking or ego is through the "Eightfold path."

'The eightfold path then is a course of treatment but it is not external treatment passively accepted by the patient as coming from outside as a matter of faith. It is not treatment by pill, or cult, or grace. It is treatment through training. The driving force behind the Buddhist ethical system is not the commandment and associated sense of sin or punishment, but the way of knowledge and compassion. If you do not steal, then it is not because of fear of sin/hell or expectation of reward/heaven, but because fear and craving themselves are the cause of suffering. The eightfold path is summarized as: 1-Right knowledge; 2-Right aspiration; 3-Right speech; 4-Right behavior; 5-Right livelihood; 6-Right effort; 7-Right mindfulness; 8-Right absorption.

"Right behavior" is further broken down into five steps: Do not kill; Do not steal; Do not lie; Do not be unchaste; Do not drink intoxicants.

What is a Buddha mind? As a not-enlightened person, one can only speculate. Suppose a mind has searched within itself and is able to recognize and neutralize all the self-ego and ego-tinted vision, then whatever is left, as a bright conscience without any tint or mental block, perhaps is the Buddha mind.

CHAPTER 45
WAR HAS COME TO INDIA!

After years of agitation over possession of Kashmir, fighting has broken out in the land of the Himalayas. Pakistan has longed for possession of the Kush and is now fighting to take it from India. The Hindu Kush is a formidable area of mountains that extends 500 miles, with a 200-mile stretch forming the southern boundary of Afghanistan.

We have been ordered to return to New Delhi; if this war escalates, our isolated situation in rural India could be dangerous. It is June, and we are busy packing. I have been worried about Gillie and decided we must take her along, as there is no way of knowing how long we will be away. Rafiq will bring her on the Jeep. Traveling with her is not an easy thing, as she is a very big dog with a long tail and wants her way. She is sweet and affectionate, but often slaps any article within the reach of her tail.

With India's current economic and internal problems, the Pakistanis feel they can get possession of this long disputed land. To make matters worse, Russia threatens to join Pakistan. *The Times of India* reports that thousands of demonstrators have stoned the U.S. Consulate in Lahore, West Pakistan. The American Counsel's car windows were smashed. Prime Minister Bhutto has flown to New York to appear before the United Nations.

Another menace rose its shaggy head when the New China News Agency reported a warning to India to stop all "intrusion and provocation" on the

Sino-Indian border. China claims that India "intruded into Dumchele and fired on the Chinese on duty there."

This is not the first border conflict there in recent years. In 1963, the Chinese in a diplomatic note accused Indians of seizing 800 sheep and 59 yak on the Sino-Indian border. To the astonishment of New Delhi residents, motorists and pedestrians found themselves surrounded by hundreds of goats and sheep. Deciding to take a hand in things diplomatic, the citizenry drove a herd of bleating sheep and goats through Cannaught Place and Barkhamba Road (the center of New Delhi's business district) to the Chinese Embassy on Litton Road. The animals wore placards with colorfully painted slogans, such as "Eat Us, But Save The World" and other signs.

The protest, which was captured on film by two Chinese cameramen, resulted in China's Second Secretary announcing that his nation was not interested in the sheep or the note of apology that would be handed to the Chinese.

In a recent article about China's aim, Chalmera M. Roberts, a writer and authority on Southeast Asia, claimed, "India and Pakistan are really pawns in a game." He reported that Peking sees the United States as having "weakened itself. It is weakened by occupying so many places in the world, overreaching itself, stretching its fingers out wide and dispersing its strength...." The view of Peking is that although "stronger than any imperialist in the past, everything is divisible, and so is this colossus of U.S. imperialism," said Roberts. "The fingers of the American hand, then, can be chopped off one by one—and Vietnam is the spot for the first chop." Mao first used the finger imagery during the Korean War.

We rode the Grand Trunk Train into Delhi. We were a captive audience for passengers who wanted to vent their feelings about the U.S.-built jets that Pakistan is using to bomb villages and railway lines in Kashmir, and planes making night raids over other parts of India. The Patton, Sherman and Chaffee tanks are another bone of contention. We became aware quickly of the hostility Foreign Service personnel overseas often face.

*　　　　　*　　　　　*

August has arrived, and Mark, John and I have been with the children in New Delhi for some weeks. We are sad because our dog, Gillie, has been lost. She was too big to stay in the house all the time. When we brought her in, she stayed on the roof, which is flat and built for the family's use during the summer. Light cots, called *charpoi*, are kept in a room on the roof. Gillie had room to run, as it is a large area. But she was in heat, and even from three stories, the signal went out to stray dogs that came around. She was kept on a leash with a long lead, but she jumped to a lower level, broke the leash and then jumped to the ground.

We were afraid for her, and John was upset. Dennis went out to find her, but Gillie was among rabid, pi dogs, scrawny and mangy. She disappeared.

The situation with the war has become more volatile in the last few days. Arthur, our cook, and Rampershad, our houseman, came in with news that a bright light and a big noise had awakened them. Then they heard guns going tat-tat-tat-tat, and planes flew away. Verbal reports from others confirmed the attack later. A mosque was bombed, and fifty people were killed while praying.

Word is out that paratroopers were to have been dropped in outlying districts. Two women in purdah were seen dumping bottles of liquid into a village well, after riding there on a hired scooter taxi. The police and health department arrived quickly and ordered the well emptied and cleaned thoroughly before any more water could be drawn for consumption.

Many Indians are extremely angry about U.S. planes and Patton tanks being furnished to Pakistan to fight this war with. We continue hearing reports of F-104 and F-86 Sabre jets being used in raids. Actually, both India and Pakistan have planes and tanks supplied by the U.S. The radio news does not discuss it.

*   *   *

The blackout curfew is at 7 p.m. for all Americans and dependents. All lights must be out by 7—all windows and doors completely blacked out.

The buttermilk sky is eerie as the moon shines hazily through the mist this evening. Standing alone on the roof garden of our house a little while ago, I could see hundreds of rooftops and temples. It is dark, and the moonlight is the only light. Across the street is a magnificent house with open verandas on three levels, the architecture resembling something designed by Frank Lloyd Wright.

Many people in Delhi have offered themselves as wardens, patrolling the streets even at midnight. Tonight, I watched as two men made their rounds.

Hundreds of bearded, dusty young men from America are streaming into the Embassy. They are given soap and told to bathe. They are sleeping in the hallways of buildings until they can leave the country.

We expect the worst of the danger will blow over in a week's time and things will go back to normal. Mark and I have received first-hand information that there is a shortage of fuel in India, especially for tanks. This is not discussed, even between us. We don't discuss anything in our home of a security-related nature.

*   *   *

Today, I took a taxi to the U.S Commissary, a very small business, only to find, when we turned off Chandra Guptas Marg, cars, station wagons and taxis jamming the parking lot. The U.S. military wives, always organized, had arrived first and the shelves were practically bare.

The Pakistani Diplomat and his wife, children and staff live across the road. They are under house arrest, although the children are allowed to be outdoors. They wait for me to come out of our compound, and then they run up to me and say, "Hello, Auntie. How are you, Auntie?" Bubbling with enthusiasm, they can never comprehend the problems that just being Pakistani, while living in an Indian culture, has made in their lives.

There were two alerts last night. One began at 1:30 a.m. as the wail of the alarm rose and fell, rose and fell again, piercing the night. I finally went to our bedroom and tried to sleep. Mark sat on the side of the bed, trying to find his lighter in the dark. "I can't muster very much enthusiasm for an alarm at this hour," he said glumly.

We heard today that a plane had been shot down by anti-aircraft as it approached New Delhi. Across the street from our house where the Pakistani Diplomat lives, there was great activity through the night, hammering, sawing—building crates for packing, according to our cook's evaluation. Two policemen are patrolling the street to deter any overly zealous patriots from doing harm to the Pakistanis.

Each morning lately the diplomat gets into his car, and a guard with rifle at attention can be seen in the rear seat. I expect they will be leaving soon. I will miss the lovely children.

*   *   *

On September 7, a report from Washington by the State Department claimed that the United States had suspended military aid shipments to both India and Pakistan. The State Department was concerned that both India and Pakistan were using the U. S. military equipment.

We have been on the sideline of this war and feel that it is not entirely over. We continue to have a concern for the children and ourselves.

*   *   *

A settlement pact has now been offered that may bring the fighting to an end. The cease-fire line of the pact extends northward from Chamb on the western border of Kashmir.

On September 23, 1965, the cease-fire between India and Pakistan finally has taken effect.

CHAPTER 46
A SPECIAL FLIGHT TO DELIVER A SPECIAL DOG

Several weeks after the end of the fighting, we have been able to return to Raipur. We miss Gillie, and John has been very lonesome for another dog.

I had told a friend in New Delhi about our lost pet. Her husband was director of an American corporation that had a development program in India for many years. She said they expected a litter of puppies from their Labrador retriever. Would John like one? I assured her that he would.

A few days ago, we had a cable saying that a plane would deliver the puppy and her papers. Mark sent his driver to pick her up. She arrived on a company-owned Cessna that could land in an open field near Raipur.

"What a beautiful puppy!" I exclaimed.

"How black!" John was smiling and excited as he took her in his arms. She began to lick his face, and they loved each other immediately.

Her registered name is Midnight Special.

"How are you going to say, 'Here, Midnight'? Let's name her something else," said John.. After much discussion, it was decided that Prita, meaning, "loved by all," would be an appropriate name for her. It was the suggestion of John's little friend Gatum.

John is a good teacher. Prita tries whatever he is attempting to tell her to do. She retrieves the ball, then runs from John when he tries to get it from her. The two of them have such fun romping on the floor and racing around in the big house. I love to hear his laughter. Gatum, who has never had a dog, comes to play with them and is someone else for her to tease and romp with.

*   *   *

I have been looking forward to Christmas when the children will be with us. It is a matter of days now.

Dennis arrived in Nagpur by a train that was occupied by hundreds of Indians, while the girls were picked up at the airport in Nagpur. We had been advised that it would not be a good idea for young American girls to ride the train unless accompanied by an adult. Activities got under way directly after they all arrived.

On Christmas day, Hindu friends brought beautiful leis and awakened us. It was to have been a late morning, since the children usually have to rise early. The leis had fresh flowers, bits of silver and gold foil worked into the flower design. We gave our friends baskets of fruits and nuts, and our servants were given the day off.

We were invited to the Mukerjis' home for our Christmas meal. Their guests were from various cities and included Hindus, Moslems, and Christians. One man was the head of the geological survey and mining operation. An official of the Burma-Shell Company and his father, who had been prominent in the Indian independence movement, were present. Another man had been on a plane five years ago that had a bomb aboard in an attempted assassination of the leader of Red China. He and four others survived, while fifty passengers were lost.

The dinner menu featured turkey and pork sausage that had been brought hundreds of miles.

Our meal was delicious, ham from Calcutta and candied yams, potatoes, peas, carrots and candied fruits. There were simulated "cranberries" made from pods picked and crushed that tasted much like the real berries. Wheat had been purchased, cleaned and ground for the breads. All candies were homemade. The Maurs, who are American missionaries, but are not allowed to preach, accomplished all of this work. They have been selling books. They are leaving, returning to the United States.

"Come on, have one more spoonful of this dressing," Rita, the Mukerjis' college-aged daughter, encouraged Mr. Mauhib, who is a Moslem. She piled another helping on his plate, knowing it contains pork that his religion strictly forbids. I knew that this Moslem belief is one not to be taken lightly. In fact, back in the 1800s, an oversight by ammunition manufacturers meant that certain rifle cartridges had a heavily greased patch at the end. The cartridge required biting off the end to release the powder into the barrel. News of lard being used on the cartridges got out and spread rapidly, giving anti-British plotters a reason for a war that was fought over it. It takes very little to stir up any factions who are fanatics. Yet the children of today still thought it was a fun prank to play on someone, leading the person to unwittingly break the taboo. I was afraid that some guest might disclose what he was eating and I did not know what would happen.

*   *   *

Earlier in the day we had had some unsettling news. We learned that the home of our Christian friends, Joseph and Lolita Jones, had been attacked during the night. Lighted torches were thrown, but fortunately there was little damage since the family and servants had awakened and extinguished the fire. All are safe and we did not allow it to spoil Christmas. Rita said, "Lolita asked what would these people do next."

After dinner, we gathered and spent the remainder of the afternoon discussing the problems of this country. It is a well-kept secret that India is in desperate need of fuel. China's attack on India's border is still very fresh in the minds of Indian leaders. Russia is very active in the country, and this has caused consternation.

Rice from America's farms has begun to pile up in the ports of India. It has been held in the ships' holds, waiting a deal between the U.S. Oil Company and the Indian government. Before the government takes charge of it, it is resold to grain merchants. The proceeds go into a special account to be used for a purpose agreed on between the two governments. Ten percent accrues to the U.S. government.

This rice, after months of delay, arrives broken and tasteless compared to the Indian rice with its bouquet. The food is unacceptable to the people, who just don't like U.S. rice, but it is all they have to eat to ward off starvation.

The urgency to get more irrigation projects into service for India's is Mark's grave concern. He has plots of improved rice growing in every one of his districts.

*   *   *

The farmers in Bustar are also facing a serious problem with tigers. The rice fields have been abandoned for fear of attacks. The farmers cannot thresh their wheat because of tigers taking their buffaloes, which are vital to their livelihood.

The boys are planning to accompany Mark and two of our servants on a hunt soon. They will stake out a buffalo for bait and wait for the tiger. The mashan, a platform of limbs held between tree limbs, serves as the hunters' seat while waiting. When the deer population gets low, the tigers go for anything edible. A mother tiger and two cubs in the Bustar region have killed four hundred villagers.

Dennis was able to go with Mark to visit a village nearby while at home this month. It was his first time in a village. "I am really glad that we made this journey," he said. "It has really opened my eyes as to what the world is like."

All the children have greatly enjoyed their trip home to Raipur. They met lovely young people, children and friends of our friends, who are home for the Christmas and Diwali holidays.

Our Maharaja friend and wife also invited us to bring the children over for a visit while they are out of school. It was a packed jeep that arrived at the palace, and the children were delighted to be there. After freshening up, we all came out on the veranda, where we met their astrologer, who had come for his regular visit. He wore a handsome kurta, a shirt with gold studs. Winnie asked him to tell her about herself. They moved to two chairs farther away from the conversation going on. A while after he began talking to her, I realized that tears were running down her cheeks. I did not interrupt, however, and she never wanted to talk about it. She only said that he knew her better than she knew herself.

We had a wonderful trip and returned from the palace for a few more days together at home. Connie, who is doing college level work at school, was invited to take a ride in glider piloted by Raja Brij of Rampur, who is famous for his flying in New Delhi. He asked my permission, and I gave it. The Raja is the attaché to the past President and visited our home in Raipur several times, as his children were in the College of Rajas here. Connie wants to travel more in India, but there has been little opportunity with her schedule.

The children were driven to Nagpur, 200 miles away, to get a plane to New Delhi and go back to school. The trip to Nagpur was exciting as they spent their time searching for animals and were not disappointed when they saw an enormous tiger. Rafiq, an authority, said it was ten feet from nose to the end of its tail.

*   *   *

Thieves are stealing anything they can sell or use. As we sat in our living room with two Indian gentlemen discussing plans for projects one evening, we were startled to see a youth leap onto our outside windowsill and remove the light bulb before we could get to the door and stop him. Stamps on envelopes must be securely attached else they will be removed and resold. We use fold-overs, aerograms, to be sure they reach their destination.

Mark sent me a hand-written message from his office yesterday. Although we had recently had a phone connected, he didn't want the conversation overheard.

"The Madman of Bustar is coming to town and to see us," his note said.

Mark was speaking of the Raja or prince who has a palace in a remote area of Orissa State. We had heard of him when we were in New Delhi, where the national newspapers had reported a terrible story about his cutting off a thief's hand. Left with wealth of olden times and following the ancient rules, the Raja had carried out the punishment after a servant stole from the palace.

"Why do you think he wants to stay with us?" I asked Mark.

"Doesn't everyone?" he replied.

I have no full-time cook and feel I cannot entertain a prince. "I thought that perhaps you could go away for a few days," Mark suggested. "I can arrange some trips and take John with me."

Today, I went to see Sonu to get her thoughts on this. She was sitting on a heavy teak chest with her bags spread about her. She told me she was going to Darjeeling. The heat is too much for her, she said, and Darjeeling would be wonderful. I agreed. I told her about the message and the prince's plans.

"You remember Geta, who plays bridge with us occasionally?" Sonu asked.

"Surely," I said. "She is lovely. I remember she told us about the white tigers of Bustar that were found and nurtured on their lands and forests."

"The Maharaja is a member of her family," she said.

"Mary, I have a wonderful idea," exclaimed Sonu. "Go with me to Darjeeling. We have a company-owned bungalow there." I could see that she was sincere.

"You really mean it? I would love it," I said on an impulse. "Maybe John can stay with Gatum, and visit his school."

Sonu said, "I will speak with the headmaster. I'm sure he will be happy to have him."

What a good escape from the Madman's visit, I thought. "It would be a face saver for us and we would all be happy."

Sonu agreed. "Do it, Mary!"

CHAPTER 47
CALCUTTA AND DARJEELING

We left today in the Ambassador, a car manufactured in India. It is sturdy and quite comfortable but small, containing Sonu, her husband R.C., a driver and me. The Land Rover was filled with luggage, food and supplies, with the cook-bearer and a driver riding behind us. We traveled at a slow pace.

The trip to Calcutta, where we are going on our way to Darjeeling, was spectacularly uneventful to begin with. Forest, jungle and countryside passed. The driver, Dowa, blew the horn when the cows, goats and people filled the road. We traveled through Sambalpur, the jungle area of Orissa. Sonu was unusually quiet. R.C. and I talked about the "world and her wife," but very seldom did Sonu enter into the conversation. I noticed that her thin body hardly imprinted her sari.

"There is much to enjoy in Calcutta. The *miadans*, parks, are magnificent," said R.C.. "Chittaranjan Avenue is one hundred feet wide and runs north and south through the city. Those palatial houses that face it were once grand homes; now they are used for shops, clubs and hotels. There is pollution, and it is densely populated, though— about 11 million today. It isn't an ancient city like Delhi."

He went on to tell about Job Charnock of the English East Indian Tea Company, leader of the English merchants who started trading there.

Emperor Akbar commanded that the three villages that were the first set-tlements of Calcutta would pay taxes. The English didn't like that, so they moved down the Hoogly River for a time, but eventually returned. In 1756, Suraj ud-Dowlah, the Moslem ruler of Bengal, captured Ft. William, and his forces sacked Calcutta. The English jumped into their ships and fled. The English finally named a new ruler of India, and resti-tution was made to them for the damages and losses.

Calcutta is a great center for manufacturing and shipping. "My com-pany maintains our activities there. Pilots steer the ships filled with oil up from the sea," said R.C..

He talked about the university, patterned after the University of London. We spent the night in their pleasant bungalow.

*   *   *

Today, we took the early train for the three-hundred-and-fifty-mile ride. We were then met and taken up the mountain. We watched the tiny railroad that paralleled our route, a brassbound engine puffing along, with the tender sitting on top of the boiler. R.C. had left us in Calcutta where he had business to attend to, while we went on to New Jalpaigur and to Darjeeling.

En route, we climbed through marvelous tea gardens and got to see how the tea is processed. It was a fascinatingly lovely place. Sonu noted that the heady rainfall from June to September and the cool temperatures here are the secrets to good tea growing.

"What a blessing that our company has this bungalow for the officers and families," she said. We couldn't wait to shake all the dust from our hair, nostrils and brains, it seemed.

We reached our destination at last. I was transfixed and drank in the view before me. The shimmering green valley lay with a succession of ranges. In front of us were the snowy peaks of Kanchenjunga, Nepal, a place that is 28,146 feet high. Glittering before us was a wall of snow that never changes. Below us were the swollen rivers. The Sikkim frontier stood with white peaks on either side. We stood silently taking in the view. These mountains are a different world.

There is a long spur for the railway to the town proper, as well as the cantonments of Katapahaar, Jalapahar and Lebong. The area is nearly five miles square. The lowest point of the valley is 2,000 feet below the upper point.

The weather is cold. We pulled on slacks and sweaters and were served marvelous tea.

*   *   *

We have been here several days. We have walked and talked, and explored the shops. Sonu bought two Chinese hairpins to criss-cross through the bun of hair that I wear on my neck. Then we went to Tiger Hill, from which the view of the sunrise on Mt. Everest is a must.

That morning, Sonu began telling me about her love for the young man, Raji. He is several years younger than she is. "It makes no difference to him," she said.

She spoke of his tenderness, their love of poetry. Raji has studied abroad as well and is ill suited for a life with a village Indian girl. His heart aches for Sonu.

"My husband had been away from home on business so much, and I have been lonely beyond words before you came to Raipur," she told me. Her husband had begun drinking on the long business trips abroad. They had become more incompatible. She could not think of divorce; that simply is not acceptable. She spoke of their love for their children.

Her appetite picked up in the mountain air. Our last evening was spent with a group of happy people in a Chinese restaurant. Once again, I found myself waiting for the train that would take me to Raipur. My compartment was comfortable. I read and slept. Sonu would return later.

*   *   *

When I returned home, the servants were full of talk about the Mad Raja of Bustar's visit to Raipur. He had stayed in a rest house. There, he went to a window and people gathered below.

"He threw rupees to the wind and watched people scramble for them," said Rafiq. I was greatly relieved that we had been away.

Three days later, we left on a business trip to Orissa State. Always when we travel, we take canned food from stock from Denmark and use as emergency rations. Water is always necessary, a clay jug purchased from the tribes keeps it cooler through evaporation than in a thermos jug. Lion's beer has saved us many times. We have come to enjoy *lasi*, a refreshing drink made using yogurt, lime juice, sugar and water. The yogurt is rich and tasty.

I always wear either a sari or slacks. I find the sari to be infinitely cooler than fitted Western clothes.

We departed in the late afternoon. There were the usual hordes of animals and people, except this time there was also a procession of elephants. One carried a holy man while a trumpet heralded his passing, and bells clanged with each step the elephant took. Young children darted in and out of the procession

Forty-five miles an hour was our average speed. However, the Sikh truck drivers hurled their rattling lorries by us with complete disregard for the possibility of our being forced off the road. The Sikhs are strong and take great pride in their virility. A friend told us that once he observed two Sikhs coming toward each other in their big trucks. Neither of them would give the right of way. Both went racing toward each other were battered and forced into the ditch. They climbed out of their trucks, unharmed, and with complete calm met with outstretched hands, embraced and returned to their respective trucks and drove away. This is the kind of competition one typically has on the narrow roads.

We pushed on until we reached the jungle rest house that had been reserved for us. We could not sleep well because we had an early meeting. We started out hurriedly to make up for being somewhat late. A little monkey ran under a tire of the jeep. It screamed, and suddenly monkeys by the dozens jumped from tree to tree, swung to the ground and came towards us. Two landed on top of the jeep and jumped down on the hood. They screeched and made piercing screams, showing their teeth.

Rafiq stepped on the accelerator and said, "We must go fast or else they will have us surrounded." The screams had warned monkeys throughout the jungle, and they were responding.

We arrived at the home of the Vice-Chancellor of the University in Orissa State. The following morning, Mark had a meeting scheduled with the university and district officials I attended.

We were introduced to four tribal chiefs. They were well built and handsome, tall and strong. Each wore a dhoti and a necklace with tiger claws and polished gems. One carried a once-handsome leather attaché case. No one would have guessed that they had run four hundred miles to attend the meeting.

This episode, along with our journey here and back home, proved once again that there was never a trip without the excitement of anticipating an appearance of a new temple, a festival, or an unexpected insight into the past and present.

Tribesmen of a remote hill tribe in Orissa came to a meeting at the University of Orissa, reportedly having run 400 miles to attend. Their necklaces are strung with tiger claws. More than 60 tribal groups of aboriginal people inhabit the state of Orissa on India's east coast.

CHAPTER 48
THE WORLD'S MOST BEAUTIFUL MOMUMENT

We have driven to Agra many times on our travels. There, the Taj Mahal is located on the bank of the Yamuna River, which flows past it on the northern side. The platforms of the tomb itself are faced with white marble from Makrana. We found the same marble's beauty on a boat trip through the marble caves of Makrana.

Other buildings at the palace are of redstone with marble detail. The approach from the south leads through an impressive gate and a formal garden divided by paths and ornamental pools.

We have seen the Taj Mahal at sunrise when the brilliant rose light falls on the white marble. We examined it during the daytime to explore its magnificence. We saw it again when orange sunset illumined the splendor of the divine monument.

The most propitious time to visit it is during a full moon. By moonlight, the dome seems to float suspended, the mist covering the remainder, the gardens and the reflecting pool of water. Once we took friends there late at late night and found the gates locked. The gatekeeper was not difficult to persuade to open it. We gave him a tip and had the entire grounds to ourselves. They could hardly tear themselves away from it.

The word Mumtaz-i Mahal, meaning "Chosen of the Palace," was the title given to Arjumand Banu Begum, the favorite wife and constant companion of the Mughal emperor Shah Jahan. She died in 1631 while giving birth to her fourteenth child. Shah Jahan wanted the finest monument that could be built as a mausoleum for his wife. The Council of Architects from India, Persia, and Central Asia came together to plan the Taj Mahal.

Plans were drawn, and work began in 1632. Twenty thousand workers were employed daily. It took twenty-two years to complete, at a cost of forty million rupees. Massive arches rise one hundred and eight feet.

Precious treasures from all over the world were used—jade and crystal, Turkestan, turquoise from Tibet, amber from Burma, lapis lazuli from Afganistan, crysolite from Egypt, diamonds from Golconda and quartz from the Himalayas. The palace features forty-three types of gems, including topazes, garnets, sapphire, rare shells, coral and mother-of-pearl from the sea.

The marble required ten-mile-long ramps of tamped earth and an unending parade of elephants and bullock carts dragging blocks of stone, to be hoisted by teams of mules and masses of workers. It is undoubtedly the most world's most beautiful building.

*   *   *

I have been fascinated by all there is to see and experience here, from the temple sculpture to the Ellora caves, famous for a temple that has been magnificently carved in the rock. The Ajanta caves are known for their paintings. They are located near Aurangabad.

Dr. Lokosh Chandler, Director of the International Academy of Indian Culture, has been a helpful friend in my enlightenment about India's art history.

When the Moghul King Akbar lived, Persia was the seat of artistic and literary culture of Islam and the Near East. Akbar's father, Humayun, lost his throne for a time and took his son to Persia. There he persuaded famed art masters, Abdus Samad and Mir Sayyid Alil, to return to India with him. They painted in the Persian style; small, beautiful figures, bright red and brilliant blues as in stained glass windows and Persian miniatures. Later, the style changed and became larger. The paintings were done on paper and placed in a portfolio instead of being hung.

The paintings of the Rajputs, a Hindu people descended from Kshatrija, the warrior caste, use stronger colors than those of the Moghuls. Krishna, incarnate of the Hindu god Vishnu, was always painted blue. He is either chasing or surrounded by maidens. The Kama Sutra served as the basis for the Rajput artists and acts of love are portrayed in exquisite detail.

Rajputs were fighters, and much of the art depicts the anguish suffered by their women during their absence at war. Lesbians were not overlooked in the paintings.

When Shah Jahan was imprisoned in 1658, Delhi suffered artistically and administratively. This disorganized state continued through years of ill rule, but an art revival came in the early 1700s. Then, Nadir Shah, a Persian, invaded India and seized Delhi. After killing and harming much of the population, he took numerous works of art, including the Peacock Throne. This invasion caused the artists to retreat to the valley of the Himalayas, where they did marvelous work for over a century and a half.

In Kishangarh, a Rajput state south of Jaipur, is a collection of remarkable paintings. The patron was a poet prince called Sawant Singh. It is said that his mistress was the model of the Mona Lisa-like pictures.

CHAPTER 49
A HOSPITAL FOR ALL

Mark has received an invitation from an American doctor who has a hospital in Dhumteri, an area we have not visited. It is two hours or more drive over difficult roads. We decided to go this week.

We found a city, in terms of population, but a village in character, with a road extending several blocks, houses and a pond filled with slime and mud. It was the dirtiest city I have seen. I say this without any thought of condemnation. Under the circumstances, I could not imagine any one power that could improve the conditions.

Arrows directed us to the hospital. We knew we had arrived when we saw the high wall, with a turnstile outside. Here, patients waited their turn to be seen. Relatives accompanied the patients.

The double gate swung open, and three men in white outfits greeted us. Two trotted ahead, directing us to the doctor's home. A deep verandah encircled the large stone house. Two women in white habits like those worn by Catholic sisters came to greet us.

"Welcome, I am Sister Angelina," one spoke. The other introduced herself as Sister Grace. As slightly built as the Indian women, the sisters looked severe and plainer than any American women I remembered ever seeing—until they smiled. Then they no longer looked plain, but warm yet dignified.

Hazel, the doctor's wife, led us into the dark sitting room, where we were immediately handed glasses of lemonade, cool, but iceless. The room was sparsely furnished, and a few old magazines from years back lay with a Bible on the coffee table. The bookcase was filled to overflowing with books, and photographs of smiling people stood on top. There was no fan, and no air stirring. The drapes were drawn against the heat and the room was darkened. I do this, too, at home so it did not seem unusual.

"George is at the hospital," his wife, Hazel, told us. "This is his first day at work in over three months. He has had hepatitis."

"The doctor was very sick. We felt we might lose him," said Sister Angelina. "Since there is no medicine for hepatitis, all we could do was to pray day and night."

"After fifteen years living here, he gets hepatitis," added Hazel. "We were all offered gamma globulin from Calcutta. He felt that if he was going to get the disease, he would already have done so and refused the shots." When the illness hit, he was delirious and hallucinated for days, she said.

Mark asked if the hospital had other doctors, and she told us there are two. "They are local people, Orthodox Hindus. George recognized their interest and abilities when they were boys. We were able to get scholarships to Edinburgh, Scotland. Now they are fine doctors."

"It must have been a great change for you to move here to live and work as an American, with the medical facilities at home," I said.

"When we came here we found terrible conditions. Human sacrifice had been prevalent. There were times when they offered a young son to the gods," she said. "Many times George has stopped the tragedy from happening."

Mark and I looked at each other with disbelief.

In a few minutes, the doctor entered. A tall man, he looked weak and his complexion was sallow.

"How was surgery, dear?" his wife inquired.

With an affirmative nod, he smiled. "I had to postpone some difficult cases, and today I will tackle them. My residents are fine doctors. Three heads are better than one."

The sparse supper of eggplant, tomatoes, beans, bread, butter, bananas and tea seemed to be totally acceptable by the attendees, although they were non-vegetarian. Mark was hungry.

"We have little or no meat these days," said our hostess. "The goat in the market is of poor quality. Sometimes we get a chicken. But no one ever told them that by fattening the chickens they could make more money."

During dinner, George told Mark, "I met a doctor in Pittsburgh two years ago when he was conducting a seminar. He had your last name, and an unusual first name, very Southern."

"I'll be damned— it's my brother! That is exactly where he was," said Mark. "It is a small world."

"Fine man," said George. "Tomorrow, I'll show you both the hospital. I'm still weak and can expect that to last awhile."

We went to our bed. I was restless; there was a fan, but it was not effective. I thought about these people—intelligent, dedicated to their belief in helping their fellow man in this remote area. There is no music except their own recordings, no theater except the festivals, or plays they write and read, the library is their personal collection, yet they feel their life has been enriched. Every five years, they can go back to the U.S to see their families.

The pillow and sheets became wet from sweating, and my gown stuck to me as I rolled over. I eased out of bed and poured water from a jug on the dresser into a bowl. Mark slept, oblivious to my wakefulness.

He rose early and left for his meeting. I put on a robe and joined Hazel in the kitchen. She was eager to talk about America. It was pleasant sitting at the table with cups of tea, becoming acquainted.

"We will make an inspection of the hospital and let the patients and their families meet you, if you don't mind. The last American woman who visited us was the wife of a missionary. They had two rowdy sons, and their hyperactivity caused the mother to lose patience. She did some yelling and pulled the children apart. All the commotion, unknown to the

Indian mothers, caused them to suspect that her sickness was anger," said Hazel.

"'Poor thing,' they would say, 'She has cut off all her womanly attributes of patience and long-suffering, with her hair cut.' I would like them to see your long braids."

We found things to laugh at during all the serious conversation. She has a wonderful spirit.

We walked across the campus, with the dry crackling grass and bare dirt spots beneath our feet. We talked about the mission's history. "We first built a two-room mud and stone building, adding room after room as we could afford it. We now have thirty rooms, a separate building for isolation cases and 26 wonderfully trained nurses," Hazel told me.

The patient lies on a string *charpoi* without a pillow or any cover except the gown, furnished by the hospital and kept washed by the family. Because of the caste system, the family prepares all of the patient's food. The aromas of the food with its strong spices overpower the antiseptic smell.

The outer door of each patient's room opens to the outside, where members of the family stay. The relatives sit on their haunches in a group talking softly. "They never leave their side and we don't try to move them. Even down in the isolation building where the contagious patients lie, they sit patiently awaiting word, be it good news of a recovery or death, when they take the body away."

I wondered how much the hospital charges for its care. "Something, depending on what they have. Sometimes they have a few *annas* (a tenth of a penny)," Hazel said.

The head nurse came and told us that the doctor would be in surgery soon. She said that if I wanted to come, I must scrub. I was a little hesitant but went on and prepared myself. They placed me where I could see and be out of the way.

"This poor fellow was attacked by a dog. They are a menace," said George. "We have kept the dog's head for the lab to examine it for rabies."

The overhead light went on over the table, showing a gaping hole in the man's hip and belly.

He examined the wound. "I'm proud of that light; I made it myself," he said in a moment, indicating the reflector above. "We are happy to have an air conditioner for this room, too; we've had it for a year."

After lunch and a siesta, we woke to have tea and talk. I told George about a young boy with a clubfoot, who had come to us in the jungle from a nearby village. The imprint of the foot lay along his leg. "We will get him to you if he can be located. We'd like to assist with expenses," I said. We had seen the mission's books and were surprised at the small amount of money they receive from their church in the United States.

I told the doctor and his wife about a woman who headed a family planning program and who visited me in Raipur. We had sat in my living room and talked at length about the program. They see few women, as male doctors are not trusted. Babies are born wherever the mother is at the time of labor, traditionally in her parents' home. Every year India has an increase in population that is equivalent to the entire population of Australia.

The family planning program leader said she had visited one village and asked how the program was going there. She said, "The answer was, 'Yes, the program goes very well. We received many pills.' They had been taking the pills ten months, I was told. 'Are you pleased?' I asked the village woman. 'I wouldn't say yes, and I wouldn't say no. We still have many births.'

"When I was about to leave, some girls were at the door giggling and hiding their faces in the ends of their saris. They said they did not take the pills. They did not like the idea of being told that they could not have any more children. Their husbands would be very angry with them if they knew they could not become pregnant. I asked why they had accepted the pills. The girls answered that it would not have been polite to refuse."

When we left Dhumteri, we invited George and Hazel to visit us. After we returned to our home, they were always on our minds. Knowledge, stamina and love had carved a wedge in ignorance. Their dream is to end their mission in another three years and turn it over completely to the people they have trained.

Chapter 50
RIDING A TRACTOR AGAIN

Yesterday Mark and I visited friends out in another part of Madhya Pradesh. After two and a half-hours' drive, we arrived at a farm, with fruit trees in straight rows. In the fields, paddy (rice) and wheat grew. The fences were painted, a rarity in this country.

A sign on the gate said, TRACTOR AND TRAINING CENTER OF INDIA. The compound was guarded by a chokidar, erect and distinguished looking in khaki shirt and pleated shorts, with khaki knee socks and brown shoes.

The farm is the work of Mark's friend, Dr. John Zacharias, and his wife. Dr. Zacharias came to India after receiving his Ph.D. in West Virginia in 1960. A black American mechanical engineer, Harold Jones, spent four years helping to set up this operation. Mr. Jones and his family are legends in this part of India, as evidenced by his fine work here. He has been gone for three years now.

When we stopped the jeep we found a volleyball game going on out back. Our host and hostess greeted us and introduced their son, Tommy. Their living room was filled with treasures. The red and white décor had splashes of gold, and a carpet of many colors covered the floor. A stuffed leopard, a tiger and a bear were placed about the room.

This family lives in an isolated part of the world, away from comforts and conveniences of the modern world, yet they are apparently happy in their home and with their work.

Our hosts insisted we spend the night with them rather than in a forest rest house several miles out in the jungle. Six Czechoslovakian engineers occupied the guesthouse, but they were to leave the next day.

We settled down to have a cool fruit drink and chat about our experiences. We were served a delightful dinner.

The Czechs sent a note asking that we meet them after dinner. There were two young men, one older man and one, the leader, about our age. The leader, who did all the talking, apologized frequently for his lack of English. All the answers he gave were not easily understood, as he was speaking from the desires of his culture and their needs. They appeared trustful of us. The major reason for being there is to sell farm equipment and train others in the repair and maintenance of them.

We were to arise at 1:30 a.m. to hunt for meat. It took an hour's drive to reach the jungle. We drove up a long incline paralleling a dried-up river at the base of the mountain. There we spotted a leopard, stretched full length up the side of a large mahogany tree. We found another, lying curled under a brush. They are fast, dangerous animals.

We proceeded slowly, branches and leaves crackling beneath the tires. Herds of elk, sambar, antelopes and spotted deer were grazing at a distance. They turned their heads to look at us. We almost reached the crest of the mountain just as the sun rose. It was a glorious view to see the full moon still shining brightly on one side of the mountain and the sun coming up on the other side.

Rafiq suggested we walk around the crest. Pieces of sandstone of all sizes were strewn everywhere. Das brought me a sturdy stick to assist me in walking over the stones. It was no place to slip and fracture a bone. The view of the valley and surrounding mountains was beautiful, red and orange with brown patches showing through the haze upon the valley.

As we drove down the mountainside, John, who had been sitting on top of the jeep with Rafiq, tapped on the roof, signaling us to stop. Before we came to a full stop, the rifle cracked. Rafiq leaped off with a knife and dashed to the fallen deer. The men loaded it in the canvas rack on the back, and we returned to the compound.

We went in and dropped down on our bunks and sleeping bags for a much-needed rest. The tractors woke us with the pleasant sound of work being accomplished. Our hostess had an Indian breakfast prepared. The main course was a dish made from the heart of wheat, which first was browned in *ghee*, or butter. Cumin, ginger and toasted almonds and raisins were added, along with honey from their beehives. We had bananas and oranges grown on the farm.

Lunch was more elaborate, with kabobs of vegetables and fish, crisp on the outside and tender and succulent inside. We had *chapattis*, flat cakes of bread that can be pulled apart and used to scoop up vegetables and meat.

Mark told our host and hostess that I had driven a tractor on my father's farm in the states. They insisted I get on the Czech tractor and give it a whirl. With a little orientation, I drove it around while they took pictures.

The tractor institute trains approximately 1,500 students each year, mostly farm youths who have never seen anything mechanical. Until now, they had been taught to use a bullock and wooden plow and stock.

The institute has a complete machine shop for repair and maintenance, as well as an electrical shop and paint shop. These things seem quite normal to us in America, but were the first that we had witnessed in our 20 months in India. It is always enlightening to see what progress is being made with our tax money. After ten months of study and experience at the institute, the young men are prepared to use the equipment and work in the shops.

CHAPTER 51
STRUCK BY THE "BUG"

This month, an unknown illness struck me, destroying my strength, causing nausea, sweating, chills. For several days, with the air conditioner out, I spent time wrapped in a damp sheet, lying on the veranda on a charpoi with my knees drawn up to alleviate the cramps. Much of the day was spent racing to the demonic demands of the stomach disorder.

One of the common problems with living in India is the dastardly illness of diarrhea. Amoebae also cause serious illnesses, and the only method of identifying the problem is in a laboratory. There is no laboratory here in Raipur.

I wanted to go to New Delhi for tests, trusting our American Embassy medical doctor and staff. This would require a one-day drive to reach Nagpur in the center of the country, then another day by plane if I was lucky enough to get a flight. I wasn't lucky. The jeep trip required a two-day drive to reach Delhi. The best way to get me there, it seemed, was to drive as fast as possible. I slept much of the way across the countryside. Once when I had to vomit, it was blood filled. When we rushed up to the Embassy and I saw the American flag, tears ran down my cheeks as I sat in silence.

The tests were positive. I was taken immediately to Holy Family Hospital. The treatment was intense; the medication was a prescription of poison to kill the amoebae, and depression is a side effect. I missed none of the symptoms— pain, fatigue, nausea and high fever. My doctor wanted to perform surgery on an area that had caused me recurrent ulcers, but the Embassy doctor did not approve the surgery.

The surgeon kept me on a diet of whole milk for a week, until one day I had had no milk all day. I asked him about it. He was very upset with the staff. The dietitian was very apologetic. The cows had wandered and had not come to be milked, he had been told.

When the doctor put me on a soft diet of solid food, I expected perhaps mashed potatoes and gelatin. Removing the cover, to my surprise I found a dish of minced goat with hot peppers, green peas and two hard green cherries. I have now had my family bring in cans of soup, along with a can-opener since the hospital had none, and I heated soup on a burner.

Many visitors came to the hospital. Among them were the Raja of Bunai and the Maharaja of Barundi. The staff was so thrilled, as the Raja and Maharaja here are like a celebrity would be at home. Like a number of my other visitors, these royal guests were friends we had entertained in Raipur.

After being discharged from the hospital, I spent two weeks recovering. I stayed with my American friends, a professor from the University of Chicago and his family. But I was eager to get home.

At last, the plane was scheduled to leave Palaam Airport at 9:30 a.m. At the airport, my driver went inside to check on the tickets. He rushed out with a worried look. "There is no plane for Nagpur today. All planes are being directed to Madras."

I went to the counter and asked the ticket agent to get me on a flight, any flight, as my husband and driver would be waiting for me in Nagpur. Their trip to Nagpur could take several hours depending on the roads. Only a few telephone lines covered those two hundred miles. Ours was one of the very few households with a phone.

I was told that the only plane available was flying to Madras in the far South, and returning back to Nagpur in central India at midnight. I wrote a note to the Embassy asking them to cable Nagpur and give my husband the message that I would arrive from Madras. It would be over 2,000 miles out of the way.

Finally I joined many people boarding, and I carried my purse and a box containing a frozen turkey, which was placed on the floor in front of me. I fastened my seat belt loosely and laid my head back. My battle to conquer the amoeba infection would continue for weeks. The medication I was on left a bad after-taste, and food was not palatable.

The drone of the engine eventually lulled my discomfort, and I slept. A gentleman in the next seat woke me. The steward stood by us with a tray. I waved him away and said, "Thank you, no." My seatmate told me that it is not good to fly on an empty stomach. To quiet him, I handed him my new *National Geographic*. It had arrived along with our mail through the American Post Office at the Embassy, and a friend had brought it to me.

Suddenly, he was laughing. "Look, this picture is of our daughter," he exclaimed. "She was one of sixteen girls invited to Washington, D. C. to see the President." I gave him the magazine, and he was very pleased.

I drank a cup of tea. Our conversation took many directions after that little incident. He was the Minister of Petroleum from the United Arabic Republic. I recalled that there was very little in the way of diplomacy between America and the U.A.R. these days. I did not realize that this meeting would lay the foundation for future meetings.

The plane landed in Madras some three hours late. We had flown almost the entire length of the country. My new acquaintance took my arm, assisting me down the stairs. Photographers were taking pictures of us, and a number of people reached to shake his hand.

"This is your wife?" someone asked.

"No, this is my friend," he said

I smiled and continued toward the terminal. No American driver was to be seen. I sat down near the door where I could watch for what surely would be a driver coming to take me for a rest. I had explained my problem. The box containing the turkey from the American Commissary in

New Delhi sat at my feet. It had come from the States, and I was looking forward to having a nice turkey dinner when I got well.

Another half-hour passed, but still no one came. People came by and stopped to look at me, then moved on. The turkey was melting, and the box was getting wet. I took it to the counter and sat it down while I used a phone there to call the American Consul. I inquired if a cable or call had come there from anyone about me. The Consular came on and said he had no such news. I asked if he could send for me, that I was ill, weak and tired, and had to wait until the midnight plane.

"Listen, I really am sorry, but I must dash off to a meeting," he said. "The only other vehicle is in for repair."

That was that. I needed a place to rest and some boiled and cooled water. A sign pointed to a restaurant upstairs. Taking my dripping box of turkey in hand, I walked to a corner seat and sat down to ponder my predicament. The clock showed that six hours had passed since I had left New Delhi. The climate in Madras is described as "hot and hotter."

"Where is your driver?" a voice said.

I looked into the eyes of the Arabian diplomat, who was still surrounded by people. "You said your people would meet you," he said with concern.

"They are either tied up, or out of town or busy." This was not quite a lie. I didn't want to discuss it with him. "I've been told if there were enough people, another plane would be sent."

"You aren't all right, you're sick," he said. "You haven't had anything but tea since I met you." Turning to one of his men, he told him to get me on the first flight back to Nagpur.

"It is settled. Until you leave, you will be with my people. You will be well cared for. I must take a flight out of the country." He handed me his card, and introduced me to four young men, graduate students at The University of Madras.

We went to the home of their advisor, and spent an hour there. I ate plain rice and drank tea. The turkey was refrigerated until we returned from a sightseeing tour of the city. Madras has green and lush shrubbery, flowers and reminds me of south Florida scenery with palm trees in abundance.

The young graduate students asked dozens of questions. They were interested in the United States and in our cars, discussing makes, speed and cylinders. They were under the impression that when you tired of a car, you just drove it to a parking lot and called for another one. I explained that it wasn't that way. "We have good roads that crisscross the country and go into every area. We pay taxes on gasoline to maintain them," I said. "And we are fortunate to have jobs to allow us to own things."

Our discussions gave me the first insight into their lives and their countries—Egypt, U.A.R., Yemen and Syria. They were concerned about the Egyptian Army supporting Yemen's Republic against the Royalists. They were particularly interested in my feelings about Viet Nam. "I feel that our government's known position is the only one I have from this distance," I said. "I have personal reservations about any war, about our men being there."

They asked about America's black citizens. One commented that their people had enslaved blacks for centuries. They also spoke of America's opulence and influence from across the miles.

They showed great interest in the social and economic problems facing their lands. The people are exceptionally poor, with a rare few being overly rich. This was the first indication I had seen of an intense interest among the young generation in the situation. They spent much time on their thoughts and ideas to alter their course of history. I hope they can make changes.

Their Moslem religion holds such strict discipline for women that they could not comprehend my traveling alone in a strange country. It was unthinkable. The concept that I wanted to see this country and know its people was amazing to them.

It had been a long day, and by the end, I was ready for my flight. They handed me into the plane and waited outside. I could see them by the light on the runway. They stood there until after the plane rose and we took off into the blackness of India. It was about midnight. India has very few electric lights. There are no illuminated parkways, marquees, drive-ins, department stores or fast food stores. Cars drive without lights, as they continuously blow their horns and couldn't do that if their lights were on. Whether on the road or in the air, the night is astonishingly black

*   *   *

I arrived in Nagpur about 3 o'clock in the morning. Surely our driver will be waiting, if Mark couldn't come, I thought. Searching for a familiar face, I saw no one I knew. The lights were being extinguished, and I saw that I'd better act fast. Surely the airport wasn't closing! Then I realized that it really was. I rushed over to a phone to try to find a hotel. Only one was listed, and there was no answer. This is a city of several million people and no hotels.

I saw a Roman Catholic priest, a Dravidian. He was the blackest of black with beautiful white teeth. I asked if he spoke English and found he did. I asked if he would assist me in getting help for the remainder of the night. He said he was on his way to see the Pope in Bombay but would try. He quickly ordered a man to assist me and then dashed out the door toward his plane, his cassock billowing behind him.

An airport helper ran back with two pillows and a blanket from the plane's supply room and motioned me to follow him over to a small group of men. By this time only a few lights remained in the building.

A car and driver were waiting. I sat on the back seat; the driver and two men squeezed onto the front seat. The little car headed into the night. The driver, a Sikh, wore his hair tightly bound on the top of his head in a knot under a turban. The men spoke no English. We traveled on, many miles into the night. I said nothing. I felt I was completely at their mercy.

We pulled up at the back of a large building where I was escorted through a door. A uniformed guard stayed outside. I looked around the

room, where one light burned overhead and a desk, file cabinet and three
chairs seemed lost in the room. I sat down and began to analyze my situation. A chill returned, and I wrapped myself in the blanket and closed my
eyes.

I must have slept, because dawn was breaking when I heard yelling
below the window. I recognized my name—not the normal pronuncia-
tion, but after a few calls, I got it. I stuck my head out of the window and
shouted down to the man. A guard came for my suitcase.

My rescuer was Sonu's friend, Raji, the oil company architect whom I'd
met at the Mukerjis. He speaks very good English. He gave the men some
rupees and we left for his house. I asked why Mark had not come. He said
the Embassy cable was delayed four days. It arrived only this morning, and
they began searching for me. When our neighbor, R.C., called the airport,
the manager was adamant that I could not have come from New Delhi
since no planes flew to Nagpur that day. "They went Delhi-Madras or
Delhi-Bombay; because of the Pope's visit all planes had been rerouted."
Eventually, the airport management remembered that I had been taken
from a Madras flight to their office building for the night. Raji, whose
company has offices in Nagpur, had found me.

He apologized for collecting me in the family's Land Rover. "The sedan
is in for repair and should be ready by noon. Traveling two hundred miles
in this ancient, roofless vehicle will be too much even for me," he said.

We agreed to wait, and he promised me breakfast at his home. I had
not had a real meal for two days. The house was large and attractively furnished. There were no servants in sight. His parents were in their mountain home, and most of the servants had gone with them.

Raji asked what I wanted to eat. Knowing that the British ate omelets,
I asked for one. He smiled and excused himself. Soon he brought a tray
with tea, milk, sugar and cashew nuts and a banana on it. Then he proudly
carried in a Glenn Miller album and put on "Serenade in Blue." He said
that an omelet was "'just now coming.'

He had discovered that the sedan could not be repaired today. "Let us go now." I said. "I have enjoyed the tea very much. Thank you, it was all good."

"No, the omelet is just coming," he repeated.

Another twenty minutes passed before he sat the omelet on the coffee table in front of me. He watched closely as I ate it, praising it all the while. It was perfect, light golden on the outside, creamy and with the right seasoning of minced green chilies inside.

He continued to apologize about the Land Rover, as we began the trip. I braced myself, grasping the seat with my left hand and the bar frame overhead, as there is no roof. We swung onto the metalized road leading from the city. He kept his hand on the horn, blowing as we swerved to avoid hitting cows and people. He did not slow for them and we didn't have seat belts.

Between the noise of the horns, motors and people, my deliverer began a conversation concerning rituals; cremation, burials, caskets and death in general. After awhile, I attempted to turn the conversation to other subjects but he was not to be diverted. Again and again he returned to the subject, with what seemed an obsessive insistence on gruesome details.

Finally we stopped by a stall along the road, and he brought two cups of tea. Eight hours later, we swung into the driveway and our servants opened the gate. We were home! I unclasped my grip on the car doorframe, unfolded my body from the vehicle and collapsed into Mark's arms. Home sweet home, at last!

*   *   *

The box containing the turkey, which had accompanied me all the way, was handed over to the cook. The turkey dinner was everything I had hoped it would be.

The next day when I saw Sonu, I related the saga of my adventures and my meal at Raji's house.

"Yes, Raji told me," said Sonu. "He had no one in the house that would break an egg. He had his servant search. Can you not see his cook running from house to house, asking cooks to come and prepare an omelet from an American memsahibji? They each declined, as they are Hindu. After an hour or so, they found a Moslem who accompanied the cook back and prepared your omelet."

"Yet never a word was uttered about this to me!" I was chagrined.

"He would not offend you in such a manner. That would be unmannerly. You were a guest in his home and a queen to be served whatever you wished."

Will I never learn the depth of these customs and religious practices? I wondered.

CHAPTER 52
LOTUS BLOSSOMS

It is hot as usual and the dust is swirling over the hard-packed clay. Ram Das, our third servant, asked if he could take the afternoon nap time today to go find water chestnuts and lotus blossoms. It is about two miles to the pond where they both grow. Das is a young and cheerful teenager. He must get very tired of being in the house with walls and closed doors all the time. I gave him permission if cook said it was okay. The servants have free time when they finish their chores and often do things together.

The water chestnuts can be found floating in water with roots stream-ing down from the round nuts. They must each be gathered, peeled and cleaned. They are very hard and they don't absorb water. We have enjoyed them in recipes often.

The lotus blossoms rise above the water on darker stems. Green leaves surround the firm, crisp petals that are creamy pink and white with a lovely stamen coming from the center. There are numerous ones on the water and a joy to see. The lotus is a delicate plant that lives and grows as a thing of beauty in the slimy, brackish water.

I have had lotus salad, but the flowers Ram Das found are too beautiful to eat. We shall put them in a crystal vase on the dining table. The lotus is the most sacred flower of India. Buddha is often painted with the lotus and it appears in other sacred paintings we have seen.

* * *

Yesterday, I went with Rafiq to the market to look at the selection of foods. We needed vegetables and Prem Chan bought meat for the dogs. The market was crowded as usual. We bought lentils, mangoes, and okra.

Cows milled around the center of the town, munching dry twigs that had escaped an earlier onslaught of animals that had moved on farther up the road. A "free" bull nudged a cow to the side where they proceeded to mate. The sight of roaming cows is what my friend Lolita despises. She wants to get the cows out of town. For her trouble, the city fathers accuse her of being unhappy in her marriage, or why else would she bring this "foolish complaint."

I observed the morning scene. Women with great brass pots balanced on a donut-shaped ring on top of their heads, backs ram-rod straight, walked to and from the tank, or pond, that serves water for every purpose. A woman sat beneath the shade of an acacia tree selling jackfruit. Flies covered the mouth and eyes of a baby sitting on the ground nearby. The mother flipped a dingy rag in their direction, and they rose, swarmed and settled back in the same places.

The tires spun on the sand as we circled the tank where all of life goes on. Buffaloes were being washed along with clothes, and people took baths, as women marched out of the water with their filled jugs. The water was brackish and threateningly low.

"Last week a deaf woman was killed by a truck driving past the tank," one of our neighbors, Mr. Chatterji, told us recently. "People were so outraged by the truck hitting her as she walked along the road that her family, friends and neighbors gathered to discuss it. They decided to put an end to this kind of carelessness. The next truck that passed after that was stopped, and the crowd took the driver out and beat him to death."

We remembered an orientation class where we had been told that if there ever was an accident, we were to go, as fast as possible, to the next town and report the accident to the police chief. "Don't stop, get away fast!" had been the warning.

*   *   *

When we got back from the market, Prem Chan came to talk with Rafiq, and then both left in the jeep without a word. I was becoming anxious about the time, when they finally returned, and Rafiq told me that Lazarus, our cook, owed money to most everyone in town.

During our stay in New Delhi, Lazarus had a suit made of fine silk, which had been charged to Mark. He has not paid for dog food or for food for the servants. He has spent all the money on himself that I had given him to use for food.

"Memsabji, we must have the best-dressed cook in India," Rafiq laughed.

"What will Sahib say?"

"He will need your help and the information from Prem Chan."

I told Mark that night, and we decided to talk with our neighbor, R.C. Mukerji.

This morning, we awakened to the noise from people banging on the metal gate and yelling, "Sahib will not pay us."

We had no way of knowing the amount of Lazarus's debts, but when it was added up it was 1,200 rupees, or $300. We made a complaint to the police, which cost us additional money for the colorful stamp attached to the very official looking document. We paid the bills, and sent Lazarus on his way. I am able to get part-time assistance from my friends' cook, and I will prepare breakfast and lunch myself.

CHAPTER 53
A ROYAL PRINCESS IS OUR GUEST

Today, on a blistering hot morning in late May, a big car pulled up loaded with sleeping bags and luggage. It was our friend, the Maharaja "K.," coming to call. This is a moment we have hoped for, as our visits to his palace have always been filled with long hours of conversation, enjoyable food and fascinating activities.

After we talked a few minutes, the Maharaja told us that someone would be meeting him here—a close friend and member of a political party. He calls her his "auntie," because of her endearment to him and his family.

This evening, the eastbound train arrived, carrying one of the most dynamic women I have met in India. Prabvati Raji is a princess and a crusader for higher religious values in her country.

Our first impression was that Raji, as we were told to call this royal lady, was five feet of femininity. Her trim, graceful figure was covered with a green silk sari with many beautiful gold bangles adorned her arms. Ruby and gold earrings are in her earlobes, and a cluster of diamonds on one nostril. She wears sandals with a single leather strap, and a gold ring on the second toe.

She has brought her handmaiden, her cook, bearer, and two attorneys, Mr. Singh and Mr. Peratis. I asked how many were in her party and learned there are thirteen. She said they would not need anything from me.

"Mary, my cook will tell your cook that I only eat a vegetarian menu," she said. "I am an orthodox Hindu. We are forbidden to eat any form of life. Nor do I use china, as it has bone meal in it. I use only crystal, silver or gold dishes." That statement set my mind to scrambling for an idea of what to use.

A bedroom was prepared for the princess and one for each attorney. The servants filed down the terrazzo hall with luggage and boxes on top of their heads.

Raji is reputed to be a brilliant speaker with a command of several languages. Fluent in English, she speaks Hindi, Tamil, Marathi, Malayalam, Bengali, German and others. The Maharaja told us she holds audiences all over India spellbound with her fervor, which can arouse the most unfeeling mind. She is an intellectual with clarity of thinking and ability to express very complex thoughts in the simplest and most effective words.

*   *   *

I have found Rajii's American English interesting. It is as though I were talking with an American, except for the philosophical opinions. She listens to the Voice of America and BBC World Broadcast, as we do. Her manners are perceived as Western.

I wonder how a princess brought up without formal academic education can reach such intellectual heights and achieve such insight into the spiritual and cultural past of India. She says her ancestors for centuries demonstrated the inevitable combination of religion and politics. Their religious life was based on Swadharma, the God-made law of righteousness and truth.

When asked how she acquired such astounding power of speech and scholastic supremacy, she quoted a Sanskrit verse, which purports that

"God can give speech to the speechless and make even a lame man cross the mountains."

Her legacy came from her father, His Highness Sir Tekuji Pawar, K.C.S.I., the Maharaja of Dewas, who was an ardent believer in the supremacy of religion. Brought into conflict with the then British rulers, her father ended his life in a fast until death.

"We are here not for business, but for political leadership," she told me one evening. "My father was a great believer in the people ruling themselves. He did not want the power all in the hands of a few people in New Delhi, but he was very much against socialism and especially communism. He encouraged and inspired his people to hold on to these tried and true beliefs. He saw the power that was being exerted by the few, and this caused him to take drastic measures. He began his fast.

"I am the only child and must carry on his beliefs. My plan is very simple. Yet, simple things are always more complex. Therefore, I must lay my foundation very well."

A champion for health and education, Rajii believes that education in India has deteriorated greatly in the past twelve years.

She told me that the Montessori system was begun here. "It has been tried in the cities and it works very well. When the Italian educator, Marie Montessori started her school in 1870, she wanted to educate defective children. It became so effective that she decided it would work with normal children. They start to school at three years of age. This is a dream for all, but the reality for so few," she said.

"When we got our independence, Prime Minister Nehru never ceased to stress that social and economic progress could be brought about by peaceful means. Our people have had to set their sights not as much upon their dreams, as on merely surviving.

"As you know, Mary, we cannot even wash our clothes, the water is so scarce at this time. When I say 'we,' I mean my people. Disease is rampant. We must have a leader who not only can use high sounding words and phrases but who can inspire my people. Until a person feels the desire to have more material things enough to strive for it, he or she cannot expect to have much interest in new techniques and there will be little effort on their part to accomplish this."

       *   *   *

She remained in our house for a week. Night after night, I sat with her in our living room with my feet tucked on the seat until after midnight, listening to her thoughts and experiences. Before she went to bed each night, her servant washed her hair and rubbed oil in it. She was up, saying her prayers, before the sun rose.

When she left us yesterday, the house seemed so quiet. I had come to think highly of the lady. She opened my eyes to the history of her land in ways that I would not be able to understand with her knowledge of Sanskrit. Her visit allowed me to understand better the various areas, castes and people.

The Maharaja and the princess both left as swiftly as they came. The reminder of their visit is before me whenever I see the crystal dish sitting on the table. That dish, I think to myself, held food for a woman most possibly born to rule.

       *   *   *

We received a formal invitation to attend the yearly musical concert given by students at the College of Rajas, Rajakapur College, this evening. Mark didn't want to attend. He was tired, and Indian music is not to his liking. I couldn't change his decision.

Sonu and her driver picked me up, and we rode to the bungalow on the campus where Mark and I had attended a dinner party a few weeks ago. The same group was present, with Sonu being the extra person tonight. Refreshments were served before the concert, which was set for seven-thirty.

After taking a glass of juice, my host, the chairman of the Board of Regents, invited me to join him on the veranda. We talked for a while, and then I looked at my watch and saw that it was past time for the concert to begin. I reminded him of the hour.

He said, "My dear, the concert begins when I arrive."

I then realized the power of this man.

When we reached the auditorium, it was filled. The doors swung open, everyone rose. With me on his arm, he proceeded down the aisle as the large auditorium crowd stood. He took me to the front seat on the left side of the aisle and he sat opposite on the right side. After we were seated, the audience sat. A British diplomat from New Delhi was among the guests who had come for the occasion.

The *sitar*, *tabla* and harmonium players performed many musical selections. I had heard Ravi Shankar once before, and these children have made a good beginning. Then, we were served tea and a sweet covered with edible silver. The concert continued until after midnight. When I told Mark about it the next morning, he realized that he had committed an error in our code of social etiquette or protocol by not attending.

New Delhi and Bhopal

1965-66

CHAPTER 54
RETURN TO THE CITY

Life is changing in many ways for us. Mark has been given a new title as Advisor to the Deputy Director of I.A.D.P. (Intensive Agriculture Division) for the entire country of India. We had thought we would be posted to Jabbalpur. Our friends with the Ford Foundation had lived there, and they brought us up to date on the situation.

Now we know that we will have a house in Bhopal and a house in New Delhi. We have decided that it is best for John and me to move back to New Delhi and not stay out in Raipur, because Mark will be traveling often and far distances. I will not have a vehicle at my disposal or an interpreter. I really regret leaving all the friends that we had made in the country. I have never known people that are as courteous, caring and sharing, as they all are—especially Sonu, Lolita and the Maharani.

*   *   *

Packers came in from Bombay and packed John's and my personal things to go to New Delhi. The furniture and household things have gone to our home in Bhopal.

Our house in New Delhi is three stories, but does not have the large rooms like those in Raipur. It is stucco, painted pink. The house and the neighborhood have interesting architecture, much of it Mediterranean style. The lawn is a playground for birds and monkeys. My favorite bird is a ringneck, black and white with a red collar. The lawn is small with a variety of shrubs that hug the four-foot stone fence with its iron gate that swings open, allowing the car to be driven into the garage. A Manx cat, big and fierce-looking, perches on the fence post waiting for a meal. Does it have an owner? I wonder. I have never seen children playing with animals.

While writing this, I have jumped up three times to shoo away the monkeys that are destroying the flowers in the front garden. There is a mother, her baby and a middle-sized male. The houseboy had hung clothes on the back line, and the monkeys took those. I went to the door and clapped my hands; this brought all the servants running to my aid. A camel is walking down the middle of the street. I don't see a herder for it, but feel sure there is one someplace around. This is a nice residential section of the city but daily events are amazing.

The house has two large windows opening onto the lawn. There is a fireplace, but will we ever use it? I have ordered gray slipcovers for the sofas and orchid-colored material for single chairs. I asked the *moli*, or gardener, to bring a plant that will fill the open fireplace space. He finds one to carry out the color theme and is proud of himself, as am I.

The four bedrooms are comfortable for the six of us. The servants live in their room attached to the back of the house. All servants are men, so there are no women living here. The dining room is nicely furnished with a chandelier hanging over the dining table. We have flatware and china for ten people, and more glasses and plates for cocktail parties. We are living in luxury since we have overhead fans, as well as air-conditioning.

When I get organized, and during school break., we hope to take our vacation time of two weeks and visit my cousins in Bangkok, Thailand,

      *   *   *

Last night, I attended a reception for the Minister of Trade. It was held at the home of my new friends, Pushpa and Delap, in the next block. The occasion was to celebrate the success of Pushpa's furniture manufacturing business. She has sold 1 crores worth of furniture, the equivalent of ten million rupees, since she began only two years ago.

Her handmade furniture was on display: teak chairs, bedsteads, tables and chairs of various designs sat about the house. The story of her business began when her husband, an engineer, was transferred from Calcutta to New Delhi. Knowing that travel by rail or lorry is disastrous to furniture, they sold all theirs before moving. To their chagrin they could not find suitable replacements.

After days of searching, Pushpa complained to her father, who lives in Old Delhi. His solution was for her to design what she wanted, find a competent furniture carpenter and lathe operators, buy seasoned teak and fittings and then furnish their home.

"But how can I do that, Papa?" she asked. Her father, having raised nine daughters and run a successful bakery in the city, encouraged her to try. If she failed, he said, just try again—my philosophy as well!

She has done exceedingly well. During the reception, she took me to the roof of the home, where the family sleeps at night. This evening, five men sat on cloths on the floor, each with a lathe in front. They powered the lathes by holding a strong string between the big toe and the second toe and worked the foot like a pedal. The string pulled the sharp blade that gently whittled the piece of wood into the proper shape.

Pushpa's sisters had ordered a telephone chair. When it was completed, it toppled over backwards. It was back to the drawing board for Pushpa and her carpenters. They eventually mastered the chair and went on to other things. Her eight sisters were so pleased that they each demanded one for themselves.

Now her furniture is very popular, and the French and Scandinavians are particularly fond of the designs. Pushpa has selected three very fine stores in America as outlets. Before I left her home, I ordered two chairs, two stools with rattan string seats and a beautiful wedding chair with domes and dangling bells on sides and back. I know I will always treasure my things.

CHAPTER 55
NEW DELHI SOCIAL LIFE

Our calendar is full for months ahead. We are expected to attend an average of three to five affairs a week. I am giving a dinner party tomorrow for an inspection team composed of CEO's of American businesses. One of the highlights upcoming this month is the Bolshoi Ballet from Moscow. We have tickets for the family to see this.

One evening, Mark and I invited two Indian couples for dinner. They are important, attractive people, who speak English well and expressed a desire to visit with Americans. The ladies, who appeared around 25 to 40 years old, arrived wearing beautiful saris and exquisite jewelry.

As we began with a tomato aspic appetizer, we talked about our families and our native towns. With salad, we talked about colleges and professions. With our entrée of cheese and vegetable casserole, we discussed India's economy, as one of the guests was an economist.

Dessert, cream tapioca with almonds, was served, and Mark decided to liven up the conversation with a joke or two.

"Our saying is that if you think you are a person of some influence," he said, "try ordering somebody else's dog around."

Silence.

I laughed. The Indians didn't. They had a blank look.

Mark tried again. "I've always heard that the quickest way to double your money is to fold it and put it back in your pocket."

Silence abounded except for Mark's and my chuckles.

I spoke up. "Never miss a good chance to shut your mouth."

The Indians broke up laughing! Mark was still mystified as to why one remark tickled them but not the others.

"But they don't like dogs, remember?" I said, after the guests left.

*   *   *

This week, we gave a reception and dinner party for ten Indian officials, American business executives and wives. The guests included the head of a worldwide American business organization from Europe who is making a tour of programs and relief projects that America has under way.

Arthur, my cook, arranged for help from three servants of the Prime Minister whose home backs up to the alley directly behind our house. I never knew before that it was his house. I must send a note of appreciation and a small gift to them.

Mark and I received our guests when they arrived. The last to come was an American, and he and Mark just stood and looked at each other. I wondered what this was about.

Then, Mark said, "Mary, this is Sam Madison, a college classmate of mine from the university where we worked on our doctorates." I was happy to think there would be a connection here for Mark. I noted that Mark was not particularly thrilled, but I couldn't imagine why.

"Sam, I'm delighted to meet you," I said.

"May I return the feeling," the American answered.

The dinner progressed smoothly. Afterward, brandy, coffee and mints were served in the living room. As we sipped, the conversation moved from a light strain to the more serious business at hand, getting better agriculture and food for the country. "You can save this for the office," one of the men said.

The children had come down hours earlier to be introduced and say good night, taking a plate of cookies and some milk upstairs as they left.

"Darling, let's invite Sam to dinner tomorrow night," I suggested in an aside to Mark. "You must have much to talk about."

"He is probably booked up," Mark said.

"Let's try."

Sam accepted the invitation immediately, and was the last person to leave.

Later, upstairs in our room, I was unwinding my long roll of hair from the bun confining it, when Mark walked in. "I'd say you were a bit chilly to Sam. I thought you would be glad to see him. He was glad to see you. What's wrong? Did something happen back there at the university?"

"Oh, he was sort of a BMOC (big man on campus)," replied Mark. "He had grown up as the son of a missionary doctor and speaks many languages. He was always ahead of us and since I speak very Southern, I was self-conscious, I guess."

"What do you expect? You grew up in the South," I said, smiling. "Let's just enjoy him as a friend here. Did you think it was a good party?"

"Yes. I'm tired," he said.

We went to bed, and he turned his back to me. That's a sure indication that he isn't happy. He was snoring in no time, and I went to sleep too.

CHAPTER 56
AMERICAN PRESS AND ELEGANT CLUBS

Now that the lights are on once more in New Delhi, we have decided to indulge in some nights on the town. We find the Café Chenoire on the top of the new hotel suits us. We were having a cocktail there one evening when a reporter for a popular U.S. magazine came over and asked us about the food supply and the conditions of the famine. Mark invited him to follow him around if he'd like. The reporter thought that too much of an imposition. We bumped into him several times around the city after our first encounter.

A few weeks later, I walked into our bedroom, where Mark was aiming the magazine at the waste can. He was upset by the on-the-spot interview at the café. The writer had not mentioned that his information did not come first hand, but secondhand. "The readers will think the reporters are out in the countryside seeing with their own eyes the progress we are making," said Mark disgustedly. "They are not—they are sitting at the bar here."

*   *   *

Mark's new position is requiring him to travel over a more extensive area of the country. He is gone for a week at a time, coming back and forth to New Delhi for short periods.

My friend, Eleanor, whose husband, Bill, is business director of Standard Oil of India, and calls himself a glorified bookkeeper, invited me to have dinner with the SOI president and other executives and their wives one evening. Their company's U.S. headquarters is in Indiana. They are an interesting group. Mark and I play golf with Eleanor and Bill whenever Mark is in New Delhi. I'm glad to join them for dinner, as many wives whose husbands are absent or occupied never get invitations.

The choice restaurant here is in a hotel in Cannaught Place, where the oil company president likes the chef. The main attraction, however, is the very talented belly dancer, who dances with a diamond in her navel.

After dinner, we listened to the band and one of the oil executives asked me to dance. He asked if I thought the band could play "Back Home Again in Indiana." I suspected he was feeling a little homesick. We moved near the bandleader and made the request. The pianist immediately went into the song and played several verses of it.

A few weeks later, when Mark was home, he and I joined our two friends for dinner in the hotel dining room. The moment we entered, the band struck up "Back Home Again in Indiana," while the musicians smiled at me.

Mark asked, "What in heaven's name does this song have to do with you?" I told him the story, to his amusement. I never again entered the restaurant without being serenaded with that song.

*   *   *

Wednesday mornings are spent at Governor's House for bridge, with excellent coffee served on breaks to talk, with a sherry and lunch at the end of the game. This fine old British club is the American military's setting for recreation for officers and wives, and a quiet scene for conversation at the end of the day. I enjoy being a guest. My weekly bridge partner is a beautiful French lady, wife of our senior military officer in India, General Paul Tibbets. He will be remembered as the pilot of the airplane,

Enola Gay, which flew the mission that ended the war with Japan. He is a quiet, soft-spoken man. I have had conversations with the two of them as their guests away from the club.

Teatime with my Delhi friends finds many interesting stories being shared. This afternoon, we gathered at the magnificent Ashoka Hotel, at Eleanor's invitation. She and Bill are living there until their house is ready to occupy. One of her anecdotes concerned the servant who takes care of her clothes and also draws her bath each morning.

Once Eleanor had seen a cockroach in the bath, so each day she would enter her bath saying loudly, "Out, Fred, out!" hoping she had made enough noise to frighten any unwanted creatures that might want to occupy the bath with her. Her regular servant went to the village to visit his family, and a substitute came in. The next morning, the new servant went into the bathroom and called, "Out, out!" He didn't know what spirit he was talking to, but if Memsahibji said it before, he would say it now.

*   *   *

Following their taking a residential home, another interesting episode was the arrival of Eleanor and Bill's car, which had been shipped here from Texas. When it was cleared through customs by their representative, they were told it would be delivered to their home. Being friends and neighbors, we all looked forward to their car's arrival.

Many days and weeks passed, and one day their servant ran to tell our servant that the car was here. We went to their gate to see this event. Two huge oxen were tied to a large cart with a great container sitting on it. When they stopped, a number of helpers that had walked behind the team began jockeying to get the container off. Finally they unfastened the lines on the bullocks and pushed the carton over with much noise, and it landed on its top. This dented the car in by several inches, and then it had to be turned upright. This was a disappointment for them.

*   *   *

We are members of The New Delhi Golf and Country Club, playing golf there mainly when Mark is home. The British built the course, and the greens have been watered and rolled for the past hundred years, they like to say. Huge mahogany, walnut and oak trees surround manicured gardens with flowers in glorious colors—bougainvillea, callas, cannas and marigolds. In the gardens sit white bamboo chairs and tables.

The great stone and marble clubhouse was formerly the manor house of a sizeable estate. While we were stationed in Raipur, the club was a refuge from stress and work on the occasions that we could come into New Delhi, which was usually at four-to six-month intervals. We may play more now.

Mr. Singh, the handsome bearded Sikh who is manager, is always courteous and helpful. Liveried waiters take orders for *nimbupani* or a whiskey, and at 4 o'clock, tea is served. Parakeets, canaries, mynah birds and an array of others flit about. There is never a scarcity of birds.

Ancient temples stand on parts of the golf course, which is a very difficult one. From the first tee, one must hit the ball high and 150 feet to the green over a wooded area; else it will land in the thick scrub bush, nettles and trees. Monkeys, kites, small eagles, and other birds live there and will surely grab it in their beaks, claws or paws. The sand traps are the deepest I have ever seen. If one is unfortunate to get a ball into it, it takes strength and accuracy to make the ball fly out of these four-to five-foot-deep traps.

One is required to have not only a caddy but also a fore-caddy who goes ahead watching where the balls fall, then scaring the animals and birds away. The caddies wear dhotis that reach to mid-calf, and loose shirts. They live on the premises and are proud of their skill. My usual caddy comes running when he sees me.

This week, I met two ladies from the United States, whose husbands had brought them along on their business trip. The ladies expressed a desire to play a game of golf. I arrived at the club first and was taking some warm-up swings when I heard a female voice ask, "Hey, how are you?"

After we stood chatting for a few minutes, I invited the newcomer, Felicite, to join us. I asked if she were not an Alabamian.

"Yes, I am. How can you tell?" she said.

"I was born in Alabama, I can tell."

Felicite had worked at the New York Stock Exchange after graduating from Smith College. "It was as a secretary. They did not hire women for any other work. I had to go take a secretarial course," she said. "Each morning when I walked in, the men all rose and said, 'Good morning.'"

Her husband sat on the stock exchange until recently and is in New Delhi to set up a Stock Exchange of India. "I am doing his typing. I told him I would if he would pay me in jewels. And he is," she said with a laugh.

The two other ladies joined us, but they were so excited that they could not concentrate on the game. Their caddies came back to me to say they could not complete the round with them and would get other caddies for them.

"Oh, I am so sorry," the women both said. "Is it a matter of money?"

"No," I answered. "The caddies are required to stay with players in their ranking. There was a little error, but no harm done. You will have a good caddy."

We went on with our round, chatting, but there was little serious golf played that day. Felicite and I weathered the day and it proved the start of a long friendship.

Mr. Singh, club director, was a gracious host for the beautiful New Delhi Golf and Country Club, built by the British more than 100 years ago.

CHAPTER 57
MARK WANTS ME IN BHOPAL

As the four-engine Vicount airplane wheeled to the end of the runway at Palaam Airport, the engines' roar reached a furious pitch that sent us skyward. I settled down to look out of my window and see the countryside around New Delhi. I was on my way to Lucknow and Bhopal to join Mark and the boys; John and Dennis had gone earlier to stay with Mark in our new house.

Mark wants me to get our house in condition and appearance, as we will be entertaining there as well as in Delhi. He will be staying there alone afterwards, and I will return to the New Delhi house.

The earth showed patches of bright green where the winter wheat had been irrigated. It resembled the patchwork quilt of a family whose favorite colors were those of the forest. Soon the green disappeared and brown, dry land was spread as far as I could see. The rivers had receded from their banks with only a thread of water, if any, moving over the stones that protruded through the surface. The liquid was green and stagnant, slimy and filled with debris. This is the water that people drink, the water used for washing, bathing, and feeding the livestock.

The farther south we traveled, the dryer the terrain became, marked with yawning holes. This is only the beginning of the trouble in India, I thought. We have three and a half months until the blessed monsoon is due. Tanks (ponds) and rivers will be completely dry within the next month or so.

We landed at Lucknow, population 1,500,000, and capital of the state of Uttar Pradesh. Centuries ago, this was the prominent capital of the Nawabs of Oudh, Moslem rulers who controlled a region of north central India for about a century after the decline of the Moghul Empire. Described as decadent, they lived a sumptuous life, but they were patrons of the arts, dance and music. The city is known today for its gracious living.

The plane's two hostesses were petite and beautiful, dressed in saris of brown material with dusty gold threads interwoven, but wearing their hair in the latest bouffant style of the West. Each had fragile, delicate features with a straight, aquiline nose and large luminous, almond-shaped eyes. They asked me about America, saying that Americans were friendlier than the British. They openly said that since the British had been their conquerors for two hundred years, they were "looked-down upon" because of their dark skin.

About fifteen passengers left the plane. I was the only woman on board, other than the hostesses. I had been given a seat by the window and no seatmate. When we became airborne again, a young man asked permission to sit by me for the ride to Bhopal. He was of slight build and bespectacled, with a ready, warm smile. I learned that he was a geologist and was Chief Engineer of Mines and Minerals of the Ministry of Mines in India.

"I am on my way to examine the deposits of aluminum in Madhya Pradesh," he said. He described the various ore deposits throughout India and expressed his hope of this discovery helping the country's economy. He discussed the scheme being laid out for further training of Indian students in various countries where the mining problems are similar to those of India.

When we landed in Bhopal, on the way out of the airport I introduced him to Mark. We promised to see the young geologist and his wife in New Delhi. He certainly had a good outlook and high hopes for his country. I could sympathize with him hoping to get a project started; just getting from place to place is difficult.

My bags were loaded into the vehicle and we headed out for Bhopal and our home.

*   *   *

The first evening we enjoyed the view from the veranda. Bhopal is built around a large lake, surrounded by hills. The breeze was blowing stiffly from the west and the air was chilly, causing me to ask for my stole as we viewed the scene from our hill. The stars were so near that you felt as if you were covered by black velvet, a star-studded blanket.

The dirt and crowds of the Indian city lay below us, but it wasn't difficult to imagine that we were in some other place in the world.

The morning brought an entirely different scene. The lake below us was almost obliterated from view. The cool breeze had brought dust, which had covered the furniture, chairs and floor. Our throats were dry, and we knew that summer and hot weather was on its way. This season is called the "Loo." The dust will continue to swirl and blow off the desert of Rajasthan from now until the monsoon rains come, about the middle of June.

*   *   *

Our cook, Arthur, who had accompanied Mark and the boys, packed a lunch for us today and loaded our Jeep with sleeping bags, blankets and necessities for a trip to Budni, fifty miles to the south. We drove out into the valley, along the road lined with the lavish salmon colored "flame-of-the-forest" trees.

The sight of winter wheat growing was refreshing, as there are too few places where there is real production of food grains in evidence. The farmers purchased as few as three grains of the newly developed variety of rice, and wheat, planted it, cared for it, gathering the output of many grains to

propagate the new variety, our friend Don told us. There is enough mois-
ture in this valley to grow a good crop without irrigation. Where there is
grain, though, always something is here besides people to eat it—mainly
birds, from the egrets and thousands of peacocks and peahens to the ever-
present crows.

When Mark had to leave for one of the projects, I flew back to New
Delhi. The children stayed on a while longer. They need a break, as they
stay busy with schoolwork and activities. Arthur takes good care of their
needs.

Chapter 58
INDEPENDENCE DAY
CELEBRATION

It is August, and the anniversary of India's Independence from England is a big celebration this month. Until 1947, the British had controlled 17 provinces, which are now divided between India and Pakistan. We were invited through our Embassy to view the Independence Day parade from choice bleacher seats near the front. Sam Madison was among the Americans seated in the row ahead of us.

A sea of people stretched farther than the eye could see. First in the parade came the many bands smartly outfitted, playing triumphant music. Then came the Army, dressed in khaki with colorful cummerbunds, decorations, and marvelous hats, followed by the Indian Navy. The procession moved down Raj Path, with a cavalry brigade, a camel brigade and decorated elephants that do the work.

Next to appear were the Gurkhas, fighters from Nepal, famed for their heroic exploits in battle. They stepped with precision and energy. There were tribal people in native costumes wearing strings of tiger's claws around their necks. The President rode in his white landau carriage drawn by teams of white horses and dressed in his splendid off-white silk Nehru jacket, decorated with ribbons and awards. Overhead flew airplanes in formation.

The parade was lengthy, but no one cared, for this is a time to rejoice and be receptive to the independence that had been so hard fought to win.

It is something that will be impressed on my mind for my lifetime—especially the joy, satisfaction and sense of pride showing on the faces of the Indian citizens.

A ball was held that night following the ceremonies to which we were invited. It was a black-tie affair but had its share of military brass from all the countries that have military attaches attached to the Embassies. Mark had bought another set of eveningwear from Hong Kong.

The General of the Indian Army danced with me through several numbers. He is tall and handsome, a good dancer. He complimented me by saying, "I like you because you are so tall," as he whirled me around in a fast step.

*   *   *

The most admired British couple among the people here are Viceroy Louis Mountbatten and his wife, Edwina. They lived their private lives in the 1920s and '30s and were poised, straight after World War II, to take up a role in India. With the Labor government dedicated to the swift withdrawal of British colonial rule over India, a cabinet mission visited the subcontinent and found it divided as never before. The British were loathed, and there was complete polarization of the Hindus and Moslems.

The question of the day was whether these interracial, antireligious quarrels could be reconciled by the exit of the British, or whether partition as well as the British handing over power would be the answer. Riots and murders were raging, although Gandhi was on his tours preaching peace in the worst areas.

It was a daunting task to consider edging such a precariously placed, bitter nation toward independence. Edwina, the viceroy's wife, had fallen in love with the country and viewed the prospect with interest and enthusiasm.

I know how she felt. That this is the largest democracy in the world is a fulfilling thought. Yet no place on earth will ever replace my love for my country, the United States of America where my ancestors fought to bring freedom from the British, my brothers fought in World War II and I worked with the Army Air Force as a civilian during that war.

Were they to lead a retreat out of India or work for reconciliation of the Hindus and Moslems? There were half a million dead and three times that many injured and homeless refugees. Edwina threw herself into the thick of it, bringing together nursing services, and began the task of aiding the casualties. She and her husband would, for the rest of their lives, be heroes in Indians' eyes.

*   *   *

My daughter Connie has just graduated with honors from the American International School, with young people of different national and ethnic groups, who are all different colors and whose eyes have a different slant. These children have been together for the school year and enjoy and respect the abilities and individualism of each other. It was not surprising to see tears fill and run over as they spoke with each other after the graduation exercise. They knew they are going to all parts of the world, and they wrote carefully in the address books and school annual.

Connie's yearbook noted that one classmate found it very rewarding to work with her in the leper colony. The student wrote, "When you smile upon a poor disabled leper nearby as you work, for a moment he basked in the warmth of your smile and seemed glad to be alive."

Connie has won a full college scholarship and is returning to America to enter Florida State University. For several weeks we have had more arguments and disagreements, which may be just to keep from becoming emotional in other ways. There have been people to see and purchases to make for family and friends back home. We searched for a Kashmir shawl for Grandmother and an ivory pen for Auntie, rings of semiprecious stones and vases or stones for nieces and friends. Most would cost 100 percent more for the same item at home.

Then came the problem of what direction Connie should travel and with whom she would stop along the way. I worried that some amorous Italian would pinch her, or an equally amorous Arab would follow her. After several weeks of talk and planning, it was decided that she would travel alone and stop in Tehran, Rome, Frankfurt and London, staying with our friends in these places.

"D (departure) Day" arrived at last, this week. The family didn't sleep that night since we had to leave the house at 1:30 a.m. in order to arrive at Palaam Airport in time for her to take her flight.

Many of her friends arrived at the airport to say goodbye to her. Seeing friends off is a custom with us abroad. The bus left the terminal and drove across the tarmac to where the plane sits. Connie was one of the last passengers to board the bus. She looked so small, silhouetted against the light in the otherwise black night of India. Tears streamed down my cheeks as I saw the first of my beloved children "leave the nest." Mark put his arm around my shoulder and said, "There goes a job well done."

Connie's life in India and her trip across the world to get home were covered in articles that appeared in the newspapers back home— the Dothan,AL, *Eagle* and the Tallahassee and Quincy, Fla., papers.

Graduation day: Thirteen months after we came to India, Connie receives her high school diploma from the American International School, joined by her proud family: (from left), myself, Winnie, John and Dennis.

CHAPTER 59
A HINDU WEDDING

My next-door neighbors in New Delhi are having a wedding— the oldest sister, Una, is getting married. Her mother and father were killed in the Pakistan invasion in 1947, and the children left their home in order to escape with their lives. The oldest son, Ifat, took over the family's wealth and secreted it out. Now he is head of the household, and it is his responsibility to marry off his two sisters.

He and the bride asked me to help select the jewels that would be a part of her dowry. Night after night, when Mark is away and the children are at their studies, I have been going over to meet with them and the jeweler who had brought boxes of jewels. They were spread out on a black velvet cloth on the floor, where we would all sit around, cross legs and examine them stone by stone. The gems had not yet been set. We selected diamonds, jade and pearls. After this, saris and furniture would be selected

The dowry of the girl is determined by the amount it cost to bring up the young fiance from birth and educate him, and the bride's family must meet this amount. The wealthier the groom's parents are, the more the bride's family owes. After the wedding, the bride is in control of everything the husband makes or owns, all his possessions, for the remainder of their lives.

Ifat is a gentleman. He loves to tell me about his wife who is with her parents awaiting the birth of their child. He sometimes speaks of her fair skin; the fairer the skin, the more prized a bride is to the husband. "She is almost as white as you are," he said once. He talked about the effort it took to bring her to love him. "I had to get her to fall in love with me after our marriage. I had never laid eyes on her before the wedding."

He had seen a German alarm clock that sat on our mantle and chimed. He wanted that more than anything. I decided to make them a present of it before I left New Delhi.

After a year of planning, Una and Vigra were to be married, and the family's astrologer from the very beginning had worked out the date. Nothing is done here without consulting the astrologer. The moon must be in the right quarter and the stars as well.

The day dawned clear with blue skies and coolness still in the air. The red and white striped *shamiana,* or tent, was raised on the *miadan*, park, across the street from our neighbor's home. Relatives and friends began arriving, each member greeting his or her opposite number in the other family. Excitement mounted as each arrived and each gift was registered with its donor's name, items and cost, for future reference.

For weeks prior to the ceremony, the bride had received special attention. As a daily ritual her body was anointed with oil. This shy, quiet and properly raised Hindu girl had been plump until the marriage arrangements had been complete, when she began to lose weight. By the day of her wedding she was a delicate, fragile, and blushing bride-to-be. She wore red pajama trousers, a red shirt, and a red veil. She was adorned with her dowry jewelry, gold bangles, chains and ornaments for her hair. On the morning of the wedding, she expressed her happiness at being allowed to have a bath at last, following the daily anointment of oil.

A band accompanied the groom as he rode to the bride's house where her brother greeted him. The groom, young and shy, was resplendent in his gold coat and a white Moslem brimless hat covered with white flowers, with silver bangles jangling before his eyes and a sword hung at his side. He jogged along on his rented white horse that had as much decoration as the groom. Garlands were distributed to guests.

The ceremony took place underneath the tent where a fire burned. The couple said their vows; a Brahmin recited the mantras and relatives flung spices into the fire. The bride walked slowly around the flame and touched her head to the groom's. Another turn round the flame, and her hand touched his, and the next time, she touched her head to his feet. Then they placed their feet side by side on a stone.

They made seven turns around the sacred flame, and Una was now the world's most secure wife; not to be divorced or to be set aside. Even if something happens to her husband and he dies, she will be cared for by his brothers, if not her sons.

The family has spent thousands of rupees on this wedding. Food was mounded on trays enough for relatives, friends and the poor alike. Following the meal, the bride dressed in the clothes brought along by her groom and left with him. After the wedding night, the bride will return to her family for a couple of days. Thus begins the weaning process of a bride from her own to her husband's family where she will take his ways forever.

The band played as the couple was seated on the rear seat of a Mercedes, a gift and part of the dowry. They smiled shyly as we watched them depart. The festivities continued for the remainder of the week.

*   *   *

Although literature and music speaks of the preoccupation with sex in India, both in religious and secular areas, everyday life here is so devoid of exhibitionism as to dispute this.

Movies show no kissing. Women stay with each other and girls play together with other girls. Boys stay together as friends. Cohabiting between the sexes only comes in marriage.

Una gave me a copy of the Kamasutra. The title translation means, "Pleasure Manual." The Indian classic book on love and social conduct instructs those who can afford the cost in money and time in the art of sex, etiquette and social accomplishments. Among its topics are

"Spreading and arranging beds or couches of flowers upon the ground. There is to be a proper disposition of jewels and decorations and adornment. Great attention is given to applying lotion to the body and dressing; the hair massaged with unguents, shampooed and perfumed. She is instructed in composing poems…and mastering the various ways of gambling. She must have the ability to know the character of a man from his features. They study the face so as to tell character. Acknowledgements of society's rules, and of how to pay respect and compliment others."

The Kamasutra gives these instructions about newly married life:

"For the first three days after their marriage husband and wife should sleep on the floor and abstain from intercourse.

"The next seven days they should bathe to the sound of music, adorn themselves, dine together, and pay their respects to their relatives and to the other people who attended their wedding.

"On the evening of the tenth day the husband should speak gently to his wife…to give her confidence. Vatsyayana recommends that a man should at first refrain from intercourse, until he has won over his bride and gained her confidence, for women, being gentle by nature, prefer to be won over gently.

"If a woman is forced to submit to rough handling from a man whom she scarcely knows, she may come to hate sexual intercourse, and even to hate the whole male sex…or she may grow to detest her husband in particular, and will turn to another man." *Kamasutra, iii, 2.*

* * *

I remember my friend Shashi, the Maharani, once describing to me the words spoken in her own wedding ceremony.

She said, "My groom speaks first and I answer. He says, 'I take one step that we may have strength of will.' 'In every worthy wish of yours, I shall be your helpmate,' I answer. 'I take the second step, that we may be filled with vigor,' he says. I answer again, 'In every worthy wish of yours, I shall be your helpmate.'

'I take the third step, that we may live in ever increasing prosperity.'

'Your joys and sorrows I will share,' I answer.

'I take the fourth step, that we may ever be full of joy.'

'I will ever live devoted to you, speaking words of love and praying for your happiness.'

'I take the fifth step that we may serve the people.'

'I will follow close behind you always and help you to keep your vows of serving the people.'

'I take the sixth step that we may ever live as friends.'

'It is the fruit of my good deeds that I have you as my husband. You are my best friend, my highest guru and my sovereign lord.'

"He places a sweetened wheat cake in my mouth, and I place one in his mouth, and we are pronounced husband and wife," she said.

We both sat for awhile without speaking. Then I said to her, "That is beautiful. I pray that all of your vows will come true as I pray for myself."

CHAPTER 60
TROUBLE!

I was awakened last night by a knock on the door. It was our servant, who said there were some American boys downstairs. They were all standing at attention when I hurried down the stairs and reached the living room.

"What's up?" I asked, looking at my watch.

"We are sorry to wake you. We think we may be in more trouble than we can handle alone," one teen-ager said.

"Sit down and tell me. Are you all right? Is anyone hurt?" I asked, looking around at the five young faces. I recognized three of them, but did not know the others.

"We stole the Chinese flag," a boy blurted out.

"Stole the flag! From where?" I was alarmed.

"The flag pole in front of their embassy."

"Did you hear about an American flag being stolen in South America recently?" another asked.

"You tried to go one better." I thought I understood and was trying to sound calm.

Visions of all kinds of diplomatic chaos flashed through my mind. An incident like this could be disastrous.

My thoughts went back to a group of boys from the American International School here who had told me about just going to the Chinese Embassy, "just to see it," they said. They had been told to leave in no uncertain terms. I asked my visitors if they had been in that group, and they said they had.

"You must take that flag back!" I said firmly. "We will need a plan and everyone must cooperate to the fullest. Understand me? We must put it back tonight! If they miss it, they will be on the alert, and you will probably be suspects because you were there last week."

We rehearsed a plan. Two would act as lookout while one crept as near as possible behind the shrubs to see what the guards did and when the guards made their tour. After we watched to see how long they have their backs turned and how many seconds they march elsewhere, the fastest runner among the boys would dash to the flagpole and drop the flag.

When we got to the Embassy, we carried out the plan and saw the guards playing a game on a board at the guardhouse. I dropped three of the boys off, saying, "Hold the flag as it is folded, and lay it on the ground. You had better stoop over and run as fast and as quietly as you can. Don't worry if they look up, Ned will yell and that will distract them."

The other two boys and I drove around. We could not see for the high fence. We returned and waited a block away. There had been a few trucks passing and people on foot who ignored us.

All went well. I never spoke of the incident afterward and made the boys promise to keep it to themselves, or we could still get in trouble. Five frightened boys and a frightened lady slept each in our own beds that night. I shivered to think what could have happened to us.

I am sure I would have been advised that I should leave it up to the diplomats. That would mean that the children would be frightened and the families would be upset with them. It would be an international story if it got out. There is never a dull moment in India.

Still, the children are having a wonderful time with friends. I see them at dinner and the girls are always watching their diet. Indian girls and women are petite.

*   *   *

I miss my friends back in Raipur and have eagerly awaited word from them. Today, I received a letter. It was brief but laden with sorrow.

Raji, the young architect who loved my friend Sonu, has committed suicide in his city. His death came in the home where he once played a record for me and had his servant search far and wide to find a cook that would dare crack eggs and prepare an omelet for me. He and I had spent hours together as he drove me home after the night I came to Central India by the mail plane.

Raji was alone in his parent's home when he placed a charpoi in a secluded corner of the roof and drank poison. Could I not have understood his misery more clearly as he talked about death? I was not prepared for that and my concern was to reach my son and husband safely. I am so very sorry, for he has taken his light and love from my friend. He could no longer love Sonu and live without her. In India, there are just no divorces, no matter the cause.

*   *   *

Letters in the last few weeks have brought more news from our friends around the countryside. My friend Shashi, the Maharani, told me the happenings from the Raj Mahal, their palace where we had visited.

Shashi wrote:

"I would have replied to your letter earlier but I wanted to send an invitation with the letter, for the marriage of my sister-in-law. I had to wait, as the dates of the ceremony were not decided upon.

"Well, John, Winnie and Connie did see a wild and free panther after all. [I had written to tell her about the children's return trip from Raipur to New Delhi, when they saw the big cat.] Bad luck they did not have a gun with them. If luck favors, then surely Mark will get one, next time you all are here.

"Remember the place where we all went for a futile beat? Two weeks back, there were three kills within four days in the small valley where we sat for the second beat. We did not go there, as my husband is too busy to spare any time, due to the Gram Panchayat Election that will take some more time to end.

"The cook managed to bake the pie. It was simply delicious, although we were a bit late in baking it. Thank you very much for all the things you gave.

"My husband sends his affectionate regards to you all. We would have visited you by this time but we cannot just yet leave Kawardha. I often think and speak of you. For are you not our friend and it is said that to gain a friend is to gain happiness and prosperity.

"P.S. We produce our own "skippy" now. Thanks. It has the same taste."

I smiled as I remembered how we had once taken them a jar of Skippy peanut butter. I answered her letter right away telling our missing her and thanking them for all of the happy and peaceful times that we had shared with them.

                    *   *   *

In another letter, headed, "Palace of Kawardhi, Durg District," Shashi said:

"My dear Mary, I have wanted to write to you before, but due to laziness I was not able to do so. Yesterday Mark came here. We were very happy to know from that your health is better and you are recovering but that the doctor wants you to stay in Delhi. And thank you very much for your letter. From it we came to know that Connie has gone back to the U.S.A and about the interviews in the papers. We shall be very glad to get a copy of the same.

"On the 1st of this month we were blessed with a son. I only hope you will be able to pay us a visit before you return home, and see him. Mark was quite annoyed and said that I should have told you before. But you see, what to tell. All of us are well and happy. We usually think of you all.

Give Winnie, Dennis and John our love. Give Connie our love when you write to her.

"Best wishes to you all, and we pray that God give you a complete recovery from your ulcer problem. Don't worry, for worry is a disease in itself, and peace and happiness is only there when there is no worry. After all, worry cannot remove unpleasantness. Our beliefs should influence you. Leave everything in the hands of God, and in his goodness. Happiness and sadness is the fruit of our past Karma."

I was so pleased to hear from Shashi. We had had wonderful times and had become fast friends. I know that I will miss her and all that she has taught me will always be with me.

CHAPTER 61
WOMAN SWEEPER

We try to keep dust and sand from our home, by tacking a strip of rubber to the bottom of the door to seal it as much as possible. It still comes in.

We had not employed a woman to work for us since we arrived in India. Recalling my excellent help in Florida, and my belief that women are good workers, I wanted a woman on my staff. Having a woman cook was out of the question as men are the only employed cooks. It is a highly sought-after vocation.

I inquired of my servants and friends' servants. One day I was told that a woman sweeper had been found. The exciting day arrived.

Genra appeared through the back door with one of our housemen. She was a petite, lovely, and shy young woman. She was not sure how old she was. Arthur, my cook, was the interpreter. She was barefooted, and wore a sari with many shades of red in it. There were many, many silver bangles on her arms, and rings on the second toe on each foot. Bracelets fitted around both her ankles. She wore long silver earrings, and had the red streak down the center part of her head and the red dot on her forehead signifying a married woman. While she stood in front of me, she kept the end of her sari over her head.

I asked her what she would charge to work every day except the sixth and seventh day of the week. She wanted to work Saturdays. I suggested she have a half day off then. The salary was agreed upon—the same that I had paid my male sweeper before, with a raise in a month if she is happy and I am happy. We agreed.

Genra appeared each morning hours before I awoke. She scrubbed the dust and dirt from all the floors, including the veranda, the garage drive and floor, and cleaned the bathrooms. Sweepers are not allowed, by their caste, to touch anything from the bottom of the cushion of the chair upward. It is absolutely forbidden.

The new servant was silent and never spoke until spoken to. She would not smile until I had smiled at her. We were all pleased to have her. She would speak to Dennis since he has learned quite a lot of Hindi. He is always cheerful and wants to be understood.

Last week, Mark and I went on a trip and left the children with the trusted servants. Dennis, a stickler for cleanliness, noticed that the crystal chandelier over the dining table was dusty. He brought a cloth and told Genra to watch what he was doing. He placed newspapers on the dining room table, went from the stepladder to the table, and began dusting. She immediately disappeared.

Dennis didn't think anything of it, expecting her to return. But she did not return then or ever. Dennis did not realize that he had frightened her. Her caste could make her an outcaste if it were known that she was doing a job that my houseman did.

I owed Genra money. None of the servants would tell me anything. Dennis has been really heartsick over this incident. He asked other sweepers if they knew where our sweeper lived. It was like running into a stone wall. None of the servants would take the money I wanted to get to her. Those are the rules of the caste.

*   *   *

Since we are in New Delhi for the holidays this year, we have been enjoying the color and excitement of Diwali, the Indian New Year celebration. Last night, we were playing bridge with our friends Eleanor and Bill.

Fireworks had been going on outside all evening. We watched the show from our flat rooftop, and then returned to the game.

Prita, our labrador, who is kept in the enclosed yard, began barking. Sounding terribly upset, she continued barking non-stop and scratching the kitchen door. Mark went to calm her, but she wouldn't be calmed. She ran back and forth from the yard to the door.

Suddenly, Eleanor exclaimed, "Smoke, I smell smoke!" We all smelled it then, and began running up the stairs to the rooftop. While I called the fire department, the men got a hose and began fighting a fire that had caught on the roof. The boys took buckets and filled them. The fire was almost under control when we heard the old iron-wheeled fire engine with its boiler come chugging up to the house.

It was then that I noticed our two servants, Arthur and Babalal, had taken up their post at the front gate. They were afraid that some religious fanatics might try to throw themselves into the flames as a sacrifice to the fire god, Agni, India's oldest god. The police came and posted two men inside and outside until the smoke had drifted away. They stayed through-out the night as a precaution. Prita was our heroine.

Leaning on the wrought-iron gate, Winnie and I chat with our cook, Arthur, at our house in Defence Colony, New Delhi.

This snake walla squatted on the road in front of our home, with a basket in front of him. He played his flute and moved it back and forth to attract the cobra to rise from the basket and spread its sheath as it swayed with the flute's movement.

CHAPTER 62
DENNIS PERFORMS

Last night was a special one— the performance of the high school play, with Dennis as the star. It was "Around the World in 80 Days," and he played the lead role of Phineas Fogg, world traveler. Over the past few weeks, we had to scurry around putting together his costume. I found material for his striped pants, located a formal tail jacket, and borrowed a top hat from the Irish Ambassador, our friend.

The show was a rousing success and Dennis was terrific. The Ambassador, whose hat he wore, said, "I'm glad I've come to know this young man." We all attended a reception following the play.

Dennis often goes to Roosevelt House on the weekends. It is the official residence of the Ambassador, though they do not live in the big house. He and Dennis spend hours talking as they sit by the pool. Dennis is interested in political and philosophical information and is a good conversationalist. He also met Lord Mountbatten when he came to India from Burma.

I attend many embassy affairs, always with an escort. Dennis is now a tall young man, courteous and enjoyable, and he is often my escort.

The Ambassador of Saudi Arabia knows of me because of my encounter with the Arabian director of petroleum on the plane to Madras. Dressed in flowing black robes, he always comes to the embassy functions without his wives. Mark seems amused at this. One day, I mentioned that

I wished he would attend with me, but he said, "No, thank you." It was not brought up again.

*   *   *

We have added another member to our household—Charlene, whose parents live in Thailand where her father is a Foreign Service officer. They had sent their daughter to board in the hostel in Delhi, the nearest American International School. Dennis came home one night and asked, "If Charlene can stay with us now that Connie has gone to college?"

We asked Winnie if she minded sharing her bedroom and she graciously accepted Charlene, whom both of our children know from the school. John loves her because she plays catch with him. We are getting along fine. She is a joy to have.

*   *   *

Today was a busy day, with some unusual activity. We had an unexpected electrical fire in the electric meter boxes, which are attached to a wooden panel in a recessed area of the wall, providing three-phase power. I rushed out to see flames leaping two feet high. Our golf bags and Mark's food box were sitting in front of the door to the fire extinguisher, so that I couldn't get to it. Our ever-faithful cook, Arthur, with main force shoved the things aside and grabbed the extinguisher. Each wire was shooting flames, but he extinguished the fire, although he got burned in the meantime.

Thank heavens the house is constructed of concrete and metal, or repairs would be a problem, due to a grave shortage of wood. I left thirty-five people, engineers and peons from the Embassy housing staff working to sort out.

After the excitement of the fire I went to sing. I joined the choir members of the Cathedral of the Holy Redemption for the opening of the new parish house. I arrived just in time for the affair. I dashed into the

Cathedral Choir room to dress in the choir sari and was out in fifteen minutes.

The President of India officiated at the event. He and I had a few moments to exchange greetings. We had met and talked at other times. The program was one of great pomp and ceremony, yet with simplicity at the same time. No one knows how to make things as colorful as the Indians. I believe it is their salvation in a drab world.

There are no other Americans in the choir. I feel honored to be a member, as they have a fine choirmaster and the singers are highly talented.

Our song was the national anthem, a prayer for all religions of India as is sung in the second line.

"*Aharaha tava pracharita, suni tava udara vani*
Hindu-Buddha-Sikha-Jaina-Parasika-Musalama-Khristani
Jaya he, jaya he, jaya he, jaya, jaya, jaya, jaya he."

A dance followed the anthem with a presentation telling the story of Mary Magdalene and her conversion. The dancers were beautiful; each had complete control of the facial muscles, head and body.

*   *   *

Mark called from Bhopal to say that he would not be able to make the ambassador's reception being held tonight for Dr. Frank, the director of the fertilizer team. He will be having dinner and a few drinks with one of the specialists, who specializes in taking a lot of drinks after dark. I had met this man once and realized that he wants a drinking buddy. I don't like the idea of Mark getting too close to him.

As I went through the reception line at the Embassy this evening, I was complimented on the work that my husband is doing and thanked for my work as well.

Dr. Subermaniam, India's Minister of Agriculture will be leaving directly for a meeting with the U.S. Secretary of Agriculture in Washington, D.C. My husband's co-worker and our friend will be accompanying Mr. Subermaniam to be sure that our side of the Indian program is represented.

I feel sorry that Mark has missed so many of the official gatherings, but I have learned in these two years of marriage that he does not care to attend them and is happy to have me take his place. He would rather come home, get a drink in hand and sit quietly. He is a quiet man, needing nothing more than a book in his hand and a glass by his chair. However, I am often complimented on his work, which is obviously outstanding.

CHAPTER 63
DIGNITARIES ARRIVE

Prime Minister Shastri, who held this office following the death of Mr. Nehru, has now died suddenly while in Tashkent, Russia, on diplomatic business. This week, he lay in state before his cremation.

Representing the United States were Hubert H. Humphrey; Vice President Dean Rusk; and Secretary of State John Kenneth Galbreath, former Ambassador. We were invited to meet these men at a garden tea. They spoke to us as a group and individually. Mr. Humphrey was natural and sensitive to the occasion. It is his first cousin's wife who has been my mentor here in India. Dean Rusk was not forthcoming and seemed somewhat distant. Whether it was his natural manner I do not know. Mr. Galbreath's intellectual discourse was lightly interested and interesting as he mentioned a repertoire of experiences.

Dennis wanted to go the Prime Minister's cremation service. His friend, the son of a British official, offered to have him join them in their family's car. Taking a movie camera loaded in 16-millimeter film, they left. A large crowd was expected.

Dennis is fifteen now and weighs one hundred and thirty-five pounds. I tried to assuage my anxiety by remembering that he is in good physical shape. When he returned from the event, he was exhausted and disheveled.

"Mom, you could have never gotten through that crowd, a million and a half. People were knocking each other down, walking on people. It was mass hysteria in pockets," he said.

"I was worried about you and our Indian friends were also concerned," I told him.

"They should have been. I was allowed inside the ropes and sat with Lord Mountbatten's aide d'camp. I enjoyed talking with him. Lord Mountbatten came in from Burma and his man from London. He was complaining about the heat since he'd left snow in London. You should have seen their gold spurs."

We had seen the processions before, and the bodies being carried on the bearers' shoulders.

In the case of the top government official, the body was placed on the ghat (high cement platform) and a mound of wood covered it. Sandalwood is the most precious wood used because of its fragrance. It costs several hundred dollars so only the rich can afford it.

India has long used cremation, which was probably associated with the concept of purification by fire. The high caste Brahmin is placed with his face to the north. A low caste person faces the opposite direction. Whatever the caste, a bit of rice flour or banana is placed on the tongue. The oldest son sprinkles oil and holy water on the pyre, circling it seven times in the case of a Brahmin. He then lights the pyre and everyone leaves. Later, the attendants gather the ashes and give them to the family to take to the river and strew them on the water.

*   *   *

Sonu's daughter, Reeta, has sent me a letter. She entertained our daughters when they visited us in Raipur. I was delighted with her writing and her English. The children begin school at four and half years old and graduate early.

"Thank you for the lovely box of eats," Reeta wrote. "I was delighted when I saw it, for any sign of any kind of foodstuffs at any time is something more than welcome.

"I am studying hard now. On the 18th our preliminaries are beginning and exactly a month later we will be having our T.S.C. exams. I've an extensive course to complete before that, and I've just started revising really seriously.

"You must have heard of the M.R.A. (moral re-armament). Well, a group came over and set up a camp here (in Jaipur) for about 6 days. All our teenagers attended it. Boys from Maya and girls from Sophia, both in Ajmer, also attended. Various girls and boys from the surrounding colleges stayed there. We Cambridge girls could not stay at the camp, but we attended a few sessions. The rest of the time we studied.

"The M.R.A are teenagers, hardly any older than us (13). They have devoted their lives for the good of India. Their chief aim actually is to change ideas of the people and the people themselves, so that India's present conditions may be improved. They and the camp was so fascinating that we decided to change and if possible attend the next camp. We might join the M.R.A. for a little while because we will be at loose ends for 6 months after school. The next camp may be held in Delhi, if so, I'll be seeing you.

"My love to everyone. With love, Reeta."

          *   *   *

Holi, the festival of fertility, is an exuberant celebration of spring, and we are in the midst of it now. It is a favorite holiday for the children, as it gives them a chance to pelt grown-ups with red and green tinted water. Everyone, including us, wears old clothes, and the children have a great time squirting, sprinkling and dunking paint all over all passersby. A parade is part of the scene, and music instruments were played, with drums and other noisemakers getting louder and louder. It is a remembrance of Lord Krishna's erotic play with the milkmaids.

Teej is another celebration, this one honoring the goddess Parvati, who was the beautiful and charming consort of the Lord Shiva. It is particularly important in homes and palaces that observe *zenana* (separation of the women). These women live much as in the story of Hindu mythology, where Parvati had meditated for years and years in order to win Lord Shiva as her husband. This is the legend told the children. During Teej, the unmarried women pray that they "will always be dressed in red," instead of the white that widows wear.

As part of the celebration, the replica of the goddess Parvati is taken out into the street and carried in procession through the town. Only eunuchs, castrated men, are allowed to be near the women, and they lead the way.

The festival features entertainment for everyone—swings, merry-go-rounds, and endless rows of stalls selling trinkets, sweets and clay dolls to the jostling, good-humored crowd.

Children and adults all dress in their finery. The animals are washed and decorated with garlands of yellow geraniums and red blossoms. They all parade before an appreciative crowd. Music fills the air. As the sun fades, the music— which has become more acceptable to our ears during our years here—dies away. The image of the goddess has been returned to wait another year until her next celebration.

CHAPTER 64
CALLAN CALLS

Our servant brought me a letter and a box a few days ago. I took the box, opened it and found a lovely bouquet of yellow roses. The card read, "I so look forward to your acceptance. Callan." The invitation was for a reception at an embassy.

I always wonder what lies ahead when we receive an invitation. We have experienced some rather amazing and delightful occasions in the past.

The French Ambassador gave one party that I won't forget, for other reasons. A wonderful wine was served with every course. Although I sipped it very slowly, I became very ill at the table. I forced myself to continue sitting and listening to the remarks from one dinner partner. "My dear, you aren't eating your food," he said.

I was too busy swallowing to open my mouth, so I smiled with pursed lips. As soon as I could, I rushed to the powder room to relieve my poor stomach. I learned early that I cannot drink more than one cocktail and that very slowly, and that my limit is one glass of wine with my meal. Since the servant at the dinner continued pouring into the wineglass, I never knew when the glass should have been emptied.

*   *   *

Mark did arrive back in Delhi in time for the embassy reception that Callan's note had invited us to attend. He looked handsome in his white linen jacket, black trousers and white tie. I wore a black silk fitted dress that has flesh colored net bordered with black embroidered flowers around the off-shoulder top. My hair was piled high with a beige silk flower tucked into it. I attached a rosebud to a black ribbon for my wrist.

The evening was a delightful affair, done up splendidly, as European parties can be. Mark seemed to enjoy himself. Several embassy wives and young women gave him a great deal of attention. He deserved it, and I thought that perhaps he would come around to enjoying social gatherings.

I was wrong, or so the scene that followed when we arrived home indicated. He took off his black Italian trousers and threw them in the wastebasket.

"That is the last time I will cozy up to a bunch of people who say nothing, but continue to talk endlessly," he said.

"Darling, you cannot take that as an indication of their intellect," I said. "This was a very casual, social event, welcoming new diplomatic staff, not a business meeting."

I didn't get very far. He poured a drink, sat on the edge of bed and drank it silently, then fell over and went to sleep.

I thought about his actions for awhile. He is out in the country, loving the independence of his work and the fact that he is really doing something very worthwhile, yet jealous of the people who are working and living in New Delhi with their families.

I wondered if he was jealous of me, and spent some time thinking about my life. I am required to do whatever is possible for better relations between Americans and the nationals and representatives of other nations here. It's true, since I live with the children in New Delhi, that I am most involved in their activities. There is swimming, tennis for John, rugby for Dennis, dinner and homework.

I am kept busy representing the U.S. government and what we stand for, and I often have senators and top American business executives come for dinner or cocktails. I must admit that it gets a bit old having parties where people don't say much of importance. But getting to meet each other is important. I am not finding life in New Delhi as fulfilling as I had our journeys throughout the vast Indian countryside. However, I did join our German friends last week to see Humayan's tomb by the full moon. It was another spectacular sight.

During the days I have become involved in various projects. The Dali Lama now resides in India. There is an on-going project to help as many Tibetans escape as possible. Several times a month, I go to the Tibetan House where we listen to some poor soul who has just escaped Chinese torture. Most days we work on moneymaking projects, collect clothes or blankets at some of our homes, then send the items to the organization with connections to incoming Tibetans, who have escaped and traveled for days through snow-covered mountains to reach India.

When I am called by the social secretary of our embassy, I am told how many will be present and given the date, and I begin preparing for the occasion. I have entertained and been invited on a number of occasions by the president of a New York banking company. I have spent many evenings with the president of the international oil company and have socialized with wives and the other officials and teams who come to inspect the Embassy. These people are outstanding in their field. I am the extra one out, usually. But I am treated very graciously and never have anyone suggest outside meetings.

I had felt guilty at times, thinking of the kindness and attention Callan had given me on whatever occasions he was present. I wished that Mark would treat me in the same manner. Callan and I enjoy talking to each other. He wishes to visit us in the United States, and I told him that we'd be delighted to see him.

Now, I do not feel guilty by Callan's attention. Mark has seen us together and never complained or mentioned anything about having any concern.

One day, Calian called Mark and asked to take us to dinner. We accepted and after dinner returned home to have a nightcap, which turned into an all night sit-up. Callan and Mark talked for a while, and then

Callan included me in the conversation. None of us went to bed that night. This is not at all uncommon I learned. We had breakfast together after awakening the cook.

*   *   *

The dinners, receptions and holiday celebrations in New Delhi at each embassy, particularly other National Days when there are special obser-vances, such as our Fourth of July, have been such a pleasure. It is like being in a storybook setting that I had never dreamed of living. The embassy events are when Americans that are invited meet nationals and internationals (Third Country, as we called ourselves). At one last week, the Indian general found his way to our table asking for a farewell dance. He is going to attend to his army's mission at a destination unknown to me. He has a solemn demeanor, but very charming.

One of the secretaries at the American Embassy arranges an escort for me if Mark is out in the country, which he most often is, since agriculture scientists have no work in the cities. Sometimes my escort is a Foreign Service Officer assigned to the Embassy in some capacity whose wife is away, or it may be a single man. All is done very properly. It is the respon-sibility of each of us to meet, greet and become acquainted with the other guests. One does not gravitate to another American for conversation; that is not our purpose for being there.

I usually see a few familiar faces. Callan attends a few affairs, and hav-ing to fly across the country to get there does not seem to be a problem for him. He is an activist for the rights of Indians, who are struggling against the bureaucracy.

"Three-quarters of India needs new institutions instead of relying on politicians," Callan remarked one evening. He occasionally talks about India's need to renew institutions and have policy reforms.

I am not here for political reasons, so I only listen. It doesn't take any special talent to know that the country badly needs an infrastructure.

Schools do not exist in the rural areas, and the shade of a mosque is used or classes are taught underneath a spreading banyan tree. There are either no roads or poor ones.

Callan and I often laugh at ourselves. He is called the "White Raja Sahib," and in Raipur I was known as "White Mother Doctor."

*   *   *

Today, a chauffeured automobile drove up to our door. The chokadar came to announce that the "Burra (big) Sahib" was here.

"Please show him in," I said.

Callan was standing there when the servant stepped aside. He had a big smile on his face. I noted his blue, blue eyes and his blonde hair that curled on his neck. He wore a white linen suit, with a tie in a pattern matching the color of his eyes. A yellow rose was in his lapel. I think he is nice.

There has never been a private moment for us, only crowds of people.

"I could not leave New Delhi without seeing you. Do you mind?" he asked.

"Of course, I don't mind, I am delighted to see you."

"Come, let us sit. I am off to London and Bern, and have little time to stay," he said. "I wish you could go with me, I have friends I'd like you to meet and you could stay with them."

"It sounds lovely to get out of the heat and dust," I told him, smiling. "I am afraid it is quite impossible. I don't think Mark would want me to go. It really is impossible, but it means so much to me to know you would like me to tag along." I was trying to put a light spin on the conversation, fearing I might do something ridiculous.

"Then I will see you when I return." He took my hands, turned the palms up and kissed both palms.

He was gone, but his masculine-scented fragrance lingered with me, as did the memory of the look in his eyes. Oh, well. There are many things to do and I must keep busy.

CHAPTER 65
STORM CLOUDS BUILDING

Mark continues to make no attempt to make love to me. I know he has been under much pressure to do the work set out for him and I am very happy that he has accomplished what he has done. I feel that he is substituting work for caring. His indifference is considerable.

I don't want the children to be disturbed by the situation as I go about my duties. I am sure now that he resents me going on with the work I've been involved in, and meeting many interesting people.

Last Saturday we were invited to the German Embassy for a dinner party. He refused to go, which is becoming a habit. When the driver brought me home, Mark was sitting on the front veranda with his eyes bloated from drink. The nearly empty bottle of bourbon and the ice pail were sitting by his chair. He had his shirt and a shoe off.

"Mark, please come inside. There are people watching us. Let's go in." I put my hand on his arm.

"I don't give a damn who's watching me."

"I'm sorry you missed the party. A number of people asked where you were." He did not answer me.

"Just leave me alone."

As he rose and stumbled to bed, I followed him and sat on the edge of the bed. "Mark, you recall that before we came, we were told that we were to be a part of the mission and that meant not only your work is important but the social interaction and contacts are as well?"

I said nothing more but recalled the concert in Raipur, and his refusal to attend that important event in the life of the royal families, a musical. There have been so many times when he chose to stay away.

Drinking never interfered with his work, though. That night he drank until I returned, then in the morning woke calling "Coffee, coffee." And by 8 a.m. he was off to work.

                    *   *   *

Today, I went down to Cannaught Circus to shop for gifts. I wanted to find a couple of rings to take home to the girls in the family. The owner of the store that I had visited once before when we were first in New Delhi came out to greet me. He spoke very pleasantly and invited me to come into his office again.

I told him that I was looking for gifts, and he began talking to me about our return to the States. I could sense that he was leading up to something, and I thought that perhaps it concerned his daughters going to college. After closing all the doors, he excused himself, rose and walked to open one door; then I heard him open an iron safe door. I could not see through the open door into his office. Soon he returned with a case and opened it.

"I want to show you something that is immensely valuable," he said quietly. "I ask you not to tell anyone that you have seen it. The stone would be recognized. Your knowing about its whereabouts could be very dangerous for you."

"Perhaps I don't need to see it," I thought. "Am I being followed? Is this going to get me in trouble?"

I had not forgotten when I was asked to meet with INTERPOL, many months ago, about jewel thefts and smuggling. I am not about to mention INTERPOL to the shopkeeper.

It was as though he read my mind. "As long as you never discuss it there is no harm in showing it to you," he said. "I wanted to share this beautiful moment with you."

At that, he took my hand and I opened my fingers. Inside, he laid a diamond that almost covered the palm of my hand. It was thick and magnificently cut. It caught all the overhead rays of light; colors sparkled. He took his hand and put my other hand over it and held it there.

"This is beautiful."

"This promise you must make to me, that you will not speak of this in any way, never say where it is or describe it if you are asked."

"Yes, yes," I exclaimed. "Thank you."

The unforgettable diamond and the night I helped the young students return the stolen Chinese flag are two secrets I have never revealed.

Chapter 66
CHANGES ARE COMING

Mark is being reassigned to Vietnam, so we will be leaving India this month. We are to arrive there on July 18th. My friend Pushpa's father, with tears standing in his eyes, pleaded with me to bring the children and live in his magnificent mansion in Old Delhi while Mark is in Vietnam.

"You are my daughter's friend. We want you and your children here with us for as long as you would like to stay. You will owe us nothing. When your husband leaves that war-torn country for a peaceful place, you go to him." He is 75 years old and has reared nine daughters.

How can I make him understand the need to keep the family together regardless of the situation we find ourselves in? Orders will be cut for me to live in Thailand, where Mark can come for visits.

We put labels on each bedroom door, marked U.S STORAGE, VIET-NAM, THAILAND, and AUBURN, AL. The boxes of our belongings are being divided. Now the packers will come and we will put our things in their capable hands.

Connie is already in the States and attending FSU. Dennis will visit a friend at the Embassy in Moscow for the summer. Winnie will be in Alabama with family members.

*   *   *

Life has not been made easier by Mark's behavior. His work seems to be all that he is interested in. He has had enormous responsibilities and demands on his time. The work he has carried out and that done by other A.I.D. staff members and contract Americans has increased productivity and helped bring about an overall rise in the economy, as well as the knowledge he and others, such as our friend Don, have imparted to the people.

Now I am wondering how life will be for Mark and me in Vietnam and Thailand. This marriage, which started off glowing with tenderness, need and hope, seems to be falling apart. He pushes me away when I only want to be held. He thinks I want intimacy more than he does. Once he said, "You'll get in trouble."

Do I really want to try to put things back together? Is it worth the effort? He couldn't have been more appreciative that I married him during the early months. He told me over and over how wonderful it would be to have all the family together. I appreciate this experience and I thank him for it. Now that he is away from the family traveling and has little interaction with us, he is colder towards me. He looks at me with quizzical expressions that seem to have a hidden meaning.

I have not found a way to reach through the shell he has built around himself. He works, reads and drinks. What will happen in the future?

Sometimes I find myself thinking of another man who was special to me in the States. Before I met Mark, I had loved J.P for three years. He had advised me during my divorce and was a friend to the children and me. I felt then that my life would be empty without J.P. Now I feel the same emptiness. He was in the midst of a divorce when I met him, a corporate lawyer/CPA, having a difficult property settlement. When I last heard from him, he had been appointed judge in Ohio. I thought he had forgotten me, so I had accepted Mark's proposal nine months before we left America.

Today, I remember a certain morning in Florida when I was preparing for the journey to India. It all comes back vividly— I had been packing dishes on our back porch when the phone rang. I rushed through the dining room, passed the lovely cherry table that I dreaded leaving, to answer it on the fourth ring.

The voice I heard was J.P.'s. "Where are you? What is going on?" I gasped.

"A friend at State Department told me you are going to India. Don't go. I know India, Mary, I know what it is like. You don't want that, darling. I flew 'the Hump' during World War II. I saw it from the air and from the ground."

"I'm married, J.P. We are on orders to go."

"Divorce him and marry me. I am no longer married. You love me; I know you do. I love you, Mary. I love the kids."

Slowly I put the receiver down. It was like a knife cutting all connection with a man I loved. Suddenly my heart ached. I went into the kitchen, picked up a piece of tissue paper and continued wrapping dishes as tears streamed down my face.

"What have I done?" I thought.

Two weeks later, we were in New Delhi.

Over two years have passed since that morning in Florida. Now, packers are coming through the door of our Delhi house. Mark is perfectly ready to go into Vietnam which means he takes a chance on being killed. Is he suicidal? He doesn't have to prove anything to me, just be the kind, loving man that I married. What is the dark cloud that hangs over his head? Maybe he has issues to deal with that I don't understand. He is a complex person and his life has been different from mine.

But for now, the feeling between us appears to be one of indifference. As my thoughts circle endlessly around, I wonder. What has become of J.P, should I try to find him? Must I follow Mark?

*   *   *

Now I must say goodbye to the members of the choir, the embassy group, to my friends, sisters Umi and Nemi. They and their parents have been so cordial and hospitable to me. Their father had been the Director of Department of Medicine. Umi's husband was a captain in the Indian Navy. Her brother Ved Mehta wrote for the *New Yorker Magazine.* There are many other friends made during almost three years in India who will be missed.

The children and I have received benefits, they liked their friends, their school and the adventure of seeing the country. They are happy about having lived here. I really do not think that Mark has any emotional ties for anything he has encountered here.

As I pack, I review my thoughts. What strength it takes to live in this country, a new democracy. What passion to continue the customs and build a life on the ruins of stones of antiquity. I better understand Gandhi's staunch determination to bring independence to the country. He put the nation on the road to self-realization, and only now can it be seen if the land can progress.

I feel there is no shortage of capabilities among the people. The philosophy that most of them espouse is different from mine. I find it unfathomable that they can hold to the rule of passivity, yet allow children to die from starvation because of their strict dietary rules. Millions of families live here with dignity, honor, pride and infinite concern for every aspect of their family life. Children dream and laugh and play in the midst of poverty, filth and unbelievable hordes of people.

Yet, where do you begin making changes, when beliefs are the most difficult to change? Do the people want to change? Are they happier as they are now? Many questions still remain in my mind.

The challenge is for the nation to meet modern-day needs of feeding and caring for a population. I believe our programs and the work done by the many specialists from the U.S. and other countries will greatly change opportunities for growth if they are complied with. The tools and methods must be relearned, while people are still using the same methods of thousands of years ago.

India has a world of highly intelligent, patient, strong and caring individuals. There is a splendor here that cannot be overlooked, a special feeling that cannot but stir the soul.

I leave with a strange mixture of emotions, some sorrows, many uncertainties about what lies ahead, yet also with memories that will never fade.

Namaste, Shalom, India.

You fulfilled my dreams beyond my expectations.

# # #

EPILOGUE

This chronicle was written in journals, page after page of whatever paper I could get my hands on, as paper was scarce. I laid it aside while we lived in Bangkok, Saigon, Danang, Manila and London. I then went to Egypt, Israel, Turkey, Greece, the Aegean Islands, Scotland, Mexico and other countries.

India opened up the world to our children as well as to me. We made the most of this journey.

I always feel a particular thrill when I meet old India friends in my travels. There is a special bond between us. I was never made to feel that I was a stranger who did not belong in India.

This is the hottest, the driest, and the wettest country there is on the face of the earth. The state of Assam has the heaviest rainfall. In the Himalayas blizzards rage and snow piles high. Birds and animals of infinite beauty and variety live everywhere in the land. There is an ever-changing variety of colors, scenes and moods. One has no opportunity to become bored. Encountering India causes one to come face to face with oneself.

It also is a different and difficult world. India has so many to educate. The people study beneath trees or any place that is not overly crowded. Jobs are at a premium. Now a wealthy man has begun changes when he made small loans available to women. They can start little businesses, and they are doing it successfully.

The wealthy get a fine education and hold leadership positions, or work in the United States or other countries, where they can earn more money and send much of it back home. Most of those return to their country in their later years.

We gave our best to our task in India. I wish that everyone who complains about opportunities in the United States or wants the government to give them their living could march through India and observe the people. Then they could go back to the United States and bless our Maker for the dependable seasons of rain and our government for the privilege of choosing an occupation or profession. We are blessed in our country in innumerable ways.

To me, India today has a need to be rational in government and not allow religious themes to dominate decision-making. Communication outlets must be more competitive so people can receive more points of view. Marketing and telecommunication need to be privatized, and government must work with industry and corporations. The need is great for water, roads, schools and health care.

Yet, with its problems, India remains the most fascinating country I have seen. Stay away unless you want a part of your heart to remain there.

Finis

AFTERWORD

INDIAN RECIPES

We had to acquire a taste for the many spices and combinations of them in Indian cuisine, but once we did, there is not a member of my family today that won't choose these as the food of preference. Indian food is prepared to satisfy the taste and to heal the body and spirit. There are numerous excellent Indian cookbooks. I have included a few recipes of personal favorites.

MULLIGATAWNY SOUP
4 cloves garlic, peeled and chopped
A piece of fresh ginger, about ½-inch cube, peeled and chopped
½ pound boneless lamb (from shoulder or leg) with fat removed; cut into ¾-inch cubes
2 tablespoons vegetable oil
1 tablespoon white poppy seeds, roasted and ground
½ teaspoon ground coriander
½ teaspoon ground cumin
¼ teaspoon ground turmeric
1/8 teaspoon salt 1/8 teaspoon cayenne pepper (optional)
1/8 tsp. freshly ground black pepper

2 tablespoons chickpea flour (can be purchased at Indian food store, or cooked and ground)

2 cup chicken broth (canned or homemade)

1 tablespoon lemon juice

2 to 3 tablespoon-cooked rice or 1 to 1-1/2 tablespoons uncooked rice (optional)

Directions: Put the garlic and ginger into electric blender with 3 tablespoons water. Blend at high speed until you have smooth paste. Set aside. Pat lamb pieces dry. Heat the oil in a 2-to 3-quart pot over medium-high flame, and add the meat. Turn and fry until the pieces are lightly browned on all sides. Remove with slotted spoon and set aside. Turn the heat off.

To the same pot, add the paste from the blender, the roasted and ground poppy seeds, coriander, cumin, and turmeric. Turn heat to medium, and fry, stirring constantly, about a minute. Turn heat to low.

Add the browned meat and any juices that may have accumulated, salt, cayenne, and black pepper. Stir and leave on low heat.

Combine chickpea flour and ¼ cup water in a bowl, mixing thoroughly until you have a smooth paste. Slowly add the chicken broth, while stirring. Pour mixture over the meat in the pot. Turn heat to high and bring soup to a boil. Add uncooked rice if you are using it. Cover, lower heat, and simmer gently for half an hour or until meat is tender. Stir in the lemon juice.

If you are using cooked rice, add it to soup 5 minutes before serving. Pour the soup into a tureen or into individual bowls. Mulligatawny soup can be served with both Indian and Western-style meals. Since it is thick and fairly filling, it can be a main course for lunch or a light supper followed by a green salad and fruit.

*   *   *

AUBERGINES

Wash eggplant, slice down center, scoop partially, mince, mix this with minced venison, tomatoes, onion, green chili pepper, fresh ginger, bound together with *ghee* (butter) and bread crumbs. Stuff and bake at 350 degrees for 30 minutes.

* * *

PEA PELAUO

Rice is washed and heated in a pan with ghee for five minutes. Then, peas and salt are added, stirring all the time, as the rice becomes sticky. Water is added, and boiled until the water is absorbed. The mixture is turned into a dish, covered and put into an oven at 275 degrees for twenty minutes.

* * *

MASALA CHAI

1-1/2 cups water
1-inch stick of cinnamon
8 cardamom pods
8 whole cloves
2/3 cup milk
6 teaspoons sugar
3 teaspoons loose powdered black tea.

Directions: Bring liquid to a boil with the spices in it. Cover and turn heat low to simmer for ten minutes. Throw in the tea, cover and turn off the heat. After two minutes, strain the tea into two cups and serve immediately. This tea is most often served at the end of the meal or at teatime, 4 p.m.

* * *

CHAPPATTIS

2 cups of wheat flour
1 tsp. salt
Water to make soft dough

Mix and let stand for half-hour. Pat into round pieces and bake in a hot skillet, turning, pressing down, turn over and over until light brown. The chappatti is used as the utensil for lifting food from the metal pan to one's mouth.

*　　　　　　　*　　　　　　　*

SOMOSA

The filling is of potatoes, peas and onion, seasoned with cumin, coriander, garlic, ginger and a spot of turmeric, a touch of cayenne pepper and bits of chopped green chilies. Pastry shells are cut in triangles, the cooked vegetables and spices added, and the packets are sealed. Then each is dropped in *ghee*, butter with the whey separated and removed. They are fried until light brown, drained and served with chutney.

*　　　　　　　*　　　　　　　*

GULAB JAMUNS

4 oz. Dried milk
2 level tablespoonS plain flour
Pinch bicarbonate of soda
4-5 tablespoons milk
8 oz. vegetable fat for frying
1 lb. sugar
2 cardamom pods
Rose water or vanilla for flavoring.

Directions: Mix dried milk, flour and soda in bowl. Add fresh milk, making smooth soft dough; make thin 2-inch-long logs. Heat the fat, then cool and put over a slow heat. Put in as many rolls as the pan will hold. Cook over a very low fire, till jamuns are pale gold and swollen twice the size.

In the meantime, put the sugar and ½ pint water in a large pan and make thick syrup. Add the cardamoms, either coarsely ground or whole, to the syrup. Drain the jamuns and add to the syrup. The syrup should be kept over low heat after adding the jamuns. Leave all jamuns in syrup for 5 minutes, then take off the fire and add the 1 tablespoon of rosewater or vanilla. The jamuns may be eaten hot or cold.

ABOUT THE AUTHOR

Mary Stickney, soon after her return from India, in one of her many saris.

Her marriage to a U.S. Air Corps captain at the end of World War II took her to Columbus, Ohio. She studied psychology and worked as Assistant to the Director/Auditorium Manager of Mershon Auditorium on the Ohio State University campus from 1959-61. She interviewed, wrote news releases and arranged receptions for artists performing at the Auditorium. She became acquainted with ballet directors, pianists, symphony conductors, singers and other well-known personalities, including baritone Richard Tucker, Eleanor Roosevelt, Trigbee Lee and Hal Holbrook, to name a few.

She had two sons and a daughter. After her marriage ended in divorce, she took her children back south to Quincy, Fla.

Later, she remarried. When her husband was offered a position with the State Department as an agronomist, she and the children went with him to India for three years.

After completing their mission in India, they lived in Bangkok, Thailand, while he went to Vietnam as an agriculture/soil specialist officer working with a pacification program. From Bangkok, she and the children moved to Manila, Philippines. When allowed, she visited her husband in Danang, Vietnam, where they had a home.

In Manila, she was a leader in the American Community and the Holy Trinity Episcopal Church, becoming involved with the needs of the street children and the elderly. As president of the Women of the Church, she helped raise money to build a Science Building at the women's college in Quezon City, now a part of Manila. She worked with the women in the countryside, traveling to Baguio and to the Mountain Provinces to the church schools.

Mary studied oil painting with Professor Gabriel Custodio, a well-known Manila artist, and still continues to paint as a hobby and an avocation.

In 1971, The State Department approved her family's move to London, England, and she worked on the American Embassy Speakers Bureau, traveling to schools, colleges, and clubs to give talks. For the British

Broadcasting Corps (BBC), she taped stories of American life and holidays that were distributed to the blind in England and Europe.

When she and her husband were divorced after returning to the United States, she returned to Florida State University where she received a master's in Clinical Social Work. She also has a bachelor's degree in Foreign Affairs.

She became a counselor with the U.S. Navy at Mayport, near Jacksonville, Fla., and worked there until after Desert Storm. Then, to be near her children, she transferred to the Veterans Administration hospitals in Perry Point, Md., once again working with veterans of all wars.

Upon retiring in 1997 and returning to her home in Atlantic Beach, Fla., Mary decided to finish the book she had begun working on two decades earlier—recording some of her experiences in India and sharing the insights she had gained into the Indian culture.

After many successful years and careers, she took on yet another adventure, the challenge of the information age, using a computer to finalize her manuscript. Having lived in primitive conditions and explored remote parts of the globe, she braved this new world of bits and bytes and downloads, a world that has kept her on her toes and pulled her dynamically into the new millennium.

She is currently working on her second book, about Vietnam, the Philippines and Thailand.

# # #

9 780595 172757